Tacit Bargaining, Arms Races, and Arms Control

Tacit Bargaining, Arms Races, and Arms Control

George W. Downs
David M. Rocke

Ann Arbor

THE UNIVERSITY OF MICHIGAN PRESS

Copyright © by The University of Michigan 1990
All rights reserved
Published in the United States of America by
The University of Michigan Press
Manufactured in the United States of America

1993   1992   1991   1990   4   3   2   1

Library of Congress Cataloging-in-Publication Data

Downs, George W.
    Tacit bargaining, arms races, and arms control / George W. Downs,
David M. Rocke
        p.   cm.
    Includes bibliographical references.
    ISBN 0-472-09450-5.   — ISBN 0-472-06450-9 (pbk.)
    1. Nuclear arms control–United States. 2. Nuclear arms control—
Soviet Union. 3. Negotiation. I. Rocke, David M., 1946–
II. Title.
JX1974.7.D795 1990
327.1'74–dc20   90-33589
                                                                CIP

For our parents:

George W. Downs Sr.
Ruth M. Downs

Sol J. Rocke
Verva C. Rocke

Preface

It has become fashionable to assert that the body of international relations theory that was created to cope with the problems of the Cold War should be swept aside with Gorbachev's reforms and the collapse of the authoritarian regimes of Eastern Europe. Whatever the general merits of this argument, there are reasons to believe that a wholesale purge would be counterproductive. The nascent theory of tacit bargaining is a case in point. While students of politics have always been sensitive to the tacit component of negotiation and political interaction, most of the theoretical work in the area has its roots in the Cold War. Thomas Schelling, Charles Osgood, and others drew much of their inspiration and many of their examples from a bipolar world dominated by the mutual antipathy of the United States and the Soviet Union. Yet despite the fact that its origins lie in a world that is (hopefully) in the process of being transformed for the better, the importance of tacit bargaining as an instrument for securing and maintaining peace has only been increased by recent events.

Whatever other characteristics it may possess, there is little doubt that this new era will be dominated by change and, not infrequently, a great deal of instability. This is precisely the sort of environment where the advantages of tacit bargaining over formal negotiation are greatest. Because tacit bargaining strategies are explicitly adaptive, they hold out the possibility of responding to changes in the political or technological environment in a matter of days or hours and continuing to do so as long as the situation changes. By contrast, formal negotiations might drag on for months and result in nothing more than an agreement that becomes obsolete as soon as it is signed. Negotiations can be re-opened but to do so is to risk the same costly delays and the same problem of obsolescence.

Unfortunately, while instability and change increase the need for tacit bargaining, they also make it more difficult to conduct by increasing uncertainty about a rival state's motives and reducing the accuracy of information about its capabilities. The resultant misinterpretation can easily provoke a spiral of punishment gestures that are far more costly than the termination of formal negotiations. The resultant dilemma posed by an environment that has simultaneously increased the relevance of tacit bargaining and the difficulty of developing effective tacit bargaining strategies is what much of this book is about.

A number of individuals made substantial contributions to this volume. Robert Jervis, Ken Oye, and Randy Siverson played a key role in encouraging the authors' interest in tacit bargaining. Steve Van Evera was of inestimable value in pointing to the relevant historical literature and providing contemporary examples. David Baron, Bruce Bueno de Mesquita, Robert Keohane, Mike McGinnis, Barry Nalebuff, and Steve Walt were all kind enough to read a prepublication version of some or all of the book and provide helpful comments. Carol Signor assisted with bibliographic work and some much-needed copyediting. We are also grateful for the patience and support of Carrie Clausen Rocke, Emily Rocke, and Miriam Rocke.

Finally, we would also like to thank the Pew Charitable Trust, the National Science Foundation, and the Center for International Studies at Princeton for their financial support.

Contents

Tables

Figures

Chapter 1

The Nature of Tacit Bargaining

We lay too much weight upon the formality of treaties and compacts.

—Edmund Burke

1.1 Introduction

When most people, including social scientists, reflect on the ways in which nations resolve their differences, they tend to think in terms of the polar alternatives of war and negotiation. While it would be foolhardy to underestimate the importance of either means of conflict resolution, this perspective ignores a third path that is no less frequently traveled. Consider the following two cases. The first is so characteristic of international relations as to almost go unnoticed; the second is unprecedented in U.S.-Soviet relations.

1. In February, 1988, the U.S. Consulate in Mukden asked for permission for its officials to visit Tan-Tung in Liaoning province. This is a railway transit point on the border of China and North Korea and consular officials are usually not allowed to travel beyond the city limits by car.

For reasons ranging from the sensitivities of North Korea to potentially compromising intelligence regarding the size of Chinese missile shipments, the Chinese refused to grant permission for the trip. In response, Washington decided to restrict Chinese consulate officials in Chicago to Cook County, unless they received permission to go elsewhere. Beijing retaliated by informing U.S. diplomats in Shanghai and Mukden that they would have to give forty-eight hours notice before traveling outside the confines of either city. On December 28, 1988, a spokesman for the State Department characterized the Chinese restrictions as "unreasonable" and charged that they went far beyond any restrictions placed on Chinese diplomats. The next day a spokesman in Beijing indignantly responded that the United States had been placing discriminatory restrictions on Chinese diplomats for years. As of January 1, 1989, the result of this familiar diplomatic Tit-for-Tat was a stalemate.

2. On December 7, 1988, General Secretary Mikhail Gorbachev announced that the Soviet Union would (a) reduce its armed forces by 500,000 men within two years; (b) withdraw six tank divisions from East Germany, Czechoslovakia, and Hungary, and disband them; (c) withdraw assault landing troops and assault crossing units from Soviet forces stationed in Eastern Europe; (d) reduce Soviet forces in Eastern Europe by 50,000 men and 5,000 tanks; and (e) reduce the armed forces and the numbers of armaments stationed in the European part of the Soviet Union. In total, the Soviets would reduce their forces on the European front by 10,000 tanks; 8,500 artillery units; and 800 aircraft. At the same time, Gorbachev hinted that the Soviet Union might be open to additional gestures of cooperation such as the dismantling of the controversial Krasnoyarsk radar station.

Although Gorbachev's move could be interpreted as a Soviet response to internal economic pressures that required no reciprocal action on the part of the United States and its allies, few experts saw matters quite so simply. John Steinbruner of the Brookings Institution described the proposals as a "significant challenge to NATO and the United States" that would make NATO's emerging arms control proposal appear ungenerous by comparison (*New York Times*, December 8, 1988, sec.

A). The *New York Times* editorial on the following day adopted a similar line:

> Breathtaking. Risky. Bold. Naive. Diversionary. Heroic. All fit. So sweeping is the agenda that it will require weeks to sort out. But whatever Mr. Gorbachev's motives, his ideas merit—indeed compel— the most serious response from President-elect Bush and other leaders. (December 9, 1988, sec. A)

These two cases are both examples of tacit bargaining. Tacit bargaining takes place whenever a state attempts to influence the policy choices of another state through behavior, rather than by relying on formal or informal diplomatic exchanges. The process is tacit because actions, rather than rhetoric, constitute the critical medium of communication. It is bargaining and not coercion because the actions are aimed at influencing an outcome that can only be achieved through some measure of joint voluntary behavior. Other examples of tacit bargaining in international relations are everywhere. A retaliatory tariff is announced in response to trade barriers. A state at war refrains from using chemical weapons or from bombing nonmilitary targets in the hope that its opponent will behave similarly. An austerity program is implemented by a financially troubled government in order to convince foreign banks that they should continue to extend credit. The list is endless.

Of course, "pure" tacit bargaining is rare. The actions of nations are often accompanied by diplomatic rhetoric, as in both the U.S.-Chinese dispute over diplomatic travel restrictions and in the Soviet announcement of force cuts in Eastern Europe. The state that institutes a retaliatory tariff inevitably announces the purposes of its actions and frequently alludes to the possibility of still greater tariffs in the future if current trade negotiations are not successful. States that refrain from attacking nonmilitary targets may make their policies public in order to encourage the other side to reciprocate and prevent it from jumping to the conclusion that its restraint has arisen out of weakness. No less frequently, states link tacit bargaining to formal negotiations. Fighting frequently intensifies between the time two adversaries agree to commence peace talks and the time the talks begin, as each attempts to achieve a stronger position from which to bargain. For the same reason, an arms race often intensifies during arms limitations talks as each state seeks a greater stock of "bargaining chips."

The fact that modern states often rely on a mixture of tacit bargaining and informal and formal negotiation should not obscure the need to understand the nature of tacit bargaining. As we shall demonstrate, tacit bargaining possesses a number of attributes that distinguish it from other forms of bargaining and its strengths and limitations are quite different. While few bargaining problems will be resolved by tacit means alone, the pure theory of tacit bargaining that is outlined here will be increasingly relevant as states rely more on actions than on policy statements and conventional negotiations.

1.2   Goals and Methodology

The purpose of this book is to evaluate the ability of different tacit bargaining strategies to bring about arms control and to maintain arms agreements. The basic idea of using tacit bargaining to promote arms cooperation is not new. Strategists like Thomas Schelling and Charles Osgood began exploring the utility of tacit bargaining as an instrument for arms control in the 1960s. The 1980s have produced another flurry of interest in the area. Prior to Gorbachev's initiatives, the erratic progress and modest achievements of formal negotiations led Kenneth Adelman, Reagan's director of the U.S. Arms Control and Disarmament Agency, to argue that the formal arms control process had created a situation where obsolete and even dangerous nuclear weapons were kept in the arsenal of both superpowers in order to bolster bargaining leverage; he suggested that the reduction of nuclear weapons could be most effectively pursued by way of unilateral or reciprocal restraint outside the context of negotiations (Adelman 1984–85). Outside the administration, physicist Richard Garwin offered a far more specific and radical tacit bargaining strategy that would call for temporarily reducing our forces by 50 percent (Garwin 1985, 44).

What distinguishes our analysis from those that have preceded it is our attempt to employ axiomatic modeling and simulation in order to generate a richer theoretical base from which policy inferences can be drawn. These formal techniques are not employed, as is sometimes the case, out of a disregard for the substantial contributions of historians and case study researchers, but *because* of two implications of their work. The first is that neither arms races nor tacit bargaining are homogeneous phenomena. It is impossible to read historical accounts of more than two arms races without being struck by their differences. For example, Germany during the 1930s and the Soviet Union during the 1950s each evidenced preferences in their respective arms races that were more characteristic of the Deadlock game than of the Prisoner's Dilemma game.[1] That is, both states appeared to prefer an active arms race with their opponent(s) to the alternative of mutual cooperation. A similar assertion can be made with regard to China during the 1960s and Iran during the 1980s.

On the other hand, there are those arms races that seem driven by preferences that correspond to the Prisoner's Dilemma, that favorite of game theorists in which mutual cooperation is preferred to mutual defection. The Anglo-German naval race in its later stages, the French-German race just before the outbreak of World War I, the Japanese, United States, and British naval race that was temporarily halted by the Washington Naval Treaty of 1923, and the U.S.-Soviet race prior to SALT I, all can arguably be placed in this category. To further confuse matters, there have been periods—some of which are referred to above—when the underlying game changed as an arms race progressed. During the last forty years, the United States and the Soviet Union have oscillated between Deadlock and Prisoner's Dilemma preferences. The Anglo-French naval race in the nineteenth century and that between Britain and Germany during the early decades of the twentieth century also appear to have been characterized by instability in the underlying game.

Case study researchers and historians often point out that such differences in historical arms races mean that the formal modeler who rigidly defines an arms race as a single game, such as a Prisoner's Dilemma, is taking a treacherous course. This admonition is entirely correct and needs to be kept in mind when choosing

---

1. Specific definitions of these games are given in chap. 3.1.3.

among tacit bargaining strategies. We will see again and again that a strategy that is successful in one circumstance may fail miserably in another. If the formal modeler ignores the fact that arms races are driven by different preferences, and compounds this mistake by making two or three comparable assumptions that are sometimes true and sometimes not, the resultant "general" model will be misleading, and parsimony will have been purchased at an excessive price.

Yet it is important to realize that such differences among arms races also affect the utility of case research and other inductive methods. The more differences that are believed to be important, the less chance of finding any convincing analog from which to draw policy inspiration in a specific case. This also means that no single case study can pretend to be a model from which generalizations can be formulated.

It may appear that one way around this problem is to acknowledge the limitations of single case studies and try to overcome them by attempting to probe, in a systematic way, the efficacy of particular tacit bargaining strategies in a variety of carefully specified circumstances. In theory, this would lead to highly conditional, but useful, results. For example, it might tell us that when the opponent has x level of resources, has Prisoner's Dilemma-like preferences, has y expectations about the future, etc., the most effective tacit bargaining strategy is "number 3."

Although superficially appealing, the problems with the last approach are also intimidating. To begin with, the number of cases is small. While there are many examples of tacit bargaining in arms races, cases where states have employed coherent and explicit tacit strategies for the purpose of promoting cooperation are few and far between. In addition, the number of variables that we have reason to believe affects the success or failure of a given strategy is larger than the number of cases. Studies of historical arms races reveal variation on a variety of dimensions that are likely to have an impact on the efficacy of strategy. Variation in the underlying preference structure has been singled-out for special attention, but variation in uncertainty, strategic doctrine, resources, and other factors are also important in determining tacit bargaining behavior. The fact that these dimensions most likely interact, in the sense that the effect of one dimension depends on the level of another, further compounds the problem.

Moreover, once we discover a clear case of tacit bargaining the problem of measurement looms. Even the most gifted team of contemporary historians would have a difficult time estimating U.S. and Soviet priorities during the last ten years, the perception each had of the other's priorities, the tacit bargaining strategy each was employing and how it was perceived, and so forth. To compile similar data about British and French naval races in the nineteenth century, or even the British-German naval race prior to World War I, would be an even more formidable task.

Given that the small number of cases and measurement problems make it impossible to statistically explore the impact of simultaneous changes in these dimensions, another form of analysis is needed that is more deductive in character. The more complex the situation, the more moves we permit each set of decision makers, and the more uncertainty and strategic misrepresentation we admit, the more likely it is that the necessary deduction will contain an explicit mathematical component. Although critics of formal modelers in general, and of economists in particular, do not like to acknowledge it, economists' adoption of ever more complicated mathematics since the 1930s was only partly motivated by "physics envy"; it was also prompted by their inability to answer complicated questions in natural language. As Donald McCloskey (1985) argues in a work that is quite critical of the excesses to which mathematics can lead, the consequence of the primitive machinery available for the conversation that represented premathematical economics was an inability to speak clearly. The same thing can be said of tacit bargaining. It is impossible to speak clearly about the advantages and disadvantages of different tacit bargaining strategies or to explore questions about the level of punishment that is "best" without some appeal to mathematics.

In a data-poor but complex decision environment, mathematics can help us explore the implications of dozens of disconnected insights. It can help specify the interaction that produces the contingent effects that suffuse national security and most areas of social science, and to forecast the implications of strategies where there is no obvious historical or reliable experimental ana-

log. Granted that there are many instances in which the key
to policy is likely to rest on factors that cannot be easily de-
duced from an axiomatic model: the consequences of a leadership
change or the domestic costs of initiating a conventional war, for
example. But there are other situations in which some sort of
quasi-axiomatic framework can be invaluable. Given the complexity and data constraints, how else is one to determine what
mixture of sanctions and forgiveness of treaty violations is optimal
in different environments or how bargaining outcomes are affected
by biased assessments of an adversary's preferences? These questions will never be answered without information that comes from
outside the narrow boundaries of the axiomatic apparatus. Intelligence assessments will inevitably play a critical role in estimating
the resources of a rival nation or how a recent transfer of power
alters national objectives. However, an axiomatic apparatus, or
some close relative, can provide powerful tools for analyzing the
strategic implications of this information.

This is not to suggest that the application of an *arbitrary* formal model will necessarily help matters. Just as case studies and
the historical analysis of arms races collectively suggest that simple inductive methods will be insufficient to generate a theory of
tacit bargaining, they also delimit the variety of formal methods
that is likely to do the job. We have already alluded to the dangers of a narrow definition of "arms race" and there are dozens of
similar problems. For example, uncertainty about the preferences
and resources of a rival has played a critical role in determining
the ways in which historical arms races unfolded. If the analysis
is restricted to one special class of arms race that ignores uncertainty, any opportunity to understand why actual arms races, as a
class of phenomena, unfold in the ways that they do is abnegated.

To avoid this trap, it is necessary to work with formal models
that are broad enough to explore the consequences of variation in
key decision variables and assumptions. This argues for the use
of simulation to supplement conventional axiomatic methods. In
chapter 4, simulation reveals why there is no single, best tacit bargaining strategy. It enables us to show in graphic detail that the
cooperative signal that a state is willing to send its rival—and by
implication its entire tacit bargaining strategy—varies according
to its estimate of the opponent's strategy, the size of the discount

rate (or the relative importance of the benefits that accrue in the future), the amount of misperception that is present, and the estimated cost of falling behind (even temporarily) in the arms race. Interestingly, many of the findings involve the sorts of threshold effects and contingencies that case study scholars complain are alien to formal methods. For example, if a state that is contemplating making a gesture of cooperation in order to reduce the intensity of an arms race believes that the probability of unresponsiveness is greater than 23 percent—a fairly low figure—the optimal size of the gesture it should offer is quite small: less than a one-year moratorium on weapon increases. In addition, if misinterpretation is a strong possibility and a nation believes that there is more than a 20 percent chance that the rival state is pursuing a Deadlock strategy, the optimal course of action is to make *no* cooperative gesture. This last finding is notable not only because it may help explain why the number of cases in which rival states have attempted to achieve arms cooperation through tacit bargaining is small, but because it is the sort of finding that would never be discovered under the assumption that all arms races are the same.

The sensitivity of formal analysis to variations in key variables argues for serious attention to the character and validity of the assumptions underlying the models. Doubtless, there are areas in science and in economics where proceeding "as if" the assumptions are true is a sensible strategy. In areas like tacit bargaining it is not. Here the empirical evidence that can substantiate the integrity of any given formalism is in short supply and small variations in assumptions can have enormous consequences in what the model predicts. When these conditions are present, the preferred approach is to employ assumptions that are justified as thoroughly as possible.

This preoccupation with assumptions is not as alien to the spirit of axiomatic modeling as the rhetoric surrounding the Samuelson-Friedman debate might suggest, and poor model performance is not the only inspiration for altering basic assumptions. Model builders in both the social and natural sciences frequently adjust their assumptions simply because they do not seem to be realistic enough. For example, economists who study oligopolistic behavior and political scientists interested in deterrence have each relaxed the assumption that decision makers have perfect information about the motives and behavior of their rivals. While this could have been inspired by poor model performance, it was not. In both realms, satisfactory empirical tests are rare and model falsification is difficult. The changes in assumptions were inspired by a combination of case studies, reflection on the problems faced by decision makers, and the development of more sophisticated methodological tools. The basic assumptions of the models used in this book—ranging from considering the decision maker a unitary actor to admitting the possibility of misperception—are scrutinized in terms of these same three sources of change.

In short, our treatment of the role of tacit bargaining in arms control attempts to avoid the twin pitfalls of formulating conclusions either on the basis of a small sample of case studies plagued with selection bias and measurement problems or from the detailed study of a single game with known utilities and perfect information. Because we attempt to explore the policy implications of a host of complicating factors, the mathematical arguments occasionally become complex, as well. We try to minimize the narrative consequences of this by relegating some of the technical material to the Appendix. However, because there is a limit to what can be safely exiled, some mathematical passages remain. Once the analysis is complete, an effort is made to summarize the policy prescriptions and the reasoning that supports them in language that is free from mathematical metaphors. Paul Samuelson may or may not have been correct when he claimed that any theory that he could not explain to his mother-in-law (and his father-in-law as well, we presume) is doomed to fail, but it is difficult to imagine national decision makers pursuing a strategy to slow the arms race or to maintain an arms treaty unless they understand the logic behind it.

1.3   Tacit Bargaining and Formal Negotiation

While tacit bargaining and formal negotiation are both varieties of bargaining (broadly defined), they possess very different strengths and limitations. Formal negotiations between nations—whether they concern territorial disputes, trade barriers, or disarmament—

often require a great deal of time to conclude. Until agreement is reached, the costs associated with the problem under consideration must be borne and any change in conditions that occurs after the formal settlement is reached will necessitate a new round of time-consuming negotiations. Unilateral efforts to deal with the problem are often postponed out of fear that they will give the state that initiates them less leverage in negotiations.

It is also difficult for formal negotiations to cope with technological innovations and other aspects of changing decision environments. Continuous innovation, for example, has been called "the most distinctive feature of the modern armaments race" (Bull 1961, 195) and few would argue with this characterization. In the past forty years, nuclear delivery systems have evolved with respect to size, warhead number and yield, accuracy, mobility, vulnerability to preemption, and a variety of other characteristics. The situation in conventional weaponry is no different. Tanks and antitank missiles, air defense and close air support fighters, communication and intelligence systems, bombers, and biological and chemical weapons have been subject to countless innovations. In every area, the pace of innovation has consistently outstripped the rate at which arms control agreements have been achieved and many of the changes have altered the cost-benefit calculus of increasing arms stocks. By providing the lure of more bang—or more policy leverage—for the buck, innovations increase the incentive to escalate an existing arms race or to violate an arms treaty. If the pace of innovation and change is fast enough, agreements/treaties become obsolete as soon as they are signed and the parties pay the high price of operating under an agreement that is suboptimal. The situation resembles that of a planned economy trying to cope with technological change and shifts in demand. Official prices and production quotas, the analogs of formal agreements, are outdated even before they are announced. The result is severe dislocations and inefficiency. Outdated treaties may have an equally bad effect.

It is difficult to believe that this pace of technological innovation will decline in any dramatic way in the near future. While it is possible to conceive of a treaty that would limit defense spending or forbid the deployment of any new weapon, the will to do so has rarely been evident and there is reason to suspect that the technological imperative cannot be easily laid to rest. An agreement that would limit the total funds that the United States and Soviets would spend on defense or on research and development has never been discussed and, if enacted, might have a smaller impact than proponents hope. The lobbies who favor increased military expenditures have sensitized everyone to the contribution that military research has made to civilian life but it is wise to keep in mind that the causal arrow runs both ways. Expenditures for ostensibly civilian purposes such as space exploration and computer technology can be used to obtain information and equipment that is useful for military purposes, and funds redirected to these ends may continue to foster a "shadow" arms race in which weapons continue to be advanced. Even if this did not occur, there is no guarantee that stable funding levels would stabilize an arms race. The relationship between R and D expenditures and the rate of weapons innovation is undoubtedly positive but progress in any applied scientific field or technical area is not simply a function of expenditure level. A host of other determinants ranging from the organization of the research enterprise, to the risk aversion of key decision makers, to the state of relevant theoretical areas, all have an impact. These variables would not be held constant simply by virtue of the fact that there was an expenditure restriction, and changes in their levels might lead to periodic breakthroughs that could rekindle an arms race.

This situation might be avoided under an arms control regime that restricted the deployment of new weapons but, once again, there is every reason to believe that arriving at such an agreement and enforcing it would not be easy. The history of arms control agreements and failed negotiations is rife with examples of emerging technologies that could not be contained. Indeed, cynics often charge that arms agreements often represent nothing more than the mutual abandonment of an old technology. A notable example is the Washington Naval Treaty of 1923, which was as conspicuous for its failure to contain agreement regarding submarines, cruisers, and aircraft carriers as its famous formula that dictated limitations regarding battleships. We call this tendency to simply divert resources and energy from a category of weaponry that is controlled by a treaty to others that fall outside its boundaries, the *displacement effect*. As we shall see, the ability of tacit bargaining to cope with the displacement effect is one of its chief advantages.

Technological innovation can also undermine an agreement by changing the cost-benefit calculations associated with a weapon system that is already controlled by a formal agreement. When the net benefit increases, the temptation to invest—to increase the pace of an arms race or to break an arms treaty—also increases. The possibility of getting more "bang for the buck" tempts a nation to spend more bucks. The successful negotiation of the ABM Treaty between the United States and Soviet Union and the stability that it initially appeared to impose were both aided by the absence of technological innovations that would permit the deployment of systems that were effective and affordable. Although it would be a gross oversimplification to argue that the Reagan administration's flirtation with violating the treaty in connection with "Star Wars" was motivated solely by subsequent technological developments, they certainly played an important role. Edward Teller's vision of what technology can now provide is argued to have played a key role in convincing the President to go forward with the program, and much of the subsequent debate in both Congress and the popular press centered on questions of feasibility rather than those of international law or the stability of the arms races.

There are times when the motivation for escalating an arms race or breaking a treaty stems from a change in internal priorities that is unrelated to technical innovation or any behavior on the part of a rival nation. Often the transformation is precipitated by a change in leadership. The arms policies of Germany during the 1930s and the United States during the 1980s both underwent dramatic changes as a result of new leaders assuming office. While weaponry evolved during these periods, it was the value placed on the weapons and on being ahead or behind in an arms race that was responsible for the change in policy. The influence of technology by itself was secondary.

Decision makers may also change their response because of domestic political conditions, independent of any change of preferences on their own part. This was the inspiration for the increase in British shipbuilding that took place during the 1870s.

The French had launched no new building program, there was no technological innovation that changed the cost-benefit calculus of increasing the size of the fleet, and the buildup did not follow the installation of a new government with different foreign policy aspirations. What did occur was a severe recession that jeopardized the economic health of Britain's steel industry and the political security of the government (Hirst 1913). More recently, domestic politics played a notable role in the arms buildup at the end of the Carter administration when the Democratic party felt itself to be vulnerable on the defense issue.

Tacit bargaining is flexible enough to permit the kind of dynamic adjustments that are necessary to cope with changes in technology and leadership. A tacit bargaining strategy that prescribes that a nation meet or exceed every increase in research or weapon deployment by its rival provides an adaptive disincentive for such behavior. While such a policy may or may not have the desired effect, its success does not hinge—as in the case of a treaty—on the ability to anticipate the evolution of technology. It is explicitly adaptive. Similarly, tacit bargaining holds out the possibility of responding to the hostile or cooperative gestures of new leadership in a rival nation in a matter of hours or weeks, instead of months or years. No Senate approval is needed for President Bush to match Soviet troop or tank withdrawals from Europe, and none would be needed to match an increase, should Gorbachev or his successor reverse such a policy.

Yet tacit bargaining also possesses a set of attendant limitations. The actions that constitute its medium of communication are expensive. Talk—the stuff of formal negotiation—is cheap. The gestures designed to promote cooperation in tacit bargaining, and most effective punishments, are not. A state that lowers a tax on imports to encourage free trade runs the risk of domestic unrest and exploitation by a trading partner that might increase exports without lowering its own duties. A state that suspends research on a critical weapons system to convince a rival state that it is serious about reducing the intensity of an arms race leaves itself vulnerable to falling behind.

Concentrating on cooperative gestures that are relatively costless may appear to avoid this problem. But there is a catch. The size of the gesture is related to the probability that it will be observed and correctly interpreted. This means that reducing the cost of a gesture reduces the odds that the intended message will be communicated. Conversely, the tacit bargaining actions that are the easiest to interpret are likely to be very costly if not reciprocated.

The cost of punishment can also be substantial. Erecting a trade barrier in response to another state's violation of free trade or initiating an ABM test program because of a suspected SALT violation are far more expensive acts than reading a position paper at the opening session of a conference. Punishment can also lead to the deterioration of an already bad situation. Formal negotiations that are broken off may leave a residue of distrust and hostility, but the likelihood is that the status quo will persist. *Tacit bargaining by its very nature changes the status quo and, when unsuccessful, produces a situation that is less desirable from the standpoint of one or both parties.*

It is all too easy to forget that most trade wars and arms races contain the potential for further deterioration. The arms races between Germany and France in the 1880s, the naval race between England and Germany prior to World War II, the export credit controversy between the United States and the OECD in the 1970s, and the recent round of retaliation of the United States against Japan all could have been more aggressively conducted had the parties chosen to do so. This potential for deterioration is present even in situations that are considered extreme. In the midst of the rampant protectionist policies of the 1930s, enough slack existed for Britain and Denmark to conduct a calculatedly small trade war. Yet initial restraint is no guarantee against the subsequent deterioration that tacit bargaining can provoke. Political scientists have long been aware that this is a risk inherent in the "bargaining chip" strategy, the tacit bargaining adjunct to formal negotiations already mentioned that involves escalating the level of policy conflict in order to make another party more responsive when negotiations begin. If it is successful, the presumption is that the resultant agreement will leave at least one, and often both, parties better off than the previous status quo, but if the ploy fails and the other party rises to the challenge, both often lose. What is true of the bargaining chip strategy will be true of most unsuccessful tacit bargaining.

A related cost of tacit bargaining stems from its susceptibility to misinterpretation. In large part, this is a function of its limited vocabulary. The extensive dialogue that surrounds the discussion of formal treaties provides a rich and sensitive medium of communication. Tacit bargaining does not enjoy this advantage. Stripped of their rhetorical libretti, economic and foreign policy gestures are crude and imperfect instruments of communication. The logic that lies behind the expulsion of the diplomats or an increased price support is not always appreciated fully by the nation to which they are directed. A cooperative gesture can be misinterpreted as an act of appeasement or weakness. An action taken in response to a supposed transgression can be interpreted as an act of aggression or attempted exploitation. A foreign policy signal can be read from a policy inspired entirely by domestic considerations.

The limited vocabulary of tacit bargaining also restricts its ability to cope with multidimensional negotiations or those that involve different types of goods. This explains why it is usually conducted in connection with a single policy output. A state that wants another state to cut its tariffs may reduce its own tariffs (a cooperative gesture) or increase them (a punishment). It rarely decides to communicate economic messages by decreasing its military budget or by violating a nuclear test ban. Should it choose one of the latter policies, the probability that the message will be correctly interpreted is small.

The defects tacit bargaining possesses by virtue of the limited language that it employs are exacerbated by the fact that most tacit strategies employ sanctions to prevent exploitation. These prescribe that a nation respond to an aggressive action or defection with a behavior of similar kind—if not necessarily the same magnitude. The choice of this type of tacit bargaining strategy means that if a state underestimates what it must do to appear cooperative in the eyes of its rival, underestimates the effect that a retaliatory gesture will have, or chooses to interpret an isolated incident of bureaucratic noise as a significant change in policy, it can easily provoke a deteriorating spiral of tacit bargaining responses that is far more costly than the breakdown of formal negotiations.

In sum, while tacit bargaining and formal negotiation both involve the iterative attempt to reach a contract point that leaves both parties better off and takes place in an environment where neither is certain of the other's utility, they differ in ways that are important for students of international relations. Tacit bargaining is capable of greater flexibility and responsiveness, but the costs of conducting it can be very high. There is a price attached to each gesture used in communication and there is the constant specter that the bargaining process will exacerbate the problem that it is attempting to solve. It will come as no surprise that both the cost of the tacit bargaining signals and the determinants of misinterpretation—misperception, control failures, utility uncertainty—will figure prominently in our evaluation of the effectiveness of tacit bargaining as a means of securing and then maintaining arms control agreements.

Chapter 2

Tacit Bargaining Research and the Achievement of Arms Control

We still work with an image of disarmament that makes it solely a peacetime (cold-wartime) process of negotiating explicit detailed agreements in a multinational context for the reduction or elimination of weapons, without adequately recognizing that, as in limiting war, limiting the arms race can be a more tacit and less formal process than the "treaty" idea implies.

—Thomas Schelling, 1960

Howard Raiffa has said that whenever he is asked where he learned something and can't remember he always answers, "Tom Schelling," and believes that he is right 69.4 percent of the time. The response is no less useful (or accurate) for anyone interested in the role of tacit bargaining in arms control. In addition to containing a wealth of original insights into the process of tacit bargaining, Schelling's books and articles set an intellectual agenda that can help us to assess the arms control implications of nearly thirty years of related research in fields as diverse as social psychology and oligopoly theory.

Although numerous political philosophers and military strategists of the premodern period and many social scientists of the first half of the twentieth century reflected on the ways in which a nation's actions can affect the behavior of another nation, Schelling was the first to emphasize the distinction between tacit bargaining and negotiation, and recognize the critical role that the former often played in arms races. One important source of inspiration was the ability of wartime antagonists to place boundaries on the magnitude of hostilities without formal negotiation. No formal negotiations were conducted to ban the use of gas during World War II or to respect the sanctity of either the 38th parallel in Korea or the Formosan Straits in China.

> The limits in limited war are arrived at not by verbal bargaining, but by maneuver, by actions, and by statement and declarations that are not direct communication to the enemy. Each side tends to act in some kind of recognizable pattern, so that any limits that it is actually observing can be appreciated by the enemy; and each tries to perceive what restraints the other is observing. (Schelling 1960, 102)

The closer one looked, the wider the range of informal cooperation that became apparent even during periods of active hostilities. Nations would take pains to confine fighting to border areas and lands not directly ruled by either country. Civilian population centers would be avoided. Weapons available in each nation's arsenals were withheld. Prisoners were spared. Little concerted effort was made to assassinate national leaders. Some of this apparent cooperation may have been epiphenomenal: the product of unilateral decisions that were made in the absence of any expectation about what the other side would or would not do. An advancing army might choose to refrain from stealing food from civilians or any number of more barbaric acts for reasons other than fears of retaliation. Still, it was clear that there were plenty of instances when expectations about the response of the other side did matter and that these expectations were shaped through tacit bargaining.

Since Schelling viewed limited war as arms control in time of war, he reasoned that tacit agreements could potentially play an equal if not greater role in peacetime arms control. There were already a number of examples of such agreements. The United States and Soviets abstained from a variety of "mischief" behaviors that afforded some short-term advantage but would have provoked a dangerous and unstable situation. Each nation avoided jamming key communication channels of the other and only conducted military maneuvers and weapons tests in areas that were unthreatening. Neither made any attempt to destroy the satellites of the other or interfere with the space program of the other. In fact, there was a gradual evolution to an "open skies" situation designed to prevent misinterpretation and misunderstandings. We were involved in a cold war with the Russians but it was an intentionally limited cold war. There was no obvious reason why a more extensive arms control regime could not be built on more of the same.

Schelling understood the ability of tacit bargaining to cope with displacement effects. While resources that would have been devoted to banned or controlled weapons systems could conceivably be used for public health projects and education, they have a way of being displaced into research and development for new weapons systems that are not covered by the formal treaty. Not infrequently, the mere suspicion that the other side might behave in such a manner provides incentive enough for politicians to accede to the pressure of the military to work away at the margins of the formal treaty.[1] Tacit bargaining provides a way to cope better with, if not break, this perverse side effect of an arms agreement. A nation can make it clear that it will hold off development—or at least deployment—of the new system if the other nation acts similarly. Without such contingent threats, Schelling realized, arms agreements will quickly become nothing more than show pieces.

Schelling and Halperin (1962) also argued that the more successful negotiators are in spelling out every possible ancillary dimension, the more likely it will be that the agreement will founder on the shoals of time. No detailed agreement is likely to stay the evolution of military technology, foresee the impact of economic changes, or anticipate any of the other factors that might effect

---

1. The modernized, follow-on version of the Lance short-range missile is supposed to have a range of 280 miles, just below the 300–3000 range for missiles that is prohibited under INF.

its attractiveness for the signatories. Decades before the Strategic Defense Initiative, Schelling and Halperin saw that technology could change in such a way that a restriction like that against the testing of an ABM system that formerly made a nation feel more secure, could suddenly be seen to stand in the way of achieving a greater level of security. At best, a rapid pace of technological events will leave negotiators in the position of constantly reopening discussions in order to catch up. At worst, the changes will make past agreements seem more like straitjackets than security blankets.

Schelling does not deal in any detail with the different tacit bargaining strategies that can be used to shape these expectations or their relative efficacy under various conditions. He does not, for example, discuss as we will in chapter 5, the relative merits of responding to a suspected violation by a violation of equal magnitude versus total treaty abrogation. He is more concerned with how intelligence and inspection strategies can minimize the need to employ such responses by reducing the possibility that a violation will go undetected. Increasing the probability of detection increases that chance of requiring a response, unless that increase in detection forces the other side to be more cautious in the first place. But he (and Halperin) recognize that the expected cost of a violation depends on the penalty that will be assessed as well as on the probability of detection, and that this expectation will be shaped by tacit bargaining as well as rhetoric. It is to be expected that nations will test each others' resolve by cheating at the margin and the action that is taken in response will determine whether the cheating will stop or increase.

Schelling and Halperin are also sensitive to several problems with treaty enforcement that are important in tacit bargaining theory generally. Every system of monitoring is imperfect and vulnerable to the problems of producing mistaken evidence of cheating and missing a real violation. The obvious consequences of the second possibility, coupled with the natural risk aversion of most decision makers, leads them to emphasize the problem of detection failures. These "false positives" can destroy any prospects for the maintenance of an arms agreement. An arms race that is propelled by successive retaliations for nonexistent violations is no less real or costly than one that is propelled by attempts to achieve superiority. More perversely, nations that believe that they will be accused of cheating regardless of what they do may decide that they have no incentive not to refrain from cheating (Schelling and Halperin 1962, 95).

Schelling and Halperin emphasized that what is needed is a balance between the two types of error: nondetection and overdetection. But where should that balance be? What should determine it? Will any balance capable of coping with purposeful violations be unstable in the long run because it is vulnerable to overdetection caused by "noise"? Should we deal with this noise problem by retaliating at a rate less than one for one or Tit-for-Tat in order that an arms race generated by overly sensitive intelligence will die out? How much interpretive bias generated by risk aversion can a treaty survive and what does this tell us about the future of arms control? These sorts of questions—with which Schelling and Halperin do not deal—require something more than qualitative reflection. They will be addressed in chapter 5.

We do not mean to suggest that the only interpretation problem lies in determining whether or not a violation has occurred. Of equal importance is the more complicated issue of what a violation actually means in security terms. An isolated violation that takes place after a long period of good relations is not likely to be interpreted the same way as one that takes place as part of a long series of violations or in time of crisis (Larson 1989). Nor is it likely to merit or provoke the same tacit bargaining response. Schelling and Halperin recognized this and stressed the role that the interpretation of intentions would have to play in treaty maintenance. The appropriate response to an apparent increase in the other side's missile production facilities or its research and development program designed to shorten the lead time if the arms race is resumed, depends on the amount of collaborative evidence that the nation has aggressive intentions.

> If it appears that the other side would be able, in a crash program, to double the number of his missiles in a few weeks by hastening assembly, by utilizing spare components, by speeding deliveries, and by intensified maintenance of the missiles that he has, this may be dangerous or not—strategically significant or not—

according as he is or is not taking other action consistent with intentions to launch an attack within some
comparable period of time. (Schelling and Halperin
1962, 117)

Any knowledge of the way that governments operate—of the
games that are played between and within agencies, of the independent actions that are sometimes taken by subordinates—
suggests that some care is needed to ensure that we not exaggerate the significance of any particular action. This dictum is easily
forgotten, particularly when the action is potentially threatening.
In part this is a consequence of the risk aversion referred to above.
It may also be the result of the "attribution bias" that leads people to attribute the actions of others to calculation and willfulness
even as they excuse comparable behavior on their own part as
the result of uncontrollable forces. A member of Congress might
point to an increase in Soviet military spending or the construction of a new facility as unmistakable evidence of an intention to
resume the arms race even as he or she justifies a similar move on
the part of the United States as a trivial consequence of a change
in membership to the House Appropriations or Armed Services
Committees. Schelling and Halperin summarize the difficulties of
interpretation quite nicely.

In the usual analogy of the detective vs. the criminal,
one gathers his evidence and springs it on the subject with all the implications of guilt. But there is a
difference between willful breaking of the law and normal bending of the rules, between tight conspiracy and
disorganized bureaucracy. In one case you indict your
enemy; in the other you argue with him. In the one
case he is either guilty or is not (whether or not you
can prove it); in the other case it is a matter of judgement, with room for genuine differences of opinion, and
with a possible gamut of motives between extremes
of willful, conspiratorial, hierarchical cheating on the
one hand, and innocently disorganized stretching of
the rules on the other. Even criminal cases have that
nice simplicity only in paperback fiction. (Schelling
and Halperin 1962, 119)

As noted in chapter 1, if uncertainty and interpretation problems are enormous, the advantages that tacit bargaining offers in relation to formal negotiation are likely to be mitigated. The benefits that it provides in dealing with a rapidly changing environment can be more than offset in a cacophony of confused and confusing signals. At best, a nation will be frustrated by the unresponsiveness of its rival; at worst the arms race will spiral in response to mutual misinterpretations and punishments. The trick is (1) to estimate what level of uncertainty and interpretation problems is so great that the dangers of tacit bargaining outweigh its advantages; and (2) to understand what conditions are associated with what degree of uncertainty and misinterpretation. Simulation in combination with game theory can address the first issue. The second requires a close reading of history.

Other aspects of the negotiation/tacit-bargaining tradeoff and, by extension, limitations of tacit bargaining are scattered through Schelling's writings. For example, he acknowledges that there is probably some correlation between the comprehensiveness and complexity of the arms agreement that is sought and the role that tacit bargaining is likely to play. When there are dozens of separate dimensions that need to be incorporated in an agreement, the vocabulary of tacit bargaining is so limited and imprecise, and the time required to conduct it so great, that it will be overwhelmed by interpretation problems. The problems will be further exacerbated if a variety of the issues involve incommensurate weapons systems or systems that might legitimately be viewed as offensive or defensive. It is not difficult to imagine the confusion of trying to establish tacitly an exchange rate by which to trade off land-based against sea-based missiles or, worse, of Soviet conventional forces against tactical nuclear weapons or cruise missiles.

In the same vein, Schelling realized that tacit agreements were probably more effective in promoting mutual restraint than collaborative action. Things that nations will do for each other—just as the benefits that management will provide for labor—will usually have to be negotiated and formalized. No country is likely to agree tacitly to the placement of seismic sensors within its boundaries or to periodic inspections of top secret bases and manufacturing facilities (except by satellite, which involves a more passive acquiescence than permitting foreign nationals access to secure facili-

ties). Understandings about the infinite variety of new initiatives
that nations might take to gain an arms advantage—like the infinite variety of behaviors that labor can use to harass management
or vice versa—are likely to be tacit (Schelling and Halperin 1962,
79). The refusal to distribute nuclear weapons to third world client
states or to place them in space requires no agreement about the
relative value of one weapon system versus another. Such refusals
require no positive actions that disrupt organizational routines
or withdraw benefits from an internal interest group, and they
involve a qualitatively distinct boundary that reduces the potential for misinterpretation. Each quality enhances the potential for
tacit bargaining.

It is now possible to place Schelling's contribution to tacit
bargaining and arms control in perspective. He did not directly
address, much less solve, all of the central questions. His under-
standable preoccupation with the task of introducing his audience
to the virtues of tacit bargaining kept him from developing a systematic theory that could guide the selection of the optimal tacit
bargaining strategy in a given context or tell us how stable the
resultant equilibrium (if any) might be. Yet his discussions of
the advantages of tacit bargaining versus formal negotiation permit the reader to infer a good deal about the character of a more
general theory. If problems of uncertainty, bias, control, and interpretation should be taken into consideration before a nation acts
to punish a suspected treaty offender, they will doubtless need to
be considered when designing (or evaluating) a theory that hopes
to explain how an arms race can be slowed in the absence of any
treaty. This is typical of his contribution and also the source of
the common impression that Schelling was the Newton of security
strategy. The questions that he inspires the reader to ask, even if
he does not address them directly, define an agenda for theoretical
and empirical research on tacit bargaining and arms control that
is remarkable for its completeness.

2.1   Prisoner's Dilemma Research

At about the same time Schelling began to reflect on the general
topic of tacit bargaining, other scholars were beginning a program of intensive experimental research on one archetypal tacit

bargaining situation: the iterated Prisoner's Dilemma. While we have argued that it does not provide the perfect model for every arms race, it almost certainly captures the incentive structure and underlying dynamic of some of them. As early as 1957, Luce and Raiffa had predicted that when the number of iterations is high, intelligent people would play a cooperative strategy. This would be true even though mutual defection could be argued to constitute an equilibrium that is undominated. They would do so because of a fear that the benefits of any defection would be outweighed by reprisals levied by a vengeful opponent. The fact that those operating in the military or political spheres acted otherwise—a point that hardly escaped their notice—was attributed to a "single play orientation" (Luce and Raiffa 1957, 101).

Experiments by Scodel et al. (1959) and Bixenstine et al. (1963) contradicted expectations of cooperation. Their findings indicated that iteration in the classic two-person, two-choice Prisoner's Dilemma resulted in increased competition rather than cooperation. Anatol Rapoport and Albert Chammah (1965) corroborated these somewhat disheartening findings where there are less than fifty iterations, but discovered that the decline in cooperation is reversed as the number of trials continues to increase. After 150 trials, 65–70 percent of the experimental pairs of subjects were cooperating. If one were to believe that the laboratory version of the Prisoner's Dilemma and the experimental subjects involved were both representative of actual arms races, this suggests that the "single play orientation" observed by Luce and Raiffa may disappear with experience. From this point of view, military and political leaders do not embrace a more cooperative strategy simply because they have not played the "game" long enough. The good news is that, when this experience is present, stable cooperation will result. The bad news is that we may be talking about a level of experience that will rarely be acquired by leaders who hold office for normal lengths of time.

For those interested in promoting cooperation in arms race environments, Rapoport and Chammah's findings are noteworthy for another reason. Among the many variables that they manipulated was the presentation of the basic matrix describing the payoffs to both players. That is, the exact nature of the game was revealed to some of the pairs of experimental subjects but not to others. Rapoport and Chammah reasoned that subjects ignorant of the structure of the game would, through simple trial and error, arrive at a state of mutual cooperation more quickly than those who knew that their opponent had a strong temptation to defect. Those ignorant of their opponent's payoffs would doubtless experiment with defection but the retaliation that this would provoke would quickly teach them the virtues of cooperation. They believed that this learned cooperation would evolve more slowly when the structure of the game was revealed because the awareness that the opponent would always stand to gain from defection would create a constant fear of exploitation. "It would be better for cooperation, we thought, if these brutal facts were not explicitly before the subjects' eyes" (Rapoport and Chammah 1965, 53).

Curiously, the results ran counter to these expectations. Subjects to whom the game was revealed cooperated twice as often as those who played the game "blind" (54). While the second group also increased their rate of cooperation as time went on, the increase was small and remained less than 30 percent after 300 iterations (101)! Rapoport and Chammah concluded that knowledge of the game's basic structure served to remind the players of the mutual benefits that were possible regardless of the formal game-theoretic prescription.

This is a finding that should provoke some second thoughts among those who hope to extrapolate the optimistic results of experimental studies where participants are informed about the payoffs to real-world situations. How often are opponents presented with a payoff structure in which they can have perfect confidence? While doubtless this happens on occasion, it is arguable that the archetypal case resembles that in which players must grope their way to an understanding of the game that they are engaged in. If subjects operating in an unbiased information environment that is structured as a perfect Prisoner's Dilemma cannot discover the benefits of cooperation, what are we to expect from national decision makers?

Experimental research quickly moved from exploring the question of how experienced subjects behave in the Prisoner's Dilemma to the relative effectiveness of various strategies in promoting cooperation. Some of the earliest studies deal with the relative efficacy of unconditional versus conditional strategies. Sermat (1964), Shure et al. (1965), and Deutsch et al. (1967) all found that a person who cooperates unconditionally will be exploited by his or her competitor. This exploitation was not universal— there were usually competitors who responded positively to such generosity—but it seemed to provide compelling testimony to the explanatory power of self-interest. More notable, from the stand-point of ending an arms race, was that very few of the players facing an opponent with a history of defection would again place themselves in a vulnerable position by experimentally cooperat-ing. A period of betrayal often seemed to breed permanent dis-trust (Rapoport and Chammah 1965).

Constant cooperation or defection do not exhaust the range of potential unconditional strategies. There are an infinite number of other possibilities. One could begin by defecting and then grad-ually become more cooperative or play some more or less complex mixed strategy where cooperation and defection are interchanged according to some rule (or randomly). Experimentalists have dis-covered that a strategy that begins with zero cooperation and gradually increases to 100 percent cooperation is more effective than a purely cooperative strategy (Scodel 1962) and that pro-ceeding from a low level of cooperation to a high level of cooper-ation is more effective than the opposite strategy (Oskamp 1971, Patchen 1987). The first finding suggests that there is value in showing an opponent that one possesses the will and the capabil-ity to inflict a penalty. Translated to the world of arms control, a nation might achieve long-term arms stability by demonstrating its short-term willingness to engage in an arms race with a rival. The second finding about the effect of less and less cooperation is consistent with the expectations that we would have developed on the basis of the work described above: a pattern of defection on the part of one subject inevitably provokes similar behavior in an opponent.

The results of natural play and the responses to unconditional strategies soon led researchers to investigate the effect of condi-tional strategies in which the choice of cooperation or defection is in some measure contingent on the behavior of the opponent. Almost immediately attention focused on the efficacy of a match-ing, or Tit-for-Tat, strategy. This was logical. Such a strategy rewarded cooperation, did not provoke retaliation, and provided a means to prevent exploitation. It was also consistent with a basic tenet of behavioral psychology: reinforce good behavior and punish bad behavior. Nonetheless, the first results of experiments designed to explore the effectiveness of Tit-for-Tat were mixed. On the negative side, Sermat (1964) found that Tit-for-Tat produced no increase in cooperation over 100 trials. Oskamp and Perlman (1965) discovered a decrease over thirty trials. And Sermat (1967) observed no change over 200 trials. Other investigators such as Deutsch et al. (1967), Komorita (1965), Rapoport (1964), Scodel (1962), and Solomon (1960) found that Tit-for-Tat did produce increased cooperativeness.

Unable to resolve the contradictory findings of these studies but convinced that the occasional superiority of Tit-for-Tat over noncontingent strategies was indicative of the advantages of contingent approaches in general, researchers began to explore other such strategies. Would a strict Tit-for-Tat be dominated by one that began with cooperation? If so, how much cooperation should there be? An initially cooperative move followed by a strict Tit-for-Tat seemed sensible, yet the Bixenstein and Wilson (1963) study had shown that it was sometimes effective to establish a pattern of noncooperation before cooperating. Once the decision was made to cooperate, how large and enduring should the gesture be? It seemed sensible that a single cooperative gesture would not be sufficient to defuse mistrust that had built up over time, but there is also a clear incentive for a nation to feign distrust for purposes of exploitation. The nature of retaliation also posed dilemmas. Should one retaliate quickly to demonstrate that one would not be taken advantage of, or more slowly in order to show that the commitment to cooperate was real? Should one attempt to reinforce the lesson that defection has its costs by adopting a revengeful strategy that responds to a single defection by defecting two or three times?

Wilson (1971) undertook the task of investigating a number of these questions. He examined what occurred when teams of two players faced (1) other teams with no prescribed strategy (natural play) and (2) artificial opponents playing four other strategies. One was a straight Tit-for-Tat. Another, more generous strategy would never defect for more than three moves without cooperating. A third would never defect for more than two moves without cooperating. A fourth strategy was more vengeful. It punished every defection with two defections of its own. Wilson further enriched the study by investigating the effects of three pretest conditions. Before players faced any of the four strategies listed above they were exposed to one of three "pretests": five defections followed by a cooperative choice, thirty defections, or a baseline condition of no preliminary experience.

The results were encouraging for proponents of Tit-for-Tat. It produced the most cooperation and the difference between it and its rivals was statistically significant. The vengeful strategy came in second, followed by the two conciliatory strategies. Natural play in which players create their own strategies came in last— something that we might have predicted on the basis of other studies. Each of the programmed strategies produced an increase in cooperation over time with Tit-for-Tat reaching a plateau rate of 80 percent cooperation after 100 iterations. The superiority of Tit-for-Tat over the more generous strategies was interesting because Tit-for-Tat was vulnerable to being "locked-in" to an endless pattern of defection from which the other strategies could escape. At least in this case, the opponents were more likely to exploit the generous strategies than to lose themselves in a pattern of endless retaliation.

The results of the pretests were provocative. Each of the programmed strategies produced the most cooperation after being preceded by five defections and one cooperation. In every case, the thirty defection pretest ranked second, and the no pretest condition came in last. Wilson acknowledged that this finding conflicted with Komorita and Mechling (1967), Pilisuk et al. (1965), Sermat (1967), and Terhune (1968). Although he could find no explanation to account for the variation in findings, he speculated that an initial pattern of defection created a baseline in regard to which subsequent cooperation seemed more attractive. This is consistent with the experimental results on noncontingent strategies that seemed to suggest that exploitation is best avoided by demonstrating a willingness to defect. On the other hand, it runs counter to the wealth of evidence that spoke to the consequences of the "lock-in" effect in which defection creates bitterness and distrust that is rarely overcome. Perhaps there is some sort of curvelinear relationship between past defections and the propensity to extend cooperation. That is, a point exists before which a history of mutual uncooperativeness makes an opponent more sensitive to the benefits of mutual cooperation but beyond which yields only resentment. If so, where is this point? How much does it vary and why?

Overall, one comes away from the experimental literature with a strong faith in the superiority of conditional over unconditional strategies, and a somewhat less strong faith in the superiority of Tit-for-Tat. It is true that Tit-for-Tat did better than two more generous and one more vengeful strategy in the first analysis. But it is also true that Tit-for-Tat preceded by various numbers of defections did significantly better. A strategy of reciprocity preceded by five defections is not the same as a strict Tit-for-Tat strategy or one that begins with a cooperative move. Despite some significant victories, the robustness of a strict Tit-for-Tat strategy versus other contingent variations in the context of a full information Prisoner's Dilemma—much less in an arms race complicated by information and control problems—was still very much in doubt.

2.2   Robert Axelrod and the Evolution of Cooperation

The stage was set for a fresh approach to the evaluation of contingent strategies, and it was realized in a series of articles and a book, *The Evolution of Cooperation*, by Robert Axelrod (1984). Part of the novelty lay in Axelrod's methodology. Instead of recording the behavior of college student subjects as they encountered a number of specified strategies, he organized two computer tournaments in which the contestants were professional social scientists, natural scientists, and mathematicians. From the standpoint of generalizing the results to arms races, this change in participants may not seem to constitute much of an improvement over the average laboratory study. It is not obvious that the national leaders responsible for conducting arms races have any more in common with professors than with college sophomores. In fact, however, the change in sample populations was almost certainly an improvement. Strategic decisions about arms policies are likely to be influenced, if not necessarily determined, by experienced and sophisticated people; it is reasonable to assume that the passage of time will produce ever more "intelligent" strategies.

The rules of the first tournament were simple. Contestants were to submit a computer program that would define a strategy that would compete with every other strategy, itself, and a random strategy that defects and cooperates with equal probability in a 200-move game. The strategy that managed to accrue the most points overall would be declared the victor.

The winner was the simplest strategy of the fourteen entered: Tit-for-Tat. Appropriately, it had been submitted by Anatol Rapoport, the individual who has probably done the most experimental and mathematical research on the Prisoner's Dilemma. Of the 600 points that are possible to achieve if both players cooperate with each other on every move, Tit-for-Tat achieved an average score of 504. The second-place winner came in with a very close 500 and even the strategy that placed eighth scored a 471. A difference of 4 (or 33) points is not that great and Axelrod was careful not to overinterpret his findings. He did note, however, that those strategies that placed ninth or lower did far more poorly than the top eight finishers. They differed from the more successful strategies in an important respect. Each of the more successful strategies possessed the virtue of being "nice," in the sense that they were never the first to defect in competition with a rival. Of the group of nice strategies, Tit-for-Tat seemed to fare best because it possessed the additional virtues of being "forgiving" and optimistic about the prospects for cooperation. By forgiving, Axelrod meant that when betrayed Tit-for-Tat did not insist on punishing the offender for more than one round. True, Tit-for-Tat could be caught in an endless series of reprisals and re-reprisals against an opponent that defected and then insisted on cooperation before it would itself cooperate. However, it avoided this "echo" problem against a strategy that tried to exploit a cooperative opponent by defecting for one or more moves prior to returning to a policy of cooperation. The reader might wonder whether a strategy that was more forgiving than Tit-for-Tat and, therefore, more likely to avoid echo problems might have done still better. The answer is yes. A strategy of Tit-for-Two-Tats would have won the first tournament.

The victory of Tit-for-Tat was interesting but it was hard to know how much to make of it. Inevitably, the performance of any strategy is a function of those it is matched against and $N = 13$ hardly exhausted the potential competition. The question remained as to how Tit-for-Tat would fare against a wider range of strategies. There was also the issue of how it would perform against strategies designed by people who were aware of the first tournament's outcome. Real-world decision makers can be expected to learn something from past experience. Iterative Prisoner's Dilemmas afford the perfect context for adaptive learning, and it would only be expected that the initial success of Tit-for-Tat or any other strategy would be observed and assimilated.

In order to address these issues, Axelrod held a second tournament designed to explore the robustness of Tit-for-Tat by increasing the diversity and sophistication of the competition. Sixty-two entries were elicited from six countries and competitors were provided with the results and some preliminary analysis of the first tournament. Each contestant knew that Tit-for-Tat had won the first round and knew that the source of its strength seemed to reside in the fact that it was both nice and forgiving. The only difference in the rules of the tournament was that the length of the contest was determined probabilistically to avoid endgame effects.

The result? Tit-for-Tat emerged victorious again. As in the case of the first tournament, it was the shortest of all of the programs entered and, although the rules permitted any contestant to submit any program, the only person to submit it was the previous winner, Anatol Rapoport. The margin of victory was close. Tit-for-Tat achieved a score of 434.73 (unending mutual cooperation throughout the tournament would have yielded a score of 453); however, the second- and third-place winners both scored over 430 and the top twelve finishers all scored over 420.

Axelrod's analysis of the results reaffirmed the lessons of the first tournament with one important addition. Each of the successful strategies possessed the virtues of being nice, forgiving, and optimistic. It also turned out to be helpful to retaliate promptly. This characteristic was important because a number of the new programs were designed to exploit "soft" echo-avoiding strategies like Tit-for-Two-Tats through occasional defection. Since these strategies were sensitive to these echo effects themselves, they would try to take advantage and then quickly back down by cooperating if they were "caught." Tit-for-Tat made them back down in a forgiving way and ended up defeating them because the advantages that they gained in exploiting more generous strategies like Tit-for-Two-Tats was less than what they lost when facing more punitive strategies that would punish them severely for their transgressions.

This finding seemed to contradict the experimental results of social psychologists like Bixenstein and Gaebelein (1971), who had found that there was profit in being slow to retaliate to acts of untrustworthiness. Yet on closer examination, it is possible that this was less a contradiction than testimony to the fact that Axelrod was tapping into the role of learning in a way that the social psychologists often were not. If Bixenstein and Gaebelein had told their subjects that slow retaliation had proved to be the most effective strategy in their experiment and then informed them that they were going to repeat it, it is quite reasonable to assume that many of their subjects would embrace such a strategy. However, it is no less reasonable to predict that some of the more cunning would anticipate this development and adopt a strategy to exploit it. Should this occur, the results would be identical to those of Axelrod. One suspects that, in a real arms race, policymakers would have the opportunity, the intellectual resources, and the incentive to behave no less cunningly than Axelrod's contestants. Axelrod's second tournament forced contestants and strategies to cope with the harsh test of strategic reflection in a way that the experiments of social psychologists did not, and Tit-for-Tat had distinguished itself by surviving that test.

The results of the second tournament increase our confidence in the effectiveness of Tit-for-Tat in different environments. Indeed, it begins to stand out in this respect. Other strategies might be able to do as well in a given environment (like the case of Tit-for-Two-Tats in the first tournament), but their success is fragile. If the composition of the rival strategies changed as it could be expected to over time, their success dropped off dramatically. Tit-for-Tat, on the other hand, seemed to insure good performance regardless of the competition. If the competitors were cooperative, Tit-for-Tat was as cooperative as possible. If they were consistently hostile, Tit-for-Tat gave away an initial advantage but nothing more. If competitors followed a mixed strategy alternating between cooperation and defection, Tit-for-Tat retaliated in such a way that it prevented exploitation.

Axelrod was aware that the performance of any strategy depended on the character of the competition, and two tournaments did not begin to exhaust the range of possible environments. Exploring the robustness of Tit-for-Tat via simulation was the obvious next step. The precise procedure that Axelrod used in his simulations is well described in the appendix of his book and need not be recounted in detail here. Suffice it to say that he first discovered that there were five "representative" strategies that accounted for most of the variance in how the sixty-three submitted strategies performed. He then used simulation to vary systematically the distribution of these five strategies to create six radically different game environments. When the strategies were pitted against each other, Tit-for-Tat won five of the six simulated tournaments and came in second in the sixth. Tit-for-Tat had passed this test of robustness with flying colors.

The history of arms control provides some isolated support for Axelrod's findings. Hirst credits a policy of reciprocity with bringing about the longest period of cooperation between the British and French during the nineteenth century (Hirst 1913, 39), and Schelling (1960) noted its role in several instances of arms restraint between the United States and Soviet Union. Unfortunately, such examples cannot be found in abundance. As we saw in chapter 1, many arms races lead to war, and most of those that were peacefully concluded were not resolved by the adoption of any specific tacit bargaining strategy. It is important to ask why this is the case. Is ignorance about the usefulness of Tit-for-Tat causing national decision makers to miss the opportunity to control mutually undesirable arms races or is something else going on? Axelrod's results could be used to support the ignorance hypothesis. His tournaments showed that experts tended to be overly competitive and that very few of them were aware of the merits possessed by Tit-for-Tat. Should it surprise us that nations do no better?

On the other hand, it is useful to recall that a number of the experts in both tournaments did employ strategies that bear a close resemblance to Tit-for-Tat. Why don't nations do the same? If they are employing Tit-for-Tat, why isn't it working as well as it did in Axelrod's tournament? It is possible that the explanation lies in the lack of expert influence in national decision making. Perhaps government decision makers are not as perspicacious as professors with a taste for game theory and contests. But it is also possible that the national policymakers are operating in a world that differs in important ways from the one in which Axelrod's contestants were competing. Indications of this problem lurk in the background of one of the book's most widely cited examples. Axelrod tells us that there were numerous instances during World War I when German and Allied soldiers established a tacit bargain based on Tit-for-Tat to stop the fighting so that they might collect the injured and dead, escape water-filled trenches, and gain a general respite from the endless shelling. These temporary truces would have persisted had it not been for orders from above or the behavior of long-range artillery troops who would choose to reengage. These anecdotes should prompt the reflective reader to wonder why the military or civilian leaders did not engage in similar behaviors. It is possible that they were ignorant of Tit-for-Tat and the possibilities that it offered. More likely, however, the explanation lies elsewhere. They probably did not use Tit-for-Tat to construct a truce because the "game" in which they were engaged differed from that which plagued the troops in the trenches. The payoff of victory may have appeared greater, the prospect and cost of loss smaller, the clarity of "signals" between the two sides more ambiguous, or a dozen other factors. Any of these factors could have resulted in Tit-for-Tat failing or, more likely, have created expectations that led to its never being seriously employed.

In Axelrod's tournament and subsequent simulations, Tit-for-Tat had proved itself to be robust across environments defined by the distribution of rival strategies. This is a singular accomplishment. However, if it is to be applied with any confidence to the problem of slowing an arms race, it must also demonstrate its robustness in coping with the complications that we discussed in the previous chapter. Would Tit-for-Tat do as well in a situation where players did not know the game they were playing? Where control and interpretation problems were rampant? Where players began, as they would in an arms race, with the knowledge that their rival had defected many times in the past? Would it have to be modified in any way when players could adopt continuous strategies that would permit varying degrees of cooperation and defection? In theory, two players using Tit-for-Tat under perfect information will begin an endless period of cooperation. How sanguine is the forecast when conditions change?

Axelrod did not explore the implications of all of the conditions that we believe distinguish arms races from laboratory Prisoner's Dilemma, but he realized that the assumption of perfect information was a potentially vulnerable point in his analysis. Misinterpretation or missed signals plague any area to which he might want to generalize his results: marriage behavior, oligopoly formation, domestic politics, or international political economy. To look at the matter more closely, he ran the first round of the tournament again with the modification that every choice had a probability of misperception of 1 percent. Axelrod was pleased to find that while this resulted in more defections, Tit-for-Tat still emerged as the dominant strategy. Interestingly, the susceptibility of Tit-for-Tat to echo effects was partly offset by subsequent misinterpretations. Just as a misperceived cooperative move could set off a pattern of mutual defections, so a misperceived defection could ignite a pattern of cooperation. Less forgiving rules suffered because they demanded more than a single cooperative gesture before they would cooperate.

Readers interested in the applicability of Tit-for-Tat to arms races might be heartened by these results, but there is still reason to be cautious. A 1 percent rate of misinterpretation departs from the assumption of perfect information but real-world rates, conditioned on histories of defection and imperfect intelligence, are probably much higher. Is Tit-for-Tat as successful when the rate of misinterpretation is 5 percent or 10 percent? There is also the problem that the rival strategies—which were weaker and less diverse in the first tournament than the second tournament—were designed to cope with a full information environment. Would Tit-for-Tat do as well against strategies expressly designed to deal with misinterpretation problems? The reader might also wonder how well the winning strategy does at promoting cooperation in this situation. Does Tit-for-Tat still end up promoting a good deal of cooperation in this degraded environment or is it only the best of a bad lot?

Tit-for-Tat's effectiveness in environments with more than 1 percent rates of misinterpretation and against strategies designed to deal with unreliable information will be explored at length in chapters 4 and 5. We can anticipate the flavor of this discussion, however, by looking at the case where there is a misinterpretation rate of 1 percent from a somewhat different perspective than did Axelrod. Recall that, as well as its relative performance, one of the most impressive aspects of the tournament results was the absolute level of cooperation Tit-for-Tat managed to inspire. This allowed Axelrod to talk about the favorable prospects for an evolution of cooperation in a variety of realms. Yet with a misinterpretation rate of even 1 percent, a game between two opponents each employing a Tit-for-Tat strategy stabilizes with at least one party defecting 75 percent of the time (Downs et al. 1985, 141). This means that the adoption of Tit-for-Tat would not only fail to end an arms race that was in progress, it would result in the initiation of a race where there had been none. Other strategies may do worse, but this is small comfort for those who hoped that tacit bargaining would provide an answer to continued arms escalation.

Fortunately, an alternative strategy immediately suggests itself. The reason for the suboptimal outcome for Tit-for-Tat under conditions of imperfect information is that each side is too willing to defect. A little more patience would seem to be called for. One way to approach the problem without departing from the basic Tit-for-Tat strategy would be to employ a probabilistic Tit-for-Tat, in which the opponent's cooperation is followed by our cooperation with probability s and by our defection with probability $1 - s$; and in which the opponent's defection is followed by our defection or cooperation with probabilities s and $1 - s$, respectively. When the opponent appears to have defected we will defect with some probability less than 1, thus being somewhat more patient. To see how this works, let us assume a more realistic misinterpretation rate of 5 percent. Suppose also that both countries decide to behave more forgivingly, treating a defection as a defection only part of the time, for example 50 percent. In that case, one or both sides will defect only 17 percent of the time, a much more satisfactory outcome. Even if only one country behaves forgivingly while the other pursues Tit-for-Tat, there is defection only

24 percent of the time. In short, a less provocable modification of Tit-for-Tat leads to considerably greater cooperation—and fewer arms races—under conditions of uncertainty.

The drawback of this less provocable version of Tit-for-Tat, of course, is that it is also more exploitable. If we calculate the long-run probabilities of each outcome between the less provocable version of Tit-for-Tat and a pure Tit-for-Tat strategy, we discover that the former will be exploited 4 percent of the time. An arms race is avoided but at a cost. This cost may be worth paying since it buys a great deal of cooperation and consequently saves defense dollars. Most liberals and others who believe that small increments of military superiority are almost meaningless would doubtless agree. Of course, many in this group would also view a higher exploitation rate (e.g., 25 percent) as also being reasonable. It is just as obvious that many conservatives would take the opposite view. There is no way to resolve this conflict without convincing one of the two groups to value marginal superiority differently than they do at present. We can, however, be explicit about the precise benefits and costs in the context of a specific model and even analytically address the important question of what implicit price the two views are placing on marginal superiority vis-à-vis cost and what discount rate they would have to employ to adopt the views that they hold. The results of this kind of analysis can lead to healthy introspection that would never be achieved if the level of discourse remained general and abstract. It is one thing to believe that MAD makes small differences in forces irrelevant and another to embrace a strategy that implies that a cumulative difference of 40 percent that occurs over time will have no policy implications. Similarly, it is one thing to maintain a belief in the virtues of superiority or absolute equality and another to acknowledge that the price of such a policy may be an endless arms race.

Fortunately, it is possible to reduce exploitation by being more clever. A nation could, for example, adopt a strategy in which the probability of response varies. If it "discovered" that the pattern of moves suggested that there was exploitation in addition to misinterpretation, it could become tougher. That is, when apparent defection on the part of the opponent exceeded some threshold, the strategy would call for defecting in response 75 percent of the time instead of 50 percent. This action would result in a greater percentage of incorrect overreactions and temporarily, at least, lead to less cooperation than was the case with the 50 percent rate. In the long run, it should increase cooperation by teaching the opponent that cheating would not go unrecognized or unpunished. Knowing precisely what strategy to adopt when there is an infinite number of shadings to choose from and conditions are complex requires careful calculation. It is equally important to be careful in deciding whether an opponent is cheating or whether one has simply underestimated the amount of misinterpretation that is taking place.

2.3 Charles Osgood and GRIT

In the early 1960s, Charles E. Osgood published a book and several articles in which he detailed a tacit bargaining–based vision of reversing the arms race and tension between the two superpowers. It was based on a strategy he called Graduated Reciprocation in Tension Reduction or GRIT for short. His general approach to arms control was motivated by two melancholy conclusions about the nature of international relations and the cold war. The first concerned the reliability of deterrence as a source of security. Osgood, like many before and after him, believed that stable deterrence was predicated on perfect intelligence information and a degree of self-restraint that might be plausible in the short run, but seemed naive in the long run. At best, miscalculations about the capabilities and intentions of the other side would lead to periodic outbreaks of arms escalation and system instability. At worst, a long time-horizon would transform any event of small probability into a likelihood and finally lead to war. To rest the future "on the shifting sands of human fallibility and hoping that it will somehow last forever" seemed to surrender passively to fate.

The limitations of deterrence inspired Osgood to search for "another alternative to war or surrender." His reflections on the history of U.S.-Soviet negotiations determined the precise character such an alternative would have to take. He believed that both sides genuinely desired peace but were equally prone to blame the other side for the absence of an arms agreement and to hold out lit-

tle real hope for progress. The last conclusion seemed inescapable
from Osgood's observations of the "woefully" inadequate technical preparations of negotiators and the corresponding absence of
government support for the study of nonaggressive solutions to
international disputes. His general, if reluctant, assessment of
arms negotiation is succinctly summarized in the 1962 book that
contains the most elaborate expression of his philosophy:

> Negotiated agreements require commitments from both
> sides prior to any action by either, and under circum-
> stances of cold war thinking commitments of any sig-
> nificance seem most unlikely; as long as both sides re-
> main chained to the requirement of prior commitment
> from the other, neither is able to take the initiative in
> moving toward a more peaceful world. (Osgood 1962,
> 84)

Contemporary readers familiar with game theory and/or the
history of the intervening 25 years would doubtless view this argument as overdrawn. To say that human fallibility makes "sta-
bilized deterrence" impossible to maintain is not to demonstrate
that periodic arms races increase the probability of war in an environment of mutually assured destruction. The history of the U.S.-
Soviet arms race provides us with instances where arms stocks
have grown or been modernized without a dramatic increase in
tension (e.g., during Reagan's second administration). Similarly,
the linkage between a finite probability of war in a given year and
the ultimate inevitability of war rests on the assumption that the
probability of war is independent across years and will not decrease over time. This may not be true. Just as success breeds
success, peace may breed peace. Arms spirals notwithstanding, it
is difficult to imagine that a prolonged arms race like that between
the United States and the Soviet Union does not reduce the perception that war is inevitable. This should correspondingly reduce
the chances that either side will engage in a war of prevention or
preemption.

There are other reasons why one or both sides may free themselves from the "chains" of the past without a prior commitment
from the other sides. Leaving aside the potential of Star Wars
weaponry that will be addressed later in this volume, innovations

can reduce sources of human fallibility such as inaccurate information about an opponent's actions and unreliable weapons control systems. National goals can also evolve in directions that might reduce the probability of war independent of any cooperative gesture. No one who has studied the arms policy of any nation for an extended length of time has failed to appreciate the extent to which it is affected by domestic politics. Arms races between the United States and Britain, and France and Britain provide compelling (if occasional) evidence that the effect can be benign.[2]

Osgood was led to advocate a tacit bargaining approach to arms control through his observations of how arms races evolved, as well as the failed attempts to bring them to an end. Like many others before and after him, he believed that arms races are propelled by a graduated spiral that was partly the product of unilateral action and partly the product of reciprocal response. The unilateral component derived from the fact that one of the nations takes the initiative to develop a new weapon or increase its stockpile. The reciprocal component of the race stems from the stimulus that this action provides the other to try to catch up and go ahead. Osgood described the process as graduated because of its dependence on continuously emerging technological innovations and the oscillating nature of the threat stimulus.

Osgood reasoned that by creatively exploiting these same attributes of unilateral initiative, reciprocity, and graduation, the spiral of terror generated by a tension-increasing system could be replaced by a spiral of trust generated by a tension-decreasing system. The key to stability was not a complicated treaty that would cut the Gordian knot of fear and distrust through abrupt and complete disarmament, but a systematic reversal of the pro-

---

2. Osgood was also too pessimistic about the potential of formal negotiation and the character of the contribution that it could make. For example, his preoccupation with the extent to which negotiations necessitate prior commitments supplied him with one of the key inspirations for his theory but it also led him to overlook an important area where this disadvantage could be helpful: future arms deployment. The very inability of the two superpowers to agree on dramatic arms reductions played a critical role in directing attention toward limitations on systems that had yet to be developed, such as space weaponry and anti-ballistic missiles, and numbers of weapons yet to be deployed. These agreements were not only significant in themselves but created modest precedents that set the stage for further agreements in much the same way as the tacit bargaining scheme that he would describe.

cess by which they evolved. This was the essence of GRIT. In practice, it called for the United States to make a unilateral gesture of cooperation and encourage the Soviet Union to follow suit. The gesture would be large enough to reveal sincerity but not so large as to make the United States vulnerable to any military action. To maximize the chances that the Soviet Union would not misinterpret that action as stemming from weakness or a lack of resolve, the motivation for the action would be well publicized. To maximize the chances that the move would be taken seriously, the promise would be held out that this was just the beginning of what could be a long and mutually beneficial process. The incentive to respond positively would be further increased by the assurance that if the offer was rejected and the Soviet Union attempted to exploit U.S. generosity, the latter would do everything in its power to return to the former status quo.

One major difference between GRIT and the proposals of many other arms control activists is its exploitation of the deterrent effects of nuclear weapons. Osgood thought it would be irrational to call for the elimination of nuclear weapons even though he agreed that the arms race mentality that called for more and more weapons was dangerous and perverse. The weapons' very destructiveness provided the United States the security that it needed to initiate unilateral gestures toward a foe that it distrusted. While it might be more emotionally satisfying to ban the bomb entirely than to reduce stockpiles to the point where each nation possessed a minimum deterrent and then—just as cautiously—reduce the size of conventional forces, this attitude ignored the enormous potential of instability that derived from the possibility of concealing nuclear weapons. It also ignored the likelihood that nuclear weapons deterred the escalation possibilities historically associated with conventional forces.

While it is easy to characterize GRIT in a few simple sentences, its sensitive implementation in a complex, political environment is not quite so straightforward. Osgood was fully aware of this. A belief in the importance of the enterprise with which he was involved, coupled with an appreciation for how easily innovative proposals can be patronized into obscurity by policymakers, led him to set out the requirements for GRIT's success in great detail. Here, for example, are some of the seventeen rules of thumb that should guide the character of unilateral initiatives (Osgood 1962, 95ff):

1. *Unilateral initiatives must be graduated in risk according to the degree of reciprocation obtained.* This keeps the relative risk of any given action virtually constant. That is, "clear reciprocation by an opponent of an earlier step makes it possible for us to take a larger step with no greater real risk than another small step would have meant before" (95).
2. *Initiatives must be diversified in nature, both as to sphere of action and as to geographical locus of application.* This increases the number of gestures that are available and diversifies the risk.
3. *Unilateral initiatives must be unpredictable with respect to their location and character.* Osgood believed that this reduced the chance of exploitation that might occur if initiatives could be anticipated. It also would help to convince world opinion that this was a gesture specifically designed to inspire cooperation rather than part of a well-established strategy that had some other end.
4. *The precise nature of the reciprocation is less important than the spirit behind it.* In some cases the invitation might be open-ended with respect to the nature of the response, and it is not unlikely that reciprocation would be "unbalanced" from a purely objective standpoint. For example, the United States should not demand that the Soviets necessarily replicate the amount of inspection that it was willing to permit.
5. *Unilateral initiatives must be continued over a considerable period, regardless of the response that they inspire.* The sincerity of our commitment to arms control is more likely to be revealed through a series of small gestures than through a single dramatic action.

Although the requirement that the nation initiating the cooperative gesture announce its intention may give it the semblance of negotiation, it should be clear that GRIT is an archetypal tacit bargaining strategy. It is inspired by the difficulties of formal negotiation; it assumes that actions have a greater potential than words for coping with the distrust that builds up during the course of an arms race; it is iterative; and the manner by which it unfolds is affected by the actions of the other party. Osgood's appreciation for these last two aspects of tacit bargaining reflect a strong intuitive appreciation for the dynamic dimension of international relations. Indeed, his appreciation for the potential of learning in both domestic and international politics led him to look forward to the early problems that the implementation of GRIT might encounter with more relish than trepidation. What better way, he reasoned, to convince an opponent that exploitation was counterproductive and to prove to those skeptics on the domestic side (whom Osgood described, more out of frustration, one suspects, than meanness, as the "Neanderthal-minded") that GRIT had nothing to do with appeasement.

Even after any early problems were ironed out, GRIT might evolve in unexpected ways. Osgood tried to capture this quality by using a musical metaphor in which GRIT is compared to jazz. Just as a jazz musician must keep an ear on what the others in the group are doing, the GRIT tactician on either side must keep a vigilant eye on the behaviors of allies and neutrals in every corner of the globe as well as on the responses of the opponent. Just as the jazz musician "selects notes not singly but in thematic sequences, not rigidly according to a preconceived plan but flexibly in terms of what he has said before and what the others are now saying to him," so the GRIT tactician "selects new initiatives of his own—not in isolation and according to some prearranged plan, but in new sequences, flexibly designed to intensify the atmosphere of mutual trust and understanding" (Osgood 1962, 119).

While Osgood's reference to playing it by ear was largely motivated by the fact that expressions of cooperation might take various forms and emerge at an unpredictable pace, it also holds obvious advantages for dealing with unpredictable changes in technology and national priorities that can render the best treaty obsolete in a short time. The advantages of a system that responds to the inevitable innovations in weaponry without necessitating a new treaty are doubtless obvious. The resources that have been released by virtue of an arms agreement can all too easily be directed toward the development of new weapons. When this occurs a quantitative arms race is simply replaced by a qualitative race, producing an international environment that is likely to be less stable than the original situation. Through its flexibility and refusal to be bound by formulas, GRIT holds out the possibility that this problem will be dealt with as it begins to emerge. A nation that keeps to the formal provisions of a nuclear test ban treaty but begins testing a new category of chemical weapons cannot help but recognize the provocative character of its act.

Despite its many virtues, Osgood's proposal possessed some problems. One stems from his general normative orientation and his limited personal experience. He was a passionate supporter of the idea that the United States and Soviet Union were trapped in an arms race by a combination of mutual distrust and a mentality in which security and policy prestige were a function of weapons stocks. This is what the more enlightened deterrence approach would replace. The possibility that one or both of these assumptions might not be true—or might not always be true—was never entertained. As a result, part of GRIT's invulnerability to exploitation is more imagined than real.

As we have argued, close scrutiny of the arms race between the United States and Soviet Union suggests that it is not a homogenous phenomenon. During some periods it has possessed the characteristics of a Prisoner's Dilemma in which both sides would have benefitted from mutual cooperation and each would have done so if it had had confidence in the other. At other times this has not been the case. This fact alone would not disturb Osgood. He would fall back on his assertion that one of the major assets of GRIT is that the costs of a very small unilateral initiative that is spurned by an unreceptive rival are negligible. Suppose, however, that the nation not interested in arms control feigned interest but argued that the size of the gesture indicated that it was likely to be insincere or a trap. Should the nation that made the unilateral gesture respond by increasing it? By what amount? What happens if the leaders of the duplicitous nation make a smaller cooperative gesture in response and argue that this tendency will have to continue in order to satisfy domestic constituencies? (Recall the argument that the initiating nation should be amenable to open-ended or proportionate responses.) Osgood doesn't take these possibilities seriously because he doesn't take small differences in nuclear—or conventional—capability seriously. Unfortunately, this view is not always shared by those in power.

The idea that this potential for exploitation can best be avoided by diversifying the substance (i.e., military, cultural, economic, etc.) and geographic location of initiatives is also problematic. It is true that diversification reduces the chances that something critical will be sacrificed in a particular sphere, but at the potential cost of creating enormous confusion. Nations rarely, if ever, act in ways that are orchestrated to perfection. The history of events leading to both world wars is filled with gestures that are both cooperative and aggressive, and recent history tells much the same story. Superpower behavior that involves decreasing the troop strength in Europe while increasing arms shipments to third world governments is the rule, rather than the exception, and the reasons range from multiple goals and the impact of prior commitments to bureaucratic ineptness. How plausible is it that something as simple as GRIT will turn this cacophony of policies into arms control? As we shall see in chapter 4, misinterpretation makes tacit bargaining difficult under the best circumstances and increasing the complexity of the task increases the potential for misinterpretation.

The prescription to diversify the GRIT initiatives and subsequent reciprocal gestures across geographical and policy space may actually blind us to the ways tacit bargaining has been used most effectively. Any review of instances where tacit bargaining has been successful—within arms control or in international relations generally—would reveal that they are concentrated in very well-circumscribed policy areas that can be decomposed from the more general relations between the two countries. It was, for example, successfully used in Berlin to guarantee free movement within the city during the Blockade. Had any linkage been attempted between the issue of free movement within the city and that of free access to the city, no such cooperative outcome would have occurred. Similarly, it is hard to avoid the conclusion that tacit bargaining was useful in developing reciprocal satellite reconnaissance because care was taken *not* to entangle the issue with others. It is no coincidence that in these and similar cases, reciprocity was easy to define. Politicians unsympathetic to arms control will doubtless be able to develop plausible arguments as to why their nation's long-range bombers or intermediate-range missiles are not the same as those of the rival nation's, but their task will be made infinitely easier if they are presented with a tradeoff involving completely different weapon systems.

Osgood was modest enough to realize that considerable research would be needed before GRIT could be implemented with any confidence. It would be necessary to understand Soviet preferences and perceptions and how they differed from those of the United States; whether GRIT had to be altered to be used in conjunction with collective versus individual decision making; what contexts formed the most conducive background for unilateral gestures; and which unilateral gestures were likely to be the most productive. We would argue for the importance of adding to Osgood's list research on the impact of complexity, misinterpretation, and possible exploitation.

Given the continued salience of arms control on the public agenda and the scarcity of imaginative proposals about how progress might be achieved, it is not surprising that GRIT inspired an enormous amount of research. There have been well over a hundred articles that have addressed one or more aspects of the general theory. While it is impossible to review more than a handful of these works here, it is useful to relate some of their findings and to convey something of their general character. As will quickly become apparent, they represent an undeniable contribution to the theory of tacit bargaining. Their chief fault, and this is all too predictable, is that their range of inquiry has been narrow. Aspects of the theory that are amenable to experimental treatment have been given a great deal of attention. Aspects requiring historical investigation or the use of sophisticated simulation have received almost none.

One of the first experimental evaluations of GRIT was conducted by Pilisuk and Skolnick (1968). Subjects were presented with a 6 × 6 matrix based on the mixed motive logic of the Prisoner's Dilemma. The number of options was increased to permit the gradual introduction of cooperation that is the centerpiece of Osgood's proposal. The game explicitly dealt with arms control in the sense that the payoffs depended on the number of missiles the players possessed at its conclusion. Subjects played the game twenty-five times but were not informed of this fact in advance.

Pilisuk and Skolnick compared the performance of subjects playing in a natural setting with no experimenter interference with others who faced a programmed opponent that employed either a matching (Tit-for-Tat) strategy or a conciliatory strategy based on Osgood's prescription. Their results provided modest support for GRIT. They found that the conciliatory strategy produced a far greater rate of cooperation than that produced by natural play but only a marginally greater rate than that of the matching strategy.

Sixteen years later, Pilisuk (1984) returned to these issues by running a series of experiments that employed the same 6×6 matrix. The major difference was that the game rules now included the options of accepting or refusing inspection and engaging in surprise attacks. Two findings are notable. First, the relative performances of GRIT–like strategies were once again only slightly superior to Tit-for-Tat. (The difference was in favor of GRIT but was nonsignificant.) Second, there was a depressing tendency for players to use inspections in a manipulative manner and to engage in preemptive surprise attacks, even when there was little chance of success. The prospect that a unilaterally adopted contingent strategy like GRIT or Tit-for-Tat would inevitably produce cooperation seemed to be fading with the addition of real-world complications. In particular, uncertainty, manifesting itself as suspicion and fear, appeared to color the game in such a way that cooperation could not be easily produced by less-than-perfect inspection schemes.

Other experimental evaluations of the relative efficacy of GRIT have yielded more positive results. Working with groups as well as individuals, Lindskold and Collins (1978) found that GRIT produced more cooperation than (1) a competitive strategy in which announcements were used to mislead the opponent; (2) a Tit-for-Tat strategy without any verbal communication; or (3) a strategy that cooperated 50 percent of the time. The significance of these results is tempered somewhat by the fact that the format of the game was a conventional Prisoner's Dilemma that did not permit the gradual introduction of cooperation that is so fundamentally a part of GRIT. Because the authors worked only with a version of Tit-for-Tat that did not cooperate on its own initiative, it is also not clear whether GRIT's superiority stems from its verbal component, its willingness to cooperate at the beginning of play, or some combination of the two. In another study constructed along similar lines, Lindskold, Walters, and Koutsourais (1983) found some evidence to indicate that GRIT was capable of winning over individuals who had previously been classified as "competitors" at a rate somewhat greater than a Tit-for-Tat strategy with no initial cooperative gesture.

These studies are representative of the experimental literature on GRIT. They have shown GRIT to be far more effective than natural play and somewhat more effective than a strategy of Tit-for-Tat that does not begin with a cooperative gesture. However, they do not take us very far in our attempt to understand the relative merits provided by GRIT's distinguishing feature of gradual cooperation. Does the opportunity to initiate a small cooperative gesture that will not result in heavy costs if rejected increase a party's propensity to cooperate? Is there a significant difference between GRIT and the initially cooperative Tit-for-Tat strategy advocated by Axelrod? Will GRIT be exploited over a long period of time when its underlying logic is uncovered? Is GRIT effective under conditions of misinterpretation and uncertainty regarding the game that is being played? How do we decide the optimal size of the initial offer, that is, the balance between visibility and risk? These questions, which are critical from a policy standpoint, remain unaddressed.

2.4   Testing Tacit Bargaining Models

Not all evaluations of tacit bargaining strategies have taken place in the laboratory. There is a rich, if much smaller, literature that attempts to draw insights directly from the historical record. The historical approach would seem to possess some obvious advantages. It need not assume that a nation's decision-making apparatus will behave in the same way as a college sophomore. And it need not work with highly stylized representations of the decision-making context that can be criticized for being incorrect (e.g., the Prisoner's Dilemma is not the model for every arms race) or dangerously incomplete (e.g., one must allow for misinterpretation).

An early analysis of a natural experiment that contained elements of both formal negotiation and tacit bargaining was that by Amitai Etzioni (1967) of U.S.-Soviet relations between June

10 and November 22, 1963. Etzioni believed that a variety of international relations problems ranging from arms races to specific crises could be illuminated by what he termed a "psychological theory of international relations." The theory, which is described in only very general language, rested on the idea that the behavior of nations was determined by strong drives that both distort the communications that they send and receive and motivate their pursuit of certain goals. Arms races were a product of spiraling misperceptions. Regardless of the political or economic reasons that may have first motivated an arms increase on the part of one nation, they are soon drowned out by the psychological dimension. "The hostility of one as perceived by the other evokes his hostility, which in turn is perceived by the first side, further increasing his hostility" (Etzioni 1967, 361). In order for the arms race to slow, one of the nations must adopt a strategy that will break this vicious cycle.

While he did not use the term tacit bargaining, Etzioni argued that formal negotiations were an ineffective vehicle for tension reduction. Almost inevitably the misperception generated by high levels of hostility would disrupt the negotiations, and the mutual recriminations that followed would only intensify the arms race. What was needed was some pattern of unilateral gestures that would defuse tensions to the point where more formal negotiation could be employed. The question was: What pattern should be used? Should the gestures be purely symbolic to avoid leaving the initiator in a vulnerable position or would such trivial or minor concessions fail because they would be seen as a trap? The extent to which reciprocity should be demanded was also not clear. It seemed to hinge on one's belief about how far tacit bargaining processes could reduce arms without formal negotiations. If one believed that an alternating pattern of unilateral gestures and reciprocal responses could lead to significant arms reductions (as Osgood had suggested), then it made sense to develop a strategy that would demand reciprocity. If, however, one believed that major arms reductions could only take place if they occurred simultaneously while carrying out the provisions of a formal treaty, then reciprocity should be ignored in favor of using small gestures. This would create an environment conducive to negotiating a formal agreement as soon as possible.

The initiatives made by Kennedy during the period under examination presented an opportunity to test the strategy of using symbolic gestures to reduce tension and promote formal negotiations. The first move was a speech delivered on June 10, 1963, entitled "A Strategy of Peace." Etzioni views this as an attempt to create a context that would increase the likelihood that subsequent gestures would be correctly interpreted. Kennedy first drew attention to the dangers of nuclear war and stressed the extent to which current problems were essentially man-made. This made them subject to solution by calm deliberation and joint cooperation. He revealed an appreciation for the dynamics of tacit bargaining by acknowledging that it was the responsibility of the United States to convince the Soviet Union that it was in its interest to put an end to the cold war. He then announced a unilateral gesture with a reciprocal requirement that was designed to accomplish this: The United States would halt atmospheric nuclear tests and not resume them unless another country did.

Etzioni argues that this gesture can be viewed as almost entirely psychological and symbolic. The United States possessed a much larger nuclear arsenal and had conducted at least twice as many atmospheric tests, including a recent series that would require up to two years to analyze. Subsequent gestures had the same quality. The Soviets ceased to jam Voice of America broadcasts and Khrushchev delivered a speech in which he stated that war was not inevitable, but a possible consequence of a dangerous arms race. To lessen that danger, he announced that the Soviets would halt the production of strategic bombers. This was viewed as comparable to the U.S. move since there was a high probability that this would have occurred in any event and no means of verification were offered. Days later, the Soviet Union removed its objection to a U.S. proposal to place U.N. observers in Yemen, and the United States reciprocated by removing its objection to restoring full voting status to the Hungarian delegation.

Neither the United States nor the Soviet Union resumed atmospheric tests, and the test ban treaty was signed on August 5. A number of proposals were made by both countries to begin formal negotiations on subjects ranging from space exploration to a nonaggression pact between NATO and the Warsaw Pact, but the next major move was tacit, symbolic, and again initiated by the United States. It came on October 9, 1963, in the form of President Kennedy's approval of the wheat sale. What made this move no less symbolic than the test moratorium was that the sale had no real commercial importance and was not tied to any reduction of trade restrictions in other areas. Later in the same month, a U.N. resolution gave formal expression to the apparently tacit agreement that neither side would place nuclear weapons in orbit.

In late October, the upward spiral toward détente suddenly halted. The United States offered no new initiatives and ceased responding to Soviet gestures. A number of explanations are suggested for the halt: the fear that more agreements would leave Democrats open to charges of appeasement if relations with the Soviets began to sour before the election, the feeling that expectations were getting too high in the West and might leave the United States vulnerable to manipulation, and the increasing misgivings of allies, particularly West Germany. Etzioni, however, is less interested in sorting out the reason why détente was arrested than in evaluating the implications of this brief episode of cooperation for the central hypotheses of his theory. He notes that a number of them were clearly supported: (*a*) unilateral gestures were reciprocated; (*b*) reciprocations were proportional; (*c*) initiatives were met with suspicion at first but accepted if they persisted; and (*d*) modest unilateral initiatives inspired more significant and formal multilateral negotiations (Etzioni 1967, 372).

Even if we acknowledge that the "Kennedy experiment" provides material that supports each of these statements, the contribution that this study makes to the formulation of a theory of tacit bargaining is far from clear. The basic problem is that the case provides a wealth of conflicting evidence that speaks more to the complexity of tacit bargaining than anything else. True, it provides us with some small assurance that symbolic reciprocity can produce results, but we are left with no confidence that it will. Take the hypothesis that unilateral gestures are reciprocated. The case details how this occurred in several instances. But what are we to make of events of late October? If someone began to test the psychological theory on October 15, would they be justified in concluding that unilateral gestures were pointless and apt to produce little response? Would they be justified in saying that persistence was apt to accomplish little?

The fact that the answer to both questions might well be "yes" is less a condemnation of Etzioni's rules of evidence than an indication that the "psychological theory" is not really a theory at all. It is the reified observation that strategy can be influenced by the "affect of context," which in turn can be influenced by gestures that are quite modest. The problem is that the "theory" has nothing to say about when small unilateral gestures will have an effect and when they will not. In this sense, it is a "sometimes" theory that sensitizes us to possibilities; at the same time it provides us with no guidance as to when these possibilities might arise. This is not necessarily a trivial contribution. It can be valuable to provide cold warriors with evidence that the arms race may be more a product of mutual paranoia than of any basic clash of interests. Nevertheless, by refusing to grapple with the basic issue of contingency, it implies that unilateral gestures constitute a sufficient condition for progress on arms reduction even as the case used to demonstrate this principle argues otherwise. Inspiring a reluctant decision maker to persist in making a number of unilateral gestures that are then ignored may have long-term consequences that are less than helpful.

A more conservative interpretation of the evidence supports only two conclusions. The first is that there are times when a strategy of unilateral, largely symbolic gestures can transform the environment in which international discourse takes place and lead to meaningful negotiations. This is consistent with Etzioni's theory. The second is that the impact of unilateral gestures is unstable and difficult to predict. The fact that some unilateral gestures failed and the fact that there was a limit to the momentum that was built up during the brief détente reinforce the suspicion that the underlying arms game is not constant. Recall the impact of both the upcoming election and the administration's belief that mutual cooperation was leading to a dangerous overenthusiasm for additional peace agreements. This is inconsistent with the prescription that you can't go wrong with unilateral initiatives, and also reduces our confidence in a momentum-based strategy such as GRIT. Just as economic theory must speak to the implications of changes in demand that spring from alterations in preferences that it cannot account for, so a comprehensive theory of tacit bargaining must make provisions for changes in perceptions of the underlying game, even if it provides no way of anticipating when they will take place. A good tacit bargaining strategy will be one that admits the possibility of failure and adjusts as this failure becomes more, or less, likely.

It would be heartening to add additional conclusions but the evidence is just not there. Consider, for example, Etzioni's optimistic hypothesis that unilateral gestures will receive proportional reciprocations. Had it received strong support it would have suggested to decision makers that they can contemplate a cooperative gesture unfettered by fears of exploitation. In fact, however, the case tells us little about the likelihood of proportional reciprocation. Several unilateral gestures were inherently reciprocal in the sense of requiring a proportional response to remain in effect. The United States made it clear that it would return to atmospheric nuclear testing if the Soviets did so, and each side suggested that their restraint in placing weapons in space could only be continued if the other side acted similarly. Moreover, the proportionality that existed is acknowledged to stem, in large part, from the symbolic nature of the gesture. It makes little sense to try to diffuse fears of exploitation by arguing that the Soviet initiative to cease bomber production was no less meaningless than the United States' unilateral moratorium on testing. There is no incentive to exploit a meaningless gesture and that is not what decision makers fear. The only way to show that the proportionality assumption is reasonable is to test it in a situation where there is both the motive and the opportunity—to put the problem in a familiar parlance—to violate the principle. In this case there was neither.

The work of Snyder and Diesing (1977) links the rigor of a deductive approach to bargaining with the richness of sixteen case studies. While oriented toward crises, it is also relevant to both the evolution of arms agreements and their maintenance. Snyder and Diesing recognize at the outset—and all of their case evidence corroborates the fact—that the underlying game is different for different crises. The Berlin Crisis in the years 1958–62 is best seen as a Prisoner's Dilemma. Evidence suggests that Quemoy and Cuba are better viewed as what they refer to as "called bluffs," a situation where one party is in Prisoner's Dilemma and the other in Chicken. By the time they are finished identifying the underlying structures of all sixteen of their crises they employ nine different games. What is more notable from the standpoint of understanding tacit bargaining in general, as distinguished from the narrower area of crisis behavior, is that there is every indication that participants could not be sure of what game their opponent was playing and, when they guessed, they often guessed wrong. The crisis of 1905, for example, occurred because Germany thought that Britain would stand aloof and that the French would be forced to play Chicken.

The importance of estimation and interpretation problems is not limited to crisis generation. They play critical roles in the phase of crises most closely tied to tacit bargaining: the evolution of strategies and expectations. Influenced by cognitive psychology and the work of Robert Jervis, Snyder and Diesing develop an information processing component to their model in which various filters operate to create misinterpretation and bias as well as introduce a lag in the rate at which expectations, strategies, and tactics are adjusted in the wake of new information. They single out six perceptual heuristics described in Jervis's *Perception and Misperception in International Politics* (1976) and show the relevance of each. One is the tendency to interpret incoming messages so that they conform with desires and expectations. In the 1905 Crisis referred to above, Germany consistently discounted British messages that they would intervene. Another heuristic is the predilection for employing analogies that mirror previous firsthand experience with little reflection as to whether the present instance is comparable. The collaborative success of Britain and Germany in defusing the Balkan crisis of 1912 led Germany to believe that Britain would prefer the role of mediator to that of fulfilling its responsibilities as an ally in the event of an Austrian-Hungarian war. Britain, for its part, used the same experience to create an expectation that Germany would collaborate in mediating a quick end to the crisis. Yet as Snyder and Diesing note, the context was dramatically different in that both Russia and Austria were far less involved in the crisis of 1912 than in that of 1914 (Snyder and Diesing 1977, 313).

Having drawn on case study material to establish that misinterpretation takes place, Snyder and Diesing next try to estimate the seriousness of the problem with greater precision. From their sixteen cases, they collect and code 350 occasions when a message was sent and classify them as correctly or incorrectly interpreted. The results are striking. Only 40 percent of the messages—both written/verbal and tacit combined—were correctly interpreted. They freely acknowledge that definitional and coding problems make this number a crude estimate but argue that there is no evidence for believing that they have overestimated the magnitude of the problem. Although there is no attempt to determine whether the misinterpretation rate of tacit communications is any higher or lower than verbal or written messages, the examples that are provided do not suggest that tacit signals are less subject to misinterpretation. The persistent Japanese overestimation of U.S. willingness to negotiate in 1940, for example, is one of many that exhibits instances of both kinds of misinterpretation. On the verbal/written side, there was the United States' rejection of Japan's provisional acceptance of the April 14 offer and proposal for a Konoye-Roosevelt meeting. On the tacit side, the United States added new embargoes in June and froze Japanese assets on July 26. That the Japanese did eventually revise their expectations and shift strategies makes these instances of misinterpretation no less important.

It is no surprise that misinterpretation and how to reduce it play a central role in much of what Snyder and Diesing have to say about tacit bargaining strategies. They stress that early efforts at accommodation are often interpreted as signs of weakness and inspire more aggressive demands. This was the German response to French accommodation in 1905, and English efforts at mediation in 1914. Meeting aggression with a comparable level of resistance seems to hold out the best prospect for leading the adversary to adjust its perception of what game is being played without creating a needlessly high probability of war. Only after the adversary has made this adjustment (indicated, one presumes, by decreased bellicosity) is it sensible to offer a cooperative gesture.

Even then the prospect that this initial olive branch will bring an end to conflict is not great, as both Jervis and Snyder and Diesing observe. In strategic terms, time is necessary for the adversary to adjust to the image of a rival willing to cooperate as well as that of a rival that cannot be bullied. To overcome the effect of decision heuristics that screen out information that conflicts with expectations, nations must be prepared to repeat the same message over and over and avoid jumping to the conclusion that the absence of a quick response means that no cooperation is possible.

Uncertainty about the game that is being played and the redundancy necessary to overcome misinterpretation would also appear to have an implication for the magnitude of the actions that will be used to convince the adversary that cooperation is possible. Although Snyder and Diesing do not discuss the issue, it is difficult to avoid the inference that these actions are likely to be modest. Too grand a gesture might lead the other side to believe that bullying will be successful, or create an irrevocable loss if it turned out that the opponent possessed Deadlock preferences and reeducation was futile. Even the suspicion that the latter might be true could have domestic political consequences that would prevent the possibility of a follow-up gesture.

The misinterpretation-sensitive strategy that emerges from the formal analysis and case studies of Snyder and Diesing thus differs from both Tit-for-Tat and GRIT. The application of Tit-for-Tat would be appropriate during the early stages of a crisis when firmness was called for, but would be disastrous during the attempt to reestablish a new cooperation-based equilibrium. It is simply not forgiving enough: a cooperative gesture would be offered, the heuristics and biases of misperception would lead to its initial dismissal by the other party, and the demands of reciprocity would then call for revenge. GRIT would fare no better in a world ruled by misperception. A crisis would arise, GRIT would prescribe a cooperative gesture to defuse it, and the aggressive party would interpret this as a sign of weakness and press for even greater sacrifices. Even if GRIT were applied after a period in which resolve was demonstrated, it would suffer from the same problem as Tit-for-Tat unless its architects were willing to accept the fact that a number of successive gestures would be needed to overcome the other side's interpretive biases.

Another effort to explore the relative efficacy of strategies that contain a high proportion of tacit behavior is that of Leng and Wheeler (1979). They examine the performance of four types of "influence strategies" (bullying, reciprocating, appeasing, and trial-and-error) using event data from twenty serious disputes in the twentieth century. Their analysis focuses on three hypotheses. The first is that serious disputes are more likely to end in war if one or both sides is employing a bullying strategy that relies on increasingly negative inducements to deal with any response short of total compliance. Not surprisingly, this hypothesis is supported by the data. Indeed, it would be more remarkable if it were not. Since each of the alternative strategies contains a cooperative component and requires that cooperation be met with cooperation, it is difficult to see how nations employing them could simultaneously obey the rules of the strategy and also go to war. In short, this is more a definitional finding than an empirical one.

Hypothesis two posits that either a reciprocating or trial-and-error strategy is the most effective means of avoiding a diplomatic defeat without going to war. Since appeasement prescribes diplomatic defeat when a bullying strategy is encountered and two bullies must continue to press their demands ever more aggressively, the empirical success of this hypothesis would also seem to be a foregone conclusion. As expected, the data supported it. It would have been more useful to investigate a more plausible variant of the bullying strategy that prescribes a negative initial response that is disproportionately strong, followed by reciprocity or a unilateral cooperative gesture. This is much closer to what negative reinforcement proponents recommend than the straw man–like bullying strategy.

Hypothesis three is not much of an improvement on the surface. It posits that when an opponent is employing a bullying strategy, the best way to avoid the twin perils of diplomatic defeat and war is to adopt a reciprocating strategy. Since, by definition, a strategy of appeasement will lead to defeat under these circumstances and bullying in return leaves little room for cooperation, the only test of interest is between the efficacy of reciprocating and trial-and-error strategies. Unfortunately, the authors found it impossible to conduct the last test because no nation employed the trial-and-error strategy. The problematic nature of the basic hypothesis does not necessarily mean that the data are without value. There is, after all, a question of absolute, as well as relative, performance. It may be a foregone conclusion that the reciprocating strategy will lead to fewer wars and diplomatic defeats than its rivals, but there is still the issue of how often it leads to compromise. It would be one thing to say that reciprocity led to compromise in 10 percent of the cases, and another to note that it did so in 90 percent of the cases. Leng and Wheeler's findings in this regard are provocative: a reciprocating strategy results in victory or compromise six times and in defeat or war only twice. Is this convincing evidence of the superiority of this strategy? Does this mean that reciprocity is always the best strategy?

The answer lies in our confidence that the cases where reciprocity was used were representative of all crises and whether or not we believe that it is possible to identify the game structure that underlies a particular crisis. Although Snyder and Diesing took great pains to identify the game that drove each of their sixteen crises, Leng and Wheeler concern themselves only with overall performance. On the surface this seems peculiar. If a strategy is invoked more frequently against nations with Deadlock preferences than are other strategies, its performance is bound to suffer in comparison. What was supposed to be a contest of relative effectiveness would actually be a study of what strategy had the misfortune to be used most often when war or capitulation were the only possible outcomes. Leng and Wheeler acknowledge that there are times when one or both parties may not want to avoid war, but argue that these instances are exceptional and make a conscious effort to eliminate them from their sample. But even if they are successful, they have only dealt with the problem of Deadlock. It is still possible that the underlying structure of the dispute varies between Prisoner's Dilemma and Chicken, and that the different strategies had to cope with a different mix of disputes. Should this be true, the selection problem would reemerge in much the same way as it would if the success of two cold-relief formulas was compared where one had the good fortune to be treating a warm and well-fed group of patients and the other had the bad luck to be used by a poorly-fed and poorly-housed group. In the context of crises, if the game is a Prisoner's Dilemma, each party will have to reduce its demands (i.e., maximum expectations) if war is to be avoided. If the game is Chicken or a related asymmetrical structure, one party can get the best of a compromise by demonstrating superiority of resolve (Snyder and Diesing 1977, 489).

There is no easy way to estimate the representativeness of the crises where reciprocity did well.[3] Even if it were perfect, however, it would not necessarily justify the selection of reciprocity in every case. A wise decision maker should no more adopt a strategy because of its overall record, than should a quarterback trying to score from the opponent's forty-five yardline elect to run a quarterback sneak because statistics show that, over the duration of an entire season, a higher percentage of quarterback sneaks result in touchdowns than any other play. The contingencies of context are at least as critical in foreign policy as they are in football. Snyder and Diesing are correct in prescribing actions based on the underlying structure of the game as well as the opponent's strategy. The only situation where the Leng and Wheeler approach is justifiable is when (1) the underlying structure (context) is the same for all cases or (2) when it varies but is so uncertain that the only sensible course is to assume that the most historically common situation holds. The first situation is improbable in either arms races or crises but the second is worth thinking about. While there is no question that secure knowledge of the underlying game will lead a rational decision maker to alter his or her tacit bargaining strategy, there is no law that guarantees that this knowledge will be present. Decision makers are notorious for misinterpreting the intentions of opponents.

It is, however, one thing to argue that a nation's estimate of the underlying game is uncertain and another to argue that it is so uncertain that the only sensible course of action is to rely on the strategy that has most often succeeded in the past. Information does not have to be perfect (certain) to be useful. Estimates of the costs and benefits that the opponent attaches to different

---

3. One possibility that might diminish this representativeness is that nations may normally use appeasement only when they believe that reciprocal strength holds little hope. For example, some of the incentive for the British to continue to try appeasement in 1939 may have lain in the fact that Britain's strength on land and in the air was so much worse than Germany's, although some incentive was clearly rooted in a belief that the Germans would be "reasonable" and that war was too horrible to be contemplated.

outcomes (i.e., what game it is playing) come from sources other than what Leng and Wheeler include through their attention to its recent behavior (revealed strategy). One has only to think of the diverse information that would be included in calculating Soviet motives for intervention in Latin America or Africa and the importance that this information would play in shaping a U.S. response. There is no question that nations make use of this sort of evidence—the only issue is how good (certain) it has to be for them to do so. Leng and Wheeler assume it is always misleading or irrelevant, but it is improbable that this is the case.

Louis Kriesberg (1987) departs from the crisis-oriented approach that dominates the events literature and examines tension reduction and dispute resolution between the United States and the USSR and between Israel and the Arab nations. Like Leng and Wheeler, he ignores the issue of what underlying game is being played and concentrates on the efficacy of alternative strategies. Is de-escalation, he asks, more likely to take place when a nation is employing an inducement strategy, a coercive strategy, or some combination like Tit-for-Tat? Kriesberg summarizes the various views. Those favoring an inducement approach, like Osgood, argue that it dissolves distrust and increases the incentive for cooperation. Those, like Herman Kahn, who emphasize the role of coercion argue for increasing the cost of noncooperation and add that positive inducements can too easily be interpreted as appeasement and lead to still greater demands. Advocates of a combined approach, like Bob Axelrod, believe that it combines the virtues of both approaches without risking appeasement or excessive provocation.

Only a small portion of Kriesberg's informal and discursive analysis deals specifically with tacit bargaining as opposed to more conventional diplomatic exchanges, but a number of his observations are notable. First, major conciliatory gestures are rarely offered although they are more likely to provoke de-escalation than any other behavior. This is probably less a paradox than it first appears because selection is almost certainly operating. Grand gestures are more successful than small gestures because they are used in circumstances where the probability of success is much higher. The rarity of grand gestures is more interesting. Kriesberg believes they are avoided because they open the door for opposition forces within the nation extending the gesture to charge appeasement. Moreover, if they are not reciprocated, the leader who made such a gesture is made to look weak and foolish. The few grand gestures that have been made have taken place when a peculiar set of circumstances acts to minimize these twin risks. The gestures Kennedy made in his 1963 American University speech came after a productive round of test ban negotiations, and Sadat's visit to Jerusalem was preceded by a similarly successful series of diplomatic communications.

A second, related point is that modest conciliatory gestures are usually not reciprocated and rarely lead to de-escalating negotiations. Kriesberg speculates that this is because it is difficult for the receiving nation to convince itself that the gesture is not simply propaganda or that it is worthy of a response. Nations are more likely to begin de-escalation negotiations with no positive or negative inducement at all. Their perceptions of their interests simply change and converge as a result of internal politics. Once again, the changing nature of the underlying game and its critical role in determining the potential for cooperation reveals itself.

2.5   Conclusion

Thomas Schelling and other theorists corroborate the arguments made in the first chapter for expanding the role of tacit bargaining in arms control. The flexibility of tacit bargaining combined with its ability to manipulate positive and negative incentives hold out a potential for coping with a variety of problems that have historically plagued formal treaties. These include the tendency to "displace" resources from controlled to uncontrolled weapon systems, the problem of a treaty being rendered obsolete by technological advances, and the countless difficulties posed by treaty enforcement.

There is far less consensus about the relative effectiveness of specific tacit bargaining strategies, what determines that effectiveness, and how they can be best evaluated. In large part, this is due to the fact that most theorists were interested in narrower questions than arms control or had a vision of arms behavior that eliminated much of its complexity. There is no reason to expect experimental research on the Prisoner's Dilemma to simultaneously investigate the consequences of uncertainty about the underlying game and information problems, and it has not. Nor is it surprising that such a seminal exploration of tacit bargaining within the context of arms control as Charles Osgood's was motivated by a highly personal vision of arms races that relegated issues concerning exploitation, misinterpretation, and complexity into the background.

Yet if the true potential of tacit bargaining is ever to be revealed in theory, much less realized in practice, complicated questions about the relative effectiveness of different strategies in different environments must be addressed. The work described in this chapter convinces us that the range of potential tacit bargaining strategies is enormous and that they are sensitive to assumptions about a rival's objectives, control and information problems, the rate of weapon obsolescence, and expectations about how long the arms race might last or the "shadow of the future." It would be foolish to underestimate the importance of simply identifying this list of relevant dimensions, but a policymaker faced with the decision of whether to extend a gesture of cooperation to the Soviet Union and how large to make that gesture needs more specific guidance. At what point should suspicion that the Soviet Union is irrevocably committed to a policy of arms expansion lead the decision maker to make no gesture? How important is it that the gesture be generous in order to be politically "notable" and how long should it be held out in the absence of a positive reply? In a world of imperfect intelligence, how much suspected cheating should be tolerated before retaliatory action is taken and what should be the nature of that retaliation?

These are the types of policy questions that have not been dealt with by previous research and which define the agenda of the next three chapters. In trying to obtain some preliminary answers, we will address some positive questions as well. For example, if tacit bargaining is as commonplace in international affairs as it appears and possesses so many advantages, why doesn't it more frequently serve as a basis for arms cooperation? Do the limitations described in the first chapter combine to restrict its usefulness? Does it require a level of institutional learning, cognitive sophistication, or policy coordination and continuity that cannot be expected of most states? Is it only likely to emerge in an arms race that has been going on for a long time? Questions like this are not only intrinsically interesting for anyone interested in the utility of tacit bargaining for arms control, they provide an indirect check on the realism of the models that are used. If they can provide a convincing explanation for how and when tacit bargaining is used, their prescriptions will be more credible.

Chapter 3

Arms Races and Formal Modeling

This chapter discusses some of the formal foundations upon which the models developed in the succeeding chapters rest. It begins with a brief discussion of previous approaches to modeling arms races and how they relate to the model employed here. There is no pretense to comprehensiveness: the arms race literature is vast and countless models have been devised. Our goals are to persuade the reader that history impels the use of a very general model and then to specify and explain the model we choose.

After presenting our formal model of an arms race, we move on to a discussion of three other assumptions relating to the rationality of actors, the role of bias and uncertainty, and the reasonableness of treating a state as a unitary actor. As noted in chapter 1, we think such a discussion is necessary because key assumptions are always important, and this importance increases still further when a scarcity of data makes it difficult to test a model's predictive power.

Finally, the chapter concludes with a brief review of two research traditions in oligopoly theory and industrial organization that have shaped our approach to tacit bargaining and arms control. The first focuses on uncertainty about underlying utilities; the second deals with uncertainty about action (e.g., has a particular firm attempted to exploit other members of the oligopoly by increasing production?).

Readers who are uncomfortable with technical material can skim the more mathematical sections without a serious loss of continuity.

3.1   What Is an Arms Race?

3.1.1   Introduction

The term *arms race* has a variety of meanings in common parlance. For the purposes of this book, we will interpret this term to mean a situation in which a nation (or nations) increases its arms expenditures partly as a result of arms-related actions of another nation and in which the rate of building is higher than some contextually determined level that represents some form of restraint. This definition is extremely broad since the observed arms increases in such a situation may be small or large. A constant level of arms expenditures may be interpreted as a tacit arms treaty or as an arms race, depending on the size of the expenditures and on previous expectations. If expenditures by both sides in an arms race are reduced to half their previous level and kept there, this could easily be interpreted as cooperation in the form of a tacit treaty, even if this new rate of expenditure was much higher than either nation's rate ten years previously. In the earlier period, a jump to the same level would have been interpreted as an intensified arms race.

This viewpoint has a number of consequences. It means that modeling arms decisions as a series of dichotomous choices is not feasible since a number of gradations is possible for the choice to be made in an individual period. Another implication is that arms races can vary in degree of severity, and an existing arms race can often become more intense.[1] Just because the opponent is "defecting" by building some amount of arms does not mean that state should feel free to arm as it wishes—the arms race could still intensify. By extension, when one side contemplates retalia-

---

1. Richardson's (1939, 1960) models require that arms increases either converge to a stable pair of increases or accelerate. Wallace (1982) uses extreme rates of increase or acceleration as criteria to identify cases in which arms races preceded wars. However, such definitions are inconsistent with the U.S.-Soviet strategic arms race that has evolved over a period of decades.

tion, there is the possibility of counter-retaliation, and so on. This means that the "game" representing the arms race has a complex set of strategic considerations. No state can act unilaterally without consideration of possible responses—departures from norms must result in calculated retaliation, not arbitrary retaliation.

In the next sections, we examine some previous approaches to the problem of modeling arms races and arms control, including Richardson models and two-by-two repeated games. Then we outline the characteristics that a model of arms races and arms control must address and suggest some modeling strategies that we will use. Because much of the inspiration for these models comes from oligopoly theory in economics, as well as related modern game theory, this literature will also be briefly addressed.

3.1.2   Richardson-Type Arms Race Models

Richardson's original model was that the rates of change ($\dot{x}$ and $\dot{y}$) of the annual arms expenditures (x and y) of two nations A and B are determined mechanistically by current levels of these variables, as in the following differential equations:

$$\dot{x} = a_x y - b_x x + c_x$$

$$\dot{y} = a_y x - b_y y + c_y.$$

In this equation, a represents the response to the opponent's actions, b represents the cost of weapons as a containing influence, and c is a term reflecting the level of hostility/friendliness between the two nations. To understand the strengths and weaknesses of Richardson's original model as well as the many extensions and alterations that have been proposed in the intervening years,[2] it is helpful to begin with a significant generalization of the model and see what specializations are necessary in order to arrive at Richardson's model. This is useful because examination of this enlarged version of the model helps distinguish between problems that are inherent in the method of attacking the problem and those that belong to specific formulations.

---

2. A good review of the literature in this area up to 1985 is found in Isard and Anderton (1985). A more recent comprehensive treatise is Isard (1988).

Let $\mathbf{X}_t$ be a vector in which the ith component is the arms expenditure of nation i at time t (taken to be an instantaneous rate). Let $\mathbf{S}_t$ be a state matrix whose i^{th} column contains a list of current conditions for nation i, which may consist of the current or past arms expenditure or arms stock as well as domestic factors, and which may itself evolve stochastically. Suppose that the rate of change of arms expenditures is determined by

$$\dot{\mathbf{X}}_t = \mathbf{R}(\mathbf{S}_t) + \mathbf{e}_t, \tag{3.1}$$

where $\mathbf{e}_t$ is a stochastic error term.

Even this very general model involves a number of questionable assumptions that might need to be altered before it can be applied to historical, as opposed to ideal, arms races. Perhaps the most important is the absence of any intentional behavior in this model. This presents us with something of a paradox. If arms expenditures were determined by such a model and the characteristics were known to all sides, then the future course of the arms race would be essentially preordained (the stochastic terms would not disturb the basic course of the arms race). But if nations knew of this unfavorable outcome, they would be foolish not to act differently in order to produce a different result. Without consideration of the "gaming" aspects of the situation, such a model can, at best, serve as a warning of what might occur if nations behave in this fashion.[3] It has no normative value, since it does not reveal what a good course of action might be; its positive value is also questionable, since it implies that nations behave essentially without consciousness of the consequences of their own actions.

Even if we accept this general approach, the problems with Richardson-type models do not end here. We can see this by examining the specializations in Equation (3.1) necessary to arrive at Richardson's model. First, in Richardson's model, the state matrix $\mathbf{S}$ consists only of the current arms expenditures by the various nations. This means that past behavior and domestic factors cannot be taken into account, except as they affect the value of coefficients. Thus exogenous or endogenous changes in

---

3. Richardson sometimes adopted this view in his writings. For example, "the process described by the ensuing equations is not to be thought of as inevitable. It is what *would occur if instinct and tradition were allowed to act uncontrolled*" (1960b, Richardson's italics).

economic conditions or political leadership cannot be reflected in changes in the dynamics of the arms race.

Second, the function **R** is taken to be a linear function with constant coefficients that depends only on the arms expenditures. This is an extremely important problem with the model, especially when one is considering asymptotic behavior (i.e., eventual behavior after a long time). To see this problem, suppose that **R** is a more general nonlinear function and view the Richardson model as approximating **R** by a linear function. In general, for any such function **R**, one may approximate the function **R** by a Taylor series at the point $\mathbf{S}_0$ and arrive at the following expression:

$$\dot{\mathbf{X}}_t \doteq \mathbf{R}(\mathbf{S}_0) + \left(\frac{\partial \mathbf{R}(\mathbf{S})}{\partial \mathbf{S}}\right)(\mathbf{S}_t - \mathbf{S}_0) + \mathbf{e}_t.$$

This approximation is valid in a neighborhood around $\mathbf{S}_0$. If $\mathbf{S}_0$ is a potential equilibrium point, then this expansion can help in determining the stability of the equilibrium. If, on the other hand, one is examining a situation in which the trajectory $\mathbf{X}_t$ does not tend to a point, then one would expect the Taylor series approximation to become increasingly inapplicable. This raises the possibility that the linear Richardson model can be useful in examining local behavior around an equilibrium, but really says little about what happens when the trajectory implied by the linear model tends toward infinity. Mere projection of current trends is often an unreliable forecasting method. A model that seems to imply that an arms race will go out of control, leading perhaps to war, may become invalid when arms stocks or increases have passed some critical point, and the situation may stabilize.

To better appreciate this point, consider the system

$$\dot{x} = 2y - x + 10$$

$$\dot{y} = 2x - y + 10,$$

which is not supposed to represent genuine parameter values of arms races, but rather to illustrate in an easy numerical fashion the nature of nonequilibrium behavior in the Richardson model. The particular parameter values do not matter since nonequilibrium behavior is essentially the same across a wide set of parameter values. Returning to the two-equation system, the only

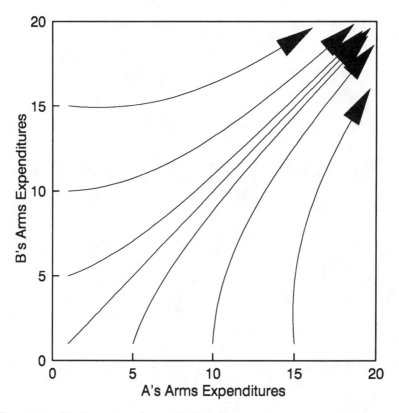

Fig. 3.1. Trajectories for a Richardson arms race model in the expenditures plane

equilibrium is at $(-10, -10)$, as can be seen by setting $\dot{x} = \dot{y} = 0$ and solving for x and y. Yet, even this equilibrium is unstable, since whenever the system is near the equilibrium but not exactly there, it evolves away from the equilibrium rather than toward it. For example, if the system is at $(-10, -10+\epsilon)$ (just "north" of the equilibrium), then the direction of movement is given by $\dot{x} = 2\epsilon$ and $\dot{y} = -\epsilon$, so that the system evolves "south" and "east." Since it moves "east" faster than it moves "south," the system does not return to equilibrium. Typical trajectories in the first quadrant of the expenditures plane are shown in figure 3.1, while the same trajectories in the arms stock plane are shown in figure 3.2.

The prediction of this model is that arms will increase without bound—even the rate of arms increase increases without bound.

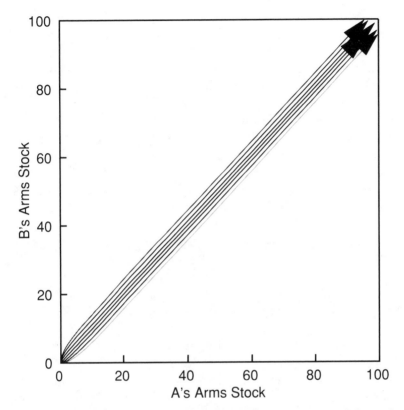

Fig. 3.2. Trajectories for a Richardson arms race model in the arms stock plane

It is notable that this acceleration is not a consequence of the parameter values, realistic or unrealistic, but of the basic structure of the Richardson model. This can be examined analytically for the case where x and y are equal, which is always asymptotically true in this model. In this case, solutions to the differential equations are of the form

$$x(t) = ce^t - 10$$

while the arms stock (with depreciation rate α) evolves as

$$S = (1 - \alpha)^{-1}ce^t - 10\alpha^{-1} + de^{-\alpha t}.$$

These trajectories can hardly represent a real arms race, since the model predicts that the rate of arms building will increase without limit. In other words, instead of representing a growth rate of 5 percent per year or 10 percent per year, this model predicts that the rate of growth itself increases without bound, rising to 20 percent, 50 percent, 100 percent per year and higher. This unrealistic prediction is caused by the assumption that behavior will be constant over an extremely wide range of conditions.

While it may be reasonable to assume that a linear, constant-coefficient, first-order differential equation could model arms race dynamics over a small region, it is unreasonable to expect such a model to work over wide ranges of the variables. The predictions of disastrous consequences if the parameters of the model predict nonequilibrium are predicated on the unremarkable and marginally relevant "fact" that, since unlimited arms races cannot occur, war will intervene. It might be as realistic to predict that a child will have eaten 400 Big Macs by Tuesday because she ate two in a half-hour on Saturday. Yet Richardson's model assumes that such predictions would be valid. Thus, the predictions of the asymptotic behavior of Richardson models are of little use, since the model could hardly hold over a wide enough region for these consequences to develop. If one adopts instead the more realistic assumption that the parameters of the model may differ in different regions of the arms plane, then a natural form of limiting behavior might well take over. For example, increasing costs and declining marginal benefits could lead to an automatic reduction in the rate of increases that could not be predicted by the linear projection of early stages of the arms race.

One empirical study that speaks to the validity of the Richardson model rather than assuming the model and then estimating coefficients is by Majeski and Jones (1981). They examined the time series behavior of arms race dyads and found that there was no evidence of any response to increases in the other side's expenditures in seven of the twelve dyads. The other five dyads had a variety of response modes, mostly not what was assumed by Richardson's model; for example, there were varying time lags or one-sided causality. Altogether, the time-series behavior of the set of dyads was not consistent with a Richardson type model.[4]

---

4. The Majeski and Jones analysis must be viewed with caution because the empirical analysis of arms races is fraught with difficulties. If one ob-

Any model of arms races or potential arms races must incorporate certain features of Richardson's model. Primarily, the arms behavior of one state will almost certainly depend on the previous arms behavior of the other state. However, a model in which gaming behavior is also considered is likely to have far greater normative and positive value than one in which the response depends in a mechanical way on immediate past actions. This is true because the reaction of one state to another is more likely to be a response to a real or perceived strategy (or pattern of behavior) than it is to be a response merely to the current level of expenditures. In order to be realistic, models of arms race behavior should not assume myopic, knee-jerk responses to the opponent, but allow the participants to consider the long-term consequences of their behavior and of the opponent's reactions. This is the rationale behind our extensive treatment of the largest set of game theory–oriented research in arms races—that using repeated 2×2 games.

3.1.3 2×2 Games

One common model of the arms race is the Prisoner's Dilemma.[5] In the arms race context, this game involves the choice by each side of Cooperation (by not arming) or Defection (by arming). Payoffs to each side are ordered so that the most preferred outcome is arming while the opponent cooperates, the second-best outcome is mutual cooperation, next is mutual defection, and the least preferred outcome is cooperating while the opponent defects.

---

serves arms stability, there is no way to tell whether neither side has any use for increased arms, or whether each side was deterred from arms increases by explicit or implicit threats from the other side. Contrariwise, when arms increases are observed, this may represent aggressive intentions, or retaliation for perceived violations by the other side, so that it is difficult to distinguish between Deadlock and the Prisoner's Dilemma. This makes a statistical approach to such analysis problematic. For more on the difficulty of this approach, see for example, Altfeld (1983), Ferejohn (1976), Rattinger (1976), Schrodt (1978), Wagner et al. (1975), and Weede (1980).

5. Early uses of the Prisoner's Dilemma and other 2×2 games to model the arms race include Brams et al. (1979), Jervis (1978), Snyder (1971), and Snyder and Diesing (1977). For more recent prominent work see Brams (1985), Brams and Kilgour (1988), Majeski (1984), Ordeshook (1986), and Wagner (1983).

For example, one set of payoffs consistent with the Prisoner's Dilemma is given in table 3.1. It is easy to see that each side prefers to defect, regardless of what the other side has chosen to do. The fact that mutual defection is the only Nash equilibrium for this game presents a gloomy picture of the possibility of arms cooperation. The situation brightens somewhat when one considers that the presence of arms treaties and tacit restraint in the real world suggest that either the model or the concept of Nash equilibrium requires alteration.

Even within the fairly restricted framework of 2×2 games, one could quarrel with the choice of the Prisoner's Dilemma to model the preferences of the participants. Perhaps the most important problem is that one side may prefer mutual defection to mutual cooperation—the preferences associated with the game called Deadlock. Table 3.2 shows a game with Deadlock preferences. For each side, the two favorite outcomes both involve defecting, so no strategy can induce cooperation and an arms race is inevitable. In fact, this outcome is also inevitable if only one side has these preferences. Table 3.3 shows a game in which A has Prisoner's Dilemma preferences but B has Deadlock preferences. Clearly, no strategy can induce B to cooperate. Such a situation could plausibly represent the German arms buildup in the thirties, the Soviet buildup in the late forties and early fifties, or the U.S. buildup in the eighties. No formal analysis of arms races could be complete that does not take this possibility into account.

Several other games have been used as models of arms races. Jervis (1978) considers the Stag Hunt as a model of arms races. In this game, mutual cooperation is the most preferred outcome for both parties, but if one suspects that one's opponent is going to defect, then one has an incentive to defect oneself. The preference structure for this game is given in table 3.4. Other games, such as Chicken, have been used as models in international politics, but none seems as apposite for arms race modeling as the Prisoner's Dilemma, Deadlock, and the Stag Hunt.

The Prisoner's Dilemma seems the most characteristic model for arms races. This presents the difficulty of reconciling the existence of instances of arms cooperation with the unique Nash equilibrium of mutual defection in the Prisoner's Dilemma. One possibility is to define a new idea of equilibrium so that the 2×2 Pris-

TABLE 3.1. Payoffs for One Version of the Prisoner's Dilemma

	B Cooperates	B Defects
A Cooperates	(5, 5)	(−4, 6)
A Defects	(6, −4)	(−3, −3)

TABLE 3.2. Payoffs for Deadlock Preferences

	B Cooperates	B Defects
A Cooperates	(0, 0)	(−4, 6)
A Defects	(6, −4)	(3, 3)

TABLE 3.3. Payoffs for Prisoner's Dilemma Preferences (A) vs. Deadlock Preferences (B)

	B Cooperates	B Defects
A Cooperates	(5, 0)	(−4, 6)
A Defects	(6, −4)	(−3, 3)

TABLE 3.4. Payoffs for the Stag Hunt

	B Cooperates	B Defects
A Cooperates	(8, 8)	(−4, 6)
A Defects	(6, −4)	(−3, −3)

oner's Dilemma has a cooperative solution—prominent attempts include those of Brams (1985), Brams and Kilgour (1988), Howard (1971), and Wagner (1983).

The problem with this sort of solution to the Prisoner's Dilemma formulation of an arms race is that an arms race is, almost by definition, an evolving series of arms decisions, not a static, one-shot game. This problem may be repaired by considering a game that consists of repeated plays of a Prisoner's Dilemma game, with payoffs discounted by a factor δ.[6] If the future is not too heavily discounted, then there exist equilibria of mutual cooperation, which involve strategies that retaliate for defection by the opponent (Luce and Raiffa 1957).

Another serious problem with the Prisoner's Dilemma as a model for arms races and potential arms races is the dichotomous nature of the choices in the model. In reality, a nation may choose to build virtually any level of armaments (within the economic capacity of that nation). This permits fine gradations of choice such as varying punishment for defection and also expands the range of possible strategies from what is permitted by the 2×2 Prisoner's Dilemma. For example, if one restricts oneself to strategies in which one's action is determined only by the opponent's immediately preceding action, there are just four possible strategies in the 2×2 Prisoner's Dilemma (always cooperate, always defect, Tit-for-Tat, and its reverse). If continuous responses are permitted, then a strategy that depends on the opponent's previous response can be viewed as a function from the space of previous responses (say a closed interval $[a, b]$) to the space of possible replies (say $[a', b']$). Not only are there an infinite number of such strategies, but the dimension of the space of such strategies is infinite.

One implication of the above is that continuous responses plus uncertainty in perceiving the other side's move raises the possibility of cheating on arms treaties by small amounts. This cheating is often difficult to detect, and, if it is detected, the proper response is far from clear. This is also more consistent with historical experience than the dichotomous concept found in the Prisoner's Dilemma. While nations are doubtless worried about the possi-

---

6. Formally equivalent in expected utility is an undiscounted game with some probability p of the game terminating after each move.

bility that a rival will abrogate a treaty and return to pretreaty
production levels, most of the diplomatic rhetoric and tacit bargaining behavior surrounding treaties like the Washington Naval
Treaty and SALT II have focused on incremental departures from
treaty limits and appropriate incremental responses.

Finally, continuous responses present the possibility, already
discussed, that nations may be engaged in an arms race that is
not being conducted at the greatest sustainable rate. In the 2×2
Prisoner's Dilemma, if one's opponent is defecting, one can defect
oneself with no further risk. If continuous responses are possible,
then one side may be defecting partially, and a punishment by the
other side may prompt the first side to defect completely. Except
when the opponent is already defecting at some maximum rate,
care needs to be taken in retaliation. As we have noted, few
arms races have been characterized by constant maximum levels
of defection. The United States has been locked in an arms race
with the Soviet Union for three decades. Yet for how many of
those years would we want to argue that the United States was
building arms its maximum rate?

The Prisoner's Dilemma model possesses other shortcomings.
It does not generally incorporate uncertainty by one side about
what the other side has done (an information problem) or differences between planned weapons production and actual, achieved
production (a control problem). Nonetheless, there are valuable
features of the Prisoner's Dilemma model that should be incorporated in any successful model of arms races and potential arms
races. First is the inclusion of gaming aspects in arms decisions—
nations must consider what the response will be to their actions.
Second is the characteristic that each side would benefit individually from increasing its arms if the other side held steady, but
both lose when both increase arms.

3.1.4 Arms Race Models Used in This Book

As described in the foregoing sections, previous work on mathematical modeling of arms races tends to fall into one of two categories. The first, inspired by Richardson (1939, 1960), treats an
arms race as the solution to a set of differential equations, usually
deterministic. These models have the advantage of being dynamic

and of representing arms as a continuum of behavior, rather than a stark cooperation/noncooperation choice. Stable states, which might represent an arms treaty, are stable equilibria of the system of differential equations. The chief drawback of such models is that they depict the two sides in an arms race as virtual automatons. While it may sometimes be useful to think of one's opponent in this fashion, it artificially restricts the range of policy choices.

The second class of models that is often used to represent an arms race is the repeated, 2×2 game. This incorporates strategic considerations, but, as we have seen, the remainder of the model is quite simplistic. Complex gradations of choice are reduced to a binary decision on cooperation, and each move is a simple repetition of the preceding one. Like Richardson models, these game theory models rarely allow for problems of information and control[7] (Downs, Rocke, and Siverson, 1985).

The starting place for the analysis contained in this book is a model for the utility a nation associates with a given state of arms stock and arms production for both sides. This model is general in the sense that it contains a number of parameters that allow different nations to have different preferences. One concession that has had to be made to tractability is that arms stocks are treated as unitary goods, not the differentiated bundles that they really are. This abstraction is meant to represent some abstract summary measure of total military capability, rather than any physical item of arms such as a missile or a tank. The model can easily be broadened to a multivariate measure of military strength, such as nuclear and conventional, but this complication seems premature.

The evolution of arms stocks in a bilateral arms race or treaty situation proceeds as states A and B choose levels of arms production P_t^A and P_t^B, respectively, for each period t. Since it is probable that technological change as well as depreciation will reduce the value of an arms stock in the absence of additions, the

---

7. This is not so much a conclusion concerning an inherent limitation of these models as an empirical observation about past research. With some loss of realism, one could conduct an analysis incorporating information and control problems using dichotomous models. However, there seems to be little advantage in doing so.

stock S_t^A evolves by the process

$$S_t^A = \alpha S_{t-1}^A + P_t^A \qquad (0 < \alpha < 1), \qquad (3.2)$$

and correspondingly for state B. Thus, if $\alpha = .9$, each side loses 10 percent of the value of its arms stock each year to depreciation and obsolescence. If arms expenditures are constant over a long period of time, this model implies that a level of military strength (arms stock) will be reached in which expenditures for new arms are just sufficient to balance the depreciation in the existing stock. Specifically, if a constant expenditure Δ is made each year, then the level eventually reached is $\Delta/(1 - \alpha)$. On the other hand, a sudden increase in arms production will lead to large changes in the arms stock over a considerable period of time.

We assume that the utility of state A at any time t is the sum of three parts. First, there is a component due to the advantage or disadvantage in arms—we will assume this to be a linear function $a_A(S_t^A - S_t^B)$ of the difference in arms stocks.[8] This denotes nothing more than that a state gains advantage from arms superiority over an opponent that may be reflected in political and economic gains, without necessarily requiring direct use of military force. Second, there is a component $b_A S_t^A$ due to the cost of maintaining the arms stock. These costs include all of the expenditures on maintenance, repair, and staffing and might reasonably be assumed to be approximately proportional to the size of the arms stock. As the size of the arms stock increases, maintenance costs increase. Finally, there is a cost associated with changing the arms stock. Since large increases would impose considerable strain on the industrial infrastructure of the state as well as exacting political costs (at least at some point), the cost associated with an increase is presumed to be a quadratic[9] function $c_A(P_t^A)^2$ of production. Thus, the utility for side A at time t is taken to be

$$U_A(S_t^A, S_t^B, P_t^A) = a_A(S_t^A - S_t^B) - b_A S_t^A - c_A(P_t^A)^2. \qquad (3.3)$$

8. In general, of course, this function will be nonlinear. However, over reasonable ranges this linear approximation may be useful. Since future outcomes are discounted, as the nonlinearities become more pronounced they are less important.

9. Linear-quadratic models for utility in arms races have been used previously in arms race modeling, for example by Simaan and Cruz (1975) and Gillespie et al. (1977), although with many differences in detail.

One could also introduce a domestic constituency factor P_D^A, which is the optimal rate of arms production with respect to internal interest groups. The third term would then become $c_A(P_t^A - P_D^A)^2$, reflecting the fact that the least "cost" of production does not occur at zero. Nonzero values of P_D^A would occur because of internal needs to stimulate the economy, pressure from representatives of districts that manufacture arms, etc. We do not further pursue this elaboration because it did not appear to make much difference in the general character of the results.

Since any decision about production levels must also come to grips with the relative value of benefits and costs occurring at different times in the future, it is necessary to add discounting factors δ_A and δ_B. The value of the discount parameter δ_A reflects the relative weighting by A of present and future costs and benefits. Values used in this book for δ_A and δ_B are 0.95 and 0.90, corresponding to interest rates of 5 percent and 10 percent. For any realized sequence of production decisions, we assume that state A values the outcome by discounting the utility by δ_A. Thus, the total utility of this realized outcome is

$$\sum_{t=1}^{\infty} \delta_A^t U_A(S_t^A, S_t^B, P_t^A). \tag{3.4}$$

It is important to realize that the word *utility*, as it is used here, reflects the net cost-benefit of a particular sequence of actual or contemplated production decisions of both sides. This includes not only the advantage or disadvantage of the relative arms stocks, but also all the costs incurred in their production and maintenance. Utility is not isomorphic with the benefits of a given pattern of actions, but represents the net benefit after allowing for all costs.

We may summarize the foregoing discussion by the following model.

The Model. *Let the arms production at time t of states A and B be P_t^A and P_t^B and let the arms stocks at time $t = 0$ be S_0^A and S_0^B. Assume that the arms stocks S_t^A and S_t^B are given by*

$$S_t^A = \alpha S_{t-1}^A + P_t^A$$

$$S_t^B = \alpha S_{t-1}^B + P_t^B \qquad (0 < \alpha < 1).$$

Then the utility associated by A with this outcome evaluated at time $t = 0$ is

$$\sum_{t=1}^{\infty} \delta_A^t U_A(S_t^A, S_t^B, P_t^A)$$

$\Delta = $ level of prod

$$= \sum_{t=1}^{\infty} \delta_A^t \left[a_A(S_t^A - S_t^B) - b_A S_t^A - c_A(P_t^A)^2 \right]$$

and similarly for nation B.

If the two sides are roughly equivalent and the coefficients a, b, and c have the usual signs, this model has certain features in common with the Prisoner's Dilemma. If one has two particular levels of production $\Delta^A < \Delta_0^A$ and $\Delta^B < \Delta_0^B$ under consideration, then the four outcomes represented by each side choosing Δ or Δ_0 form a payoff matrix of the Prisoner's Dilemma type. In this case, each side prefers to produce more whatever the choice of the other side, but both sides would prefer mutual cooperation to mutual defection. The model we use has, however, several more realistic features. First, it allows cooperative gestures or cheating of any size, so that nations are not presented with dichotomous choices but rather choose from a continuum of production levels. Second, if the two sides are not equal in all respects, the model presents the possibility that one side may prefer mutual defection to equal cooperation; that is, if Δ_0^A was much larger than Δ_0^B, then A might be able to extract a sufficiently large positive utility from the continuing arms advantage to make up for the costs of the arms race. Thus, this model can exhibit the Deadlock-like behavior exemplified by the German arms buildup before World War II.[10] Third, and perhaps most notably, the model does not consist of a repetition of the identical game since the payoffs to a choice pair depend on the arms stocks and, therefore, on the previous choices of the participants. In prospect, each future year will look like a different game since the arms stocks of the two sides will (possibly) be different.

---

10. See Jervis (1978) and Snyder and Diesing (1977).

3.2   Basic Assumptions

3.2.1   Assumption 1: *Decision makers act rationally in pursuit of their goals.*

Those who have an intimate knowledge of the cost of arms races and the pattern of misperception, self-delusion, and stupidity that often seems to fuel them are frequently put off by a theoretical structure that is based on the premise that states behave in a "rational" fashion. They question the logic of believing that a sophisticated understanding of rational behavior can constitute the foundation for generating policies to control arms races, which they consider to be an irrational behavior. They note the absence of a market to enforce the evolution of "optimal" behavior and the absence of a common incentive such as income, which plays such a large role in microeconomic models. And they point to an increasingly rich, experimental literature in cognitive psychology (see Kahneman et al. 1982) that suggests that individuals employ a variety of decision heuristics that are inconsistent with the tenets of rationality.

Devotees of formal modeling often respond to these challenges by acknowledging that while their approach may be imperfect their critics have yet to present a coherent alternative. Whatever the defects of the rational actor model, there is no theory of the irrational actor. Scientific paradigms and models are not dislodged by criticism alone; they are dislodged by another paradigm or model that has fewer flaws or solves more problems (Laudan 1977). To date, critics of microeconomic theories of choice have produced no such model. The Carnegie School, best exemplified by March and Simon (1958) and Cyert and March (1963), probably represents the most ambitious attempt to create an alternative to microeconomics but it eventually foundered on ambiguities associated with key concepts such as "aspiration level," "satisfycing," and "sequential attention to goals."

The argument that there is no well-specified alternative may contain a certain compelling bravado, but it is too easily extendable to justifying the use of crystals as a cure for arthritis. Desperation and the fact that no other cure is available might be justification for experimenting with the procedure; it isn't justification for believing that it will work. Fortunately, the argument for employing formal modeling rests on more positive attributes. In the wake of the Carnegie School attack, microeconomics proved itself capable of absorbing certain key elements of its detractors' criticisms and emerging stronger than ever. The Carnegie School presented some compelling arguments that a model that assumes that firms behave as if there were perfect information and no role for agenda setting provides a poor basis for generating interesting normative or descriptive insights about firms (let alone nations). It erred, however, in assuming that, because early economic models possessed these assumptions, they were somehow inherent in formal analysis. Economic models developed in the wake of the Carnegie School critique quickly demonstrated that many of their limitations could be overcome by including information and resource constraints. The seemingly absurd assumption that individuals or firms omnisciently maximize utility evolved into little more than the assumption of purposive action under specifiable constraints to which there is little alternative. This sequence of criticism and theory adaptation has occurred many times—if not quickly enough or frequently enough to satisfy every detractor.

The flexibility of formal models also forms the core of a response to the criticism that it is naive to believe that formal theory can be used to understand a behavior that seems to incorporate a large irrational element. Two of the bases for this criticism are that national leaders exhibit ambitions that seem perverse (e.g., Hitler, Khomeini) or pursue policies that seem not in the best interest of the decision makers who are responsible for them. A formal modeling perspective can easily cope with the perverse preference point by simply acknowledging that a high degree of preference variation exists. Trying to understand a phenomenon is easier if the analyst can assume that all participants have the same preferences, but it is not a prerequisite for formal analysis. This should be clear from our insistence that the arms race behavior of some nations is motivated by Deadlock rather than Prisoner's Dilemma preferences and that the possibility that this is true is a major determinant of arms race and treaty behavior. This explains the generality of the arms race model that we employ. The inability to assume consistent preferences has a cost, of course. It means that in order for a policymaker to use the results of our analysis to shape an arms decision, he or she will have to make an estimate of the preferences of rival decision makers. This may be difficult, but it is a difficulty that characterizes most bargaining situations. A theory that provides insight into how to bargain most effectively against negotiators with different characteristics is valuable even if the theory cannot predict what sort of adversary one will encounter.

A formal model is only a theory of choice; it does not explain the origins of national ambition. Nor does it explain the propensity to take risks, or predict that every choice will produce desirable results. Just as axiomatic modeling can deal with the existence of different goals, it can incorporate assumptions that are consistent with risk-seeking behavior and large amounts of uncertainty. Under these conditions, models that still warrant the term *rational* will predict that decision makers will frequently adopt policies that appear irrational to an outsider, in the sense that they lead to poor outcomes. Indeed, formal models, like statistics, can be useful in demonstrating that optimal decisions in an uncertain world do not always lead to desirable results.

The sophisticated critic may respond that, while one can incorporate variation in the utility function of decision makers, different risk functions, and large amounts of uncertainty into formal models so that they lead to behaviors that appear irrational, the *frequency* of suboptimal decisions suggests that they are inspired by decision heuristics that belie the microeconomic ideal. Because the existence of such heuristics is supported by such a wealth of experimental evidence, this challenge to formal modeling deserves to be taken very seriously.

Consider, for example, the tendency of individuals to view the concessions they make during bargaining as being greater than those that they receive in return (Ross and Sicoly 1979, 322–26). This will obviously make any kind of negotiation difficult because equitable treatment is a widespread norm. In the context of tacit bargaining, each side will view the other as greeting its cooperation with a modest degree of defection or exploitation. Not surprisingly, this is likely to reduce the magnitude and frequency of cooperative gestures. To the extent that each side "punishes" anything less than an equitable response, the relationship will slowly spiral downward. The rate of this downward spiral will be increased by a corresponding tendency to view the punishment that each receives for genuine defection to be excessive.

The misinterpretation-inspired process of deteriorating relations that can take place even in an environment where the underlying preferences of both sides are consistent with a cooperative outcome can be further exacerbated by what psychologists refer to as the "fundamental attribution error." This refers to the inability of an individual to appreciate the extent to which an opponent is simply responding to the individual's own behavior or to elements outside the opponent's control (Ross and Anderson 1982). Decision makers, like people in general, believe that they act aggressively because they are forced to do so, while their opponents act aggressively because they want to do so. The fundamental attribution error reduces the chances that the *source* of the confusion described in the previous paragraph will ever be discovered. Instead of attributing the rival's behavior to a difference in perception or to conditions that lay outside its effective control—the behavior of a third nation or the effect of economic turmoil that impels decision makers to follow a policy course that they would prefer to avoid—each state will attribute the increased aggressiveness (or decreased cooperativeness) of the other as a calculated effort at exploitation and respond accordingly.

Still another bias that further reinforces the tendency toward misinterpretation and exacerbates the biases just discussed concerns the interpretation of new evidence. Social psychologists have produced experimental evidence showing the limited ability of individuals to evaluate objectively new information that conflicts with their deeply ingrained predispositions. People not only tend to dismiss high-quality information that contradicts their position in favor of information from more suspect sources that supports their views, but they often use conflicting evidence to support their position (Nisbett and Ross 1980). If, because of a combination of ideology and experience, national decision makers share this tendency, it will be difficult for a state to accept any "signal" other than the one that is anticipated, and the ability of a nation to communicate a willingness to improve relations will be slim.

These heuristics appear to undermine the basic logic of formal analysis because they suggest that decision makers cannot be expected to behave in a way that maximizes any utility function. It is not difficult to show that a decision maker can be made better off by abandoning the fundamental attribution algorithm or the tendency to dismiss information that runs counter to predispositions. Yet, even if every decision maker embraced every decision heuristic ever described, formal analysis combined with simulation could still make a contribution by investigating the precise implications of these biases. Treating the heuristic as a constraint, such analysis could tell us what tacit bargaining strategies succeed best under conditions of high information bias and something about the impact of the heuristic on traditional tacit bargaining strategies such as Tit-for-Tat. Because we believe that such heuristics can be important during the initial stages of tacit bargaining or in very unsophisticated environments, we complete such an exercise in chapter 4. Not surprisingly perhaps, a decision process plagued by large amounts of bias makes successful tacit bargaining almost impossible.

More encouraging is the argument that these heuristics may be less applicable to arms behavior than one might think. To begin with, it is impossible to avoid observing that tacit strategies do seem to work and that arms races are frequently less intense than one would predict on the basis of heuristic-driven behavior. Most arms races do not escalate at the ever-increasing pace that a simple interpretation of the fundamental attribution bias and the tendency to underestimate the value of an opponent's cooperative gesture would imply. The races between Britain and its European naval rivals did not escalate uniformly and the U.S.-Soviet race has certainly not done so. While this might be attributed to the intermittent operation of economic constraints generated by business cycles, it ignores the no less confounding fact that these races did not consume—even at their height—a portion of national income that was as large as a heuristic-driven simulation would predict.

Still another argument for not abandoning formal analysis in the face of evidence of bias-generating heuristics concerns the ability of institutions to overcome them.[11] Although it is undeniably

---

11. It should also be noted that, even at the individual level, these heuristics are not universally applied. The susceptibility to each of them—including the fundamental attribution bias—varies across individuals for reasons that are not well understood.

true that institutions are made up of individuals who employ biased decision rules, it is no less true that institutions can create procedures and incentive systems to overcome biases that are organizationally dysfunctional. Overestimating the probability of rare events is an example of one heuristic that can lead to inefficient decisions on the individual level but can be compensated for at the organizational level. The success of brokerage and insurance firms has depended on it. Should we expect less of the decision-making arm of government in relation to a heuristic such as the fundamental attribution error?

Some might respond that the key to abandoning a bias-generating heuristic is the presence of a technology that can take its place. In the case of the heuristic of overestimating the probability of rare events, the technology of actuarial science is what saved the day. Probability theory and the procedures associated with its application created an institutional standard operating procedure that insulated decisions from individual heuristics. No such technology has been developed to overcome the negative effects of the fundamental attribution bias.

There may be some truth in this argument, but we believe that it can be overdrawn. Those who write articles advocating that decision makers understand the perverse effect of the attribution bias in producing arms spirals obviously believe that it is possible to compensate for its ill effects. They are asking leaders to refrain from making an incorrect attribution and hope to motivate them to do so by describing the costs that this can have. If they succeed, they will not only have been instrumental in avoiding these costs, they will have helped produce more nearly optimal decisions that are similar to those that would be recommended by a formal model. If the rival nation possesses analysts of comparable insight and rhetorical skills, it will do the same. Ironically, the more successful psychologists and institutionalists are in accomplishing their mission of blunting the impact of biases, the weaker their critique of formal modeling will become.

Thus, even if one can point to examples of where decision making appears to be dominated by a bias-inducing heuristic, there is reason to believe that this effect will diminish over time. If a bias can be detected, its impact can be reduced through some compensatory action, and there is an incentive for national decision

makers to take the necessary actions. This is why it is incorrect to
argue that the mere absence of a market precludes the evolution of
rational behavior. The fact that scholars see fit to emphasize the
perverse effects of heuristic behavior on arms races and the occasional ability of decision makers to listen to their counsel suggests
that a market is not a necessary condition for the adoption of more
nearly optimal decision rules in the area of arms cooperation. A
market may speed the rate of convergence on optimality but the
only *necessary* requirements are the recognition that a dangerous
bias exists and an institutional capacity to eliminate its effect.

3.2.2   Assumption 2: *The presence of bias may be transient,
but the presence of uncertainty is not.*

The possibility of overcoming the dysfunctional effects of decision
heuristics that resolve uncertainty in a biased fashion does not
eliminate the underlying uncertainty. No amount of rationality
will eliminate uncertainty about the capabilities or intentions of
a rival power, the existence or nonexistence of a suspected treaty
violation, the possibility that a tacit bargaining signal will be mis-
read by a rival, or the relative utility of a weapon system to the
nation deploying it. This sort of uncertainty is endemic to tacit
bargaining and while there will be situations in which it is low,
it is unlikely ever to be eliminated entirely. Consider one of the
most simple sources of uncertainty: force estimates. These necessarily play a key role in a nation's arms policy and have often
proved incorrect. The Anglo-French naval races of the nineteenth
century were fueled by a number of forceful responses to nonexistent moves; German mobilization against France in 1875 was
precipitated by a similar combination of poor intelligence and
wild misinterpretation (Cobden 1868; Gooch 1923; Hirst 1913).
Although there is a tendency to believe that increasingly sophisticated monitoring procedures will eliminate miscalculations based
on faulty intelligence, the evidence in favor of this position is not
convincing. Controversies among intelligence agencies with regard
to Soviet capabilities were common throughout the 1970s and, on
a number of occasions, an agency's revision of its own previous
estimate has been dramatic (Lee 1977). And this is only the beginning. Uncertainty about force estimates pales in magnitude

when compared with the other sources of uncertainty mentioned above. Suspected violations have plagued arms treaties from the Washington Naval Treaty to SALT II, and debates about the objectives of other states have played a prominent role in every arms race and in the events leading to both World Wars.

Fortunately, the days are long past when formal modelers had to ignore the ubiquitousness of uncertainty and proceed on the basis of models that assumed perfect information. Recent work on deterrence by Nalebuff (1989) and Powell (1990) that is inspired by economic research on games with incomplete information are good examples of axiomatic modeling where much of the insight is driven by the explicit recognition of uncertainty. One of the important functions of arms behavior is to establish a reputation for strength that will deter and grant policy influence. Shifted to an arms race setting, Nalebuff's discussion of the impact of intervention on reputation suggests that uncertainty can produce a higher rate of arms building than would exist under perfect information. This higher rate is sustained because uncertainty provides a state with the opportunity to inflate a rival's perception of capability, not because risk aversion inspires an attitude of "better safe than sorry."

Powell's research on crisis stability is also driven by uncertainty, in this case uncertainty about both commitment and capability. Using sequential equilibrium models, Powell shows that the state with the greatest resolve will not necessarily prevail, and that an irresolute challenger may be more likely to escalate if it meets resistance. If such conclusions seem "weak" or less definitive than they would be under perfect information, this is no accident. Powell's point is that the presence of uncertainty transforms a crisis into something more complicated than a mere contest of resolve (Powell 1988, 171).

As we will proceed to demonstrate time and again, the existence of uncertainty about the goals of a rival nation and the behaviors in which it engages play a critical role in determining what tacit bargaining strategies will be used (and can be used) to slow an arms race and maintain an arms agreement. When uncertainty about motives is high, tacit bargaining becomes conservative. When uncertainty about motives is low, but it is high about specific behaviors like test violations, it suggests the use

of "trigger strategies" that consist of announced thresholds that
are carefully calculated to allow for a given level of uncertainty
but which cannot be exceeded without retaliation. When uncertainty is simultaneously high about both motives and actions,
tacit bargaining becomes problematic, at best, and may be often
dangerous.

3.2.3   Assumption 3: *It is possible to regard the decision-making apparatus of a state as a unitary actor.*

Only slightly less controversial than the assumption of rationality
is the assumption that states can be represented as unitary actors.
While international relations theorists in the realist school from
Thucydides to Waltz (1979) and Bueno de Mesquita (1981) have
found it useful to assume that a nation has a set of interests that
it pursues in a fashion identical to that of an individual, scholars
with a bureaucratic politics or bureaucratic process orientation
have argued that this characterization can be quite misleading
(see Allison 1971; Cohen and March 1976; Cyert and March 1963;
and Halperin and Kanter 1973).   They contend that priorities
emerge from organizations in such a way that they are prone to
the social choice problems that plague any quasi-legislative body
(see Arrow 1951; Ordeshook 1986). Just as no single person is fully
in charge, policy priorities cannot be dependably represented by
a single, stable utility function.

Once again, it is possible simply to assume that states behave
as if the unitary actor assumption were true and argue that the
empirical validity of the resultant model will settle the matter. If
the model correctly predicts behavior, the assumption is appropriate. The problem in the present context is that there are an
insufficient number of cases to test any theory about tacit bargaining. In this situation, the confidence that we can place in
particular assumptions is critical. Therefore, there is good reason
to be interested in the questions, "When is it possible to represent the foreign policy–making apparatus of a state as a unitary
actor?" and "How frequently do these conditions obtain?"

One set of circumstances that can justify a unitary actor assumption has its roots in the tradition of strong executive leadership in foreign policy and the structure of government that sup-

ports it. This is the basis for Bueno de Mesquita's argument in favor of the unitary actor assumption in *The War Trap* (1981). He first presents an abstract argument that demonstrates that when the vote of one member of a decision-making collective is weighted more heavily than other members, that individual can function as a necessary part of most (if not all) winning coalitions. Such an executive will play a critical "gatekeeping" role that fits in with Bueno de Mesquita's vision that the causes of war are made up of necessary, but not sufficient, conditions; that is, the leader may not have the power to thrust a nation into war unilaterally, but he or she has the power to veto anyone else's attempt to do so.

Having demonstrated the possibility that a strong executive can cause a nation to act as if it were a unitary actor, Bueno de Mesquita goes on to present some historical evidence that such executives have played a key role in making decisions about war and peace. He notes that Britain's response to a powerful enemy has often been to abandon, temporarily, its democratic procedures and that the United States has done the same. Moreover, when we think of the decision to go to war or to appease, he argues that it is usually tied to a specific executive rather than the bureaucracy or legislature: Richelieu, Metternich, Teddy Roosevelt, Chamberlain, Hitler, the list goes on and on. No leader can ignore what goes on around him or her, but ultimately it is "the responsibility of a single leader to decide what to do and how to do it" (Bueno de Mesquita 1981, 28).

The last part of the argument can be overdrawn, of course. The existence of a place where the "buck stops" does not mean that the resultant decision will be made in accordance with the preferences of the person making the decision. Still, Bueno de Mesquita has a good point. The decision to go to war seems more likely to be closely tied to the preferences of a strong leader than many of the more trivial decisions that governments make. It is difficult not to notice that the decisions that are the grist for classic expositions of the importance of bureaucratic processes on decision making ranging from Cyert and March (1963) to Allison (1971) are relatively mundane. "Standard operating procedures" that define the nature of organizational heuristics are often suspended for rare and important events, and major foreign policy initiatives are certainly not typical. Even if we move from a bureaucratic process model to a bureaucratic politics model, it often seems to be the case that critical decisions increase the impact of certain offices and institutions. While we will be dealing with arms race behavior and treaty maintenance rather than the decision of whether to go to war or not, it seems likely that these decisions will also be executive dominated. In the United States, for example, Congress has involved itself in the discussions of Soviet violations of the SALT agreements, but the presentation of the evidence that the violations exist and the definition of their significance has usually had its locus within the White House.

Speaking in terms of executive branch dominance in critical foreign policy decisions is helpful because it diverts attention away from the personality of the chief executive and makes us sensitive to the structural sources of "strong leadership." The kind of social choice mechanism that is vulnerable to Arrow's famous paradox (1951) bears little resemblance to the process that controls foreign policy decisions in any modern nation-state. The agenda setting power of executives, the hierarchical nature of bureaucracies, the ability to appoint key officials in the policymaking process, party discipline, vetoes, access to intelligence, and de jure control over associated bureaucracies like the State Department and the Office of Management and Budget all act to give the president of the United States more weight in the decision process than other "players." Comparable or greater advantages exist (and have always existed in one form or another) in every major power. Collectively, these advantages combine to make the assumption that a state's decision-making apparatus in the domain of major foreign policy decisions can be approximated by a unitary actor less naive than it might initially appear.

Strong leadership and the institutions that support it do not exhaust the rationales for the unitary actor assumption. Perhaps perversely, one motivation behind the evolution of a unitary-actor-oriented process lies in the best documented heuristic—the fundamental attribution bias. If nation A is going to ignore the plurality of forces that affect decisions and develop policies as if it were dealing with a unitary actor, then there is an incentive for nation B to develop a more unitary process in self-defense. To fail to do so would commit both nations to a history of misunderstandings in which nation A would react to a variety of tacit bargaining signals that B never intended to send. For example, a lack of control over the decision-making process would be interpreted as B's unwillingness to cooperate and could easily inspire retaliation. Depending on the foregone benefits of cooperation and the cost of retaliation, this may leave B far worse off. While it would be silly to claim that in the presence of the fundamental attribution bias a nation should—or can—abandon every semblance of pluralism in the policy process, a state acting to avoid the "costs" of sending false signals by increasing centralization and control is commonplace. It is most evident in the constant evolution of more reliable command and control systems in the military. Ten years ago, Soviet ship captains were permitted far greater autonomy in harassing U.S. fleets for the purpose of intelligence gathering or readiness exercises than they are today. One suspects that one of the main reasons for this change is that the Soviet Union has little desire to jeopardize improved relations with the United States through the existence of actions that could be misinterpreted as tacit signals of aggressive aspirations.

The evolution toward greater centralization and more unitary actor-like behavior is further fueled by the fear of exploitation. Even if the attribution bias did not exist, neither state could afford to be too generous in its interpretation of the other's motives. Not only does the Soviet Union have an incentive to exercise control over the behavior of its ship captains because it does not wish to provoke the United States, but the United States has an incentive to show a tendency to be provoked by such gestures. If the United States were to adopt a policy of "Captains will be Captains, it is important not to be provoked by such things," a calculating Soviet Union would soon find it profitable to give the impression that all of its military units were permitted maximum, decentralized discretion. An isolated test ban violation, a border skirmish, the harassment of diplomats, and a thousand other policies could be ingenuously attributed to the adventurism of uncontrollable military officers or diplomatic officials. The fact that this incentive is very real is one of the reasons why states frequently send messages that they will hold a rival nation responsible for such behavior and will not accept the excuse that it was unintended. In this way the "game" of international relations creates a situation where states have an incentive to act like a unitary actor and to treat their rivals as if they were unitary actors.

Another approach to the justification of the unitary actor assumption is through formal models. The Condorcet (1785) paradox of cyclical voting and Arrow's (1951) impossibility theorem show that majority rule with arbitrary preference distributions can have an inconsistent outcome. However, Black (1948) showed that if the decision space were one-dimensional, if each actor had a single-peaked utility function, and if the decision rule were majority rule, then the preferences of the median voter would win out, so that the decisions on this dimension would be representable by a utility function. A remarkable recent result of Caplin and Nalebuff (1988, 1989) states that the preferences of the *mean* voter will always rule if the decision criterion is 64 percent majority rule. This result requires several assumptions about the type of utility function held by each individual, about the distribution of preferences across individuals, and about the decision rule. The most important limitation is that there is a status quo that will continue to hold unless a supermajority of 64 percent of the electorate favors one single alternative. This avoids cycling, but may often lead to no decision at all when there is any substantial difference of opinion. Still, this level of consensus is often met in the areas of foreign and defense policy, which are known to enjoy a level of nonpartisan agreement that is rare in the domestic arena.

A more subtle justification for the unitary actor assumption is based on the way pluralistic preferences can plausibly combine. Suppose we have an executive and a set of advisers/influencers. The final decision lies with the executive, but each other actor may influence the decision by applying pressure on the decision maker. Such pressure incurs a cost (political, financial, etc.), and there is therefore a limit to the amount of pressure that will be applied. We show that the final decisions that emerge from this political system are those of a hypothetical aggregate actor whose preferences are a weighted average of those of all the actors, including the executive.[12]

---

12. Achen (1988) gives the sketch of a one-dimensional model somewhat similar to the one used here; however, both the results and the interpretation as directional "pushing" are new in this book.

Assume that all players have utilities derived from generalized quadratic loss from their ideal point. This is a generalization of a common assumption in the social choice literature, going back to Davis and Hinich (1967), that preferences are generated by Euclidean distance from an ideal point $\mathbf{v}_i$. Here we allow any quadratic distance function, so that the utility function is not assumed to be separable on the attribute dimensions and the individual actor can weight each dimension and combination of dimensions in any way he or she chooses.

Assume that the set of alternatives forms a convex set $X \subset \mathbf{R}^p$ containing the ideal points $\{\mathbf{v}_i\}$ of the actors. Each dimension refers to some aspect of the policy, the entire collection of which can be said to characterize the choice. Assume that the utility of $\mathbf{x} \in X$ for actor i $(i = 1, 2, \ldots, n)$ is

$$u_i(\mathbf{x}) = -\tfrac{1}{2}(\mathbf{x} - \mathbf{v}_i)^{\top} \mathbf{E}_i (\mathbf{x} - \mathbf{v}_i),$$

where $\mathbf{E}_i$ is a symmetric, positive-definite, $p \times p$ matrix—this is the generalized quadratic loss referred to above.

Now suppose that actor $i > 0$ can choose a vector $\mathbf{a}_i$ such that the quantity $\mathbf{a}_i^{\top} \mathbf{E}_0 \mathbf{x}$ is added to the utility of the decision maker (actor 0, abbreviated DM), and the quantity $\tfrac{1}{2} b_i \mathbf{a}_i^{\top} \mathbf{E}_0 \mathbf{a}_i$ is subtracted from the utility of actor i. Thus, each actor i can influence the executive in a chosen direction, but must pay a price that depends on which direction the actor pushes the executive (the direction of $\mathbf{a}_i$) and how hard the actor pushes (the length of $\mathbf{a}_i$). Note that this does not amount to an assumption of transferable utility—there is no numerical correspondence between the pressure $\mathbf{a}_i^{\top} \mathbf{E}_0 \mathbf{x}$ that actor i can impose on the decision maker and the cost $\tfrac{1}{2} b_i \mathbf{a}_i^{\top} \mathbf{E}_0 \mathbf{a}_i$ that is incurred. Rather, this is an attempt to model the fact that advisers or other independent actors in the government can "cash in some chips" in order to influence policy in a preferred direction.

Proposition 1. *Under the setup of this section, the final decision made by a rational decision maker along with rational influencers is consistent with a utility function $\tilde{u}$ defined by*

$$\tilde{u}(\mathbf{x}) = u_0(\mathbf{x}) + \sum b_i^{-1} u_i(\mathbf{x}). \tag{3.5}$$

Proof. The final utility of the DM is

$$u_0(\mathbf{x}) = -\tfrac{1}{2}(\mathbf{x} - \mathbf{v}_0)^\top \mathbf{E}_0(\mathbf{x} - \mathbf{v}_0) + \sum \mathbf{a}_i^\top \mathbf{E}_0 \mathbf{x}.$$

The first-order condition (FOC) for the maximization problem that the DM must solve is

$$0 = -\mathbf{E}_0(\mathbf{x} - \mathbf{v}_0) + \sum \mathbf{E}_0 \mathbf{a}_i$$

giving the solution

$$\mathbf{x}^* = \mathbf{v}_0 + \sum \mathbf{a}_i.$$

Note that $\mathbf{v}_0$ would be the DM's optimal choice without the pressure from the other actors.

Now the utility for actor i at the DM-optimal choice $\mathbf{x}^*$ is given by

$$u_i(\mathbf{x}^*) = -\tfrac{1}{2}(\mathbf{x}^* - \mathbf{v}_i)^\top \mathbf{E}_i(\mathbf{x}^* - \mathbf{v}_i) - \tfrac{1}{2}b_i \mathbf{a}_i^\top \mathbf{E}_0 \mathbf{a}_i.$$

The FOC for the optimal choice of $\mathbf{a}_i$ by actor i is

$$\begin{aligned} 0 &= -\frac{\partial \mathbf{x}^*}{\partial \mathbf{a}_i} \mathbf{E}_i(\mathbf{x}^* - \mathbf{v}_i) - b_i \mathbf{E}_0 \mathbf{a}_i \\ &= -\mathbf{E}_i(\mathbf{x}^* - \mathbf{v}_i) - b_i \mathbf{E}_0 \mathbf{a}_i \end{aligned}$$

so that

$$\mathbf{a}_i = -b_i^{-1} \mathbf{E}_0^{-1} \mathbf{E}_i(\mathbf{x}^* - \mathbf{v}_i).$$

Substituting this into the FOC for the DM we get

$$0 = -\mathbf{E}_0(\mathbf{x}^* - \mathbf{v}_0) - \sum b_i^{-1} \mathbf{E}_i(\mathbf{x}^* - \mathbf{v}_i)$$

so

$$\mathbf{x}^* = \left(\sum b_i^{-1} \mathbf{E}_i + \mathbf{E}_0\right)^{-1} \left(\mathbf{E}_0 \mathbf{v}_0 + \sum b_i^{-1} \mathbf{E}_i \mathbf{v}_i\right).$$

Finally, the FOC for the DM is the same as the FOC for a unitary actor with utility function

$$\tilde{u}(\mathbf{x}) = u_0(\mathbf{x}) + \sum b_i^{-1} u_i(\mathbf{x})$$

which is

$$0 = -\mathbf{E}_0(\mathbf{x} - \mathbf{v}_0) - \sum b_i^{-1}\mathbf{E}_i(\mathbf{x} - \mathbf{v}_i)$$

as asserted. ∎

We can interpret this result in the following way. Each influencer chooses a direction in the p-dimensional decision space in which to influence the decision maker. If $\mathbf{a}_i$ is the vector chosen by actor i, then the decision maker may choose freely in the space orthogonal to $\mathbf{a}_i$ (in the metric defined by the decision maker's utility) and is pushed in the direction of $\mathbf{a}_i$ with a strength that depends on the length of $\mathbf{a}_i$. The cost to actor i of exerting this influence is proportional to the squared length of $\mathbf{a}_i$, again in the metric induced by the decision maker's utility. This is arguably the correct metric, since it measures the reluctance of the decision maker to move in that direction. With these assumptions, the resulting decision is the same as that chosen by a unitary actor whose utility is a linear combination of the decision maker's utility and the utilities of the other actors. The weights depend on the policy space metric that each actor has, as well as the explicit weights b_i. Note that the "power" of each actor relative to the others can be said to depend on the direction away from $\mathbf{v}_0$ one is considering.

This treatment forms a model of bureaucratic politics with an executive. Consider, for example, the president of the United States, together with the cabinet and the leaders of the House and Senate. Suppose a particular issue is essentially to be decided by the president, as is the case with many foreign policy choices. Each of the actors will have an ideal choice that he or she would choose if the decision were left to that actor alone. Each actor can put pressure on the president because of constituencies that he or she represents and because of the need of the president for the cooperation of these actors in the future. The result just given states that such a system will produce consistent decisions that would be those of a hypothetical composite actor whose utility is a combination of the utilities of all of the actors, each weighted by the "power" of that actor. Although we may quarrel with the priorities of this composite actor, the results are still "rational" in the sense of being representable by a utility function. More complex decisions that result from voting in legislative bodies or the combined actions of the executive and the legislature are not covered by the above proposition, but the coverage is broad enough to have relevance for the modeling of foreign policy behavior.

In sum, although the unitary actor assumption is subject to criticism from a number of angles, the assumption is a better approximation of decision making than one might think at the outset. The traditional argument that foreign policy decision making is more executive centered than is domestic policymaking is buttressed by an increased appreciation for the instruments that sophisticated executives can employ to increase their control. These include agenda-setting power, the hierarchical nature of bureaucracies, the ability to appoint key officials, and privileged access to intelligence information. There are two additional arguments for this assumption. The first concerns the nature of the international relations "game." The prospect that each nation will be held accountable for its actions as if it could exert centralized control increases the incentive to develop institutional apparatuses that can provide that control. Second, the model of organizational decision making provides a plausible way in which a nation run by a group can still act with a single, overall utility function.

3.3   Oligopoly Theory

Some of the material in this book uses methods derived from oligopoly theory in economics. The analogy between an oligopoly and arms control in the international system is clear. An oligopoly is a group of firms that could profit by an agreement to restrict production. However, conditional on the restricted production of the others, each firm has an incentive to increase its own production, if it could do so without retaliation. Similarly, in many cases, all members of an international system would benefit if arms could be limited, but each nation, optimizing against fixed decisions of other nations, has a similar incentive to increase arms production. Firms that engage in this conditional optimization behavior may end up in the Cournot equilibrium, which yields less profits than cooperation—nations behaving similarly may find themselves in an arms race.

Suppose that the market for a homogeneous good is entirely supplied by n firms and that the market demand function $p(X)$

is given, where p is the price and $X = x_1 + x_2 + \cdots + x_n$ is the industry production.[13] For simplicity in this presentation, we will assume that the firms face identical cost functions $C(x) = cx + d$ with constant marginal cost c over the relevant range of x.[14] Firm i's profit is

$$\pi_i = p(X)x_i - cx_i - d$$

and total industry profit is

$$p(X)X - cX - nd,$$

which is maximized when

$$p'(X)X + p(X) - c = 0 \quad \text{or}$$

$$(p - c)/p = \epsilon^{-1},$$

where $\epsilon = -p(X)/Xp'(X)$ is the market elasticity of demand. Thus the collectively optimal action would be for the oligopoly as a whole to produce the quantity X_0 that achieves the monopoly price, and divide that output among the oligopolists. However, at that production level, the marginal revenue of the ith firm is $\text{MR}_i = p'(X_0)x_i + p(X_0)$ so that

$$\text{MR}_i - p(X_0) = -p'(X_0)x_i > 0.$$

This means that each firm individually has an incentive to raise production, so that the monopoly (cooperative) price cannot be maintained without some means of enforcement. If each firm raises its production as far as it can and still earn positive profits, then the resulting equilibrium (called the Cournot equilibrium) satisfies $[p(X) - c]/p(X) = n^{-1}\epsilon^{-1}$. This equilibrium results in a smaller markup for each firm than the monopoly price. In some sense the Cournot equilibrium is intermediate between true competition and monopoly. The key aspect from the oligopolists' point of view is to develop methods to maintain the price at higher than the Cournot level, so that profits can be increased.

---

13. This summary follows Shapiro (1987).

14. These restrictions are, of course, not necessary for the existence of the Cournot equilibrium. They are adopted for expository purposes only. See Shapiro (1987) for more general results.

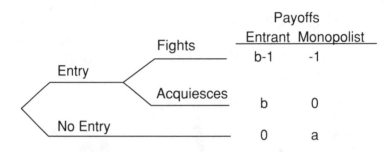

Fig. 3.3. Utilities for a weak monopolist

There are two research traditions within oligopoly theory from which we draw. The first concerns uncertainties about underlying utilities. Selten's (1978) chain store paradox concerns a situation in which a chain store extracts monopoly rents in a variety of markets. He examines a scenario where other stores contemplate entry sequentially, one into each of the markets. In each market, the potential entrant decides whether to enter the market and then the monopolist decides whether to fight or acquiesce. If the payoffs are as given in figure 3.3 (*weak monopolist*), then the potential entrant will always enter and the monopolist will always acquiesce, an aggregate outcome that is extremely unsatisfactory to the monopolist, since all the markets become less profitable. If the utilities of the participants are common knowledge, then there would seem to be little way that the monopolist could avoid this outcome. Suppose, however, that there is uncertainty in the minds of the potential entrants as to whether the monopolist has the utilities as in figure 3.3 or those in figure 3.4 (*strong monopolist*). If the monopolist had the utilities shown in figure 3.4, then the entrant would expect the monopolist to fight entry. Since this would be an unsatisfactory outcome for the potential entrant, entry would be deterred.

Clearly, if the subjective probability that the monopolist is "strong" is sufficiently high, entry will be deterred, and if it is sufficiently low, entry will be assured. For intermediate values, the solution is not immediately clear. A solution to this problem was provided by Kreps, Milgrom, Roberts, and Wilson (1982), Kreps and Wilson (1982a; 1982b), and Milgrom and Roberts (1982),

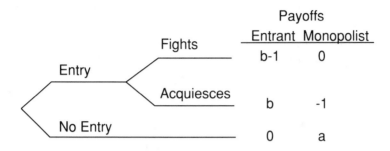

Fig. 3.4. Utilities for a strong monopolist

who demonstrated the existence of an equilibrium (with certain parameter values). In a typical outcome, the potential entrant decides not to enter in each of the first k of n decisions. After the kth period, the monopolist will fight each of the following entries for a further period of random length ℓ, and then acquiesce thereafter. The potential entrants actually enter in some of these cases (testing the monopolist) and do not in others, according to another randomization rule. This solution depends crucially on the assumption that the game is of finite length, because a critical variable is the amount of time until the last potential entry.

This method has been applied in several security examples, most notably by Powell (1985, 1987, 1988, 1990) who applies these concepts to crisis stability. A key feature of these models is the imposition, perhaps artificial,[15] of a final stage, so that the backward induction method used by Kreps and Wilson (1982a) would apply. This model can also be applied in arms race modeling, although the analysis is more complex than in the crisis stability case. In chapter 4, we present a model of this type relating to the achievement of an arms agreement by tacit means in the presence of utility uncertainty.

The second tradition of oligopoly theory that we employ involves uncertainty about actions, rather than uncertainty about

---

15. In many of these situations, there is no natural exact limit to the number of moves before the game terminates. An exact endpoint is imposed so that backward induction may be used to derive an equilibrium. However, with many games, equilibria with an exact finite number of replications are very different from those when the number of replications is unknown or indeterminate.

utilities, and involves the use of trigger strategies (Abreu, Pearce, and Stacchetti 1986; Green and Porter 1984; Porter 1983). The context is that of a repeated game in which each of n identical firms chooses a production level at each period and reaps profits that depend on its own production and on the total market production; i.e., $\pi_i = p(X)x_i - cx_i - d$. The total payoff may be computed as the discounted cash flow involved. The oligopolists collectively would profit from producing less than the Cournot equilibrium amount so an agreement to restrict production would benefit all the members of the agreement. However, given that the other members are restraining their production, each member would have an incentive to increase its own production. In this setup, the members of the oligopoly may agree to punish any defector from the agreement by defecting to the Cournot production amount for some number of periods after a violation. If the period is long enough that the net result to the defector is negative, then the incentive to defect is removed, and the agreement is enforced. It is important to note that this threat can be considered credible and, therefore, might be carried out, since it only involves reversion to the individually optimal act.[16]

Now suppose that each oligopolist knows the market demand function $p(X)$ and its own production level, but not the opponent's production level and, therefore, not the total production X. Assume also that the price determined by the aggregate demand is subject to some uncertainty—the price is random from a distribution indexed by X. Since actual production amounts are not observable in this model, this could lead to prompt reversion to the Cournot equilibrium, as each firm cheats in the knowledge that the other firms cannot detect the cheating. A trigger price strategy consists of a threat to revert for a time to the Cournot production level (or worse) if the market price is observed to fall below a critical trigger price. Even though none of the members of the oligopoly can be sure who caused the fall in price or if it

---

16. Abreu (1986) and Abreu, Pearce, and Stacchetti (1986) have shown that one may sustain even more cooperative outcomes by use of an elaborate hierarchy of punishments. There may be some doubt that these could be carried out or conveyed as threats in practice. See also Farrell and Maskin (1988), who argue that renegotiation will prevent the use of some strategies that employ punishments that hurt both sides.

was caused by accidental variations in the price level, all benefit from the periods of cooperation induced by these threats.

The equivalent problem in arms races is when both sides would benefit from an arms treaty that restricts production, although each individually would prefer to produce more arms if the other side could be held to their current production. This situation is represented by the model presented above. If actual production amounts cannot be observed exactly, then some kind of trigger strategy might be able to enforce an arms treaty. There are many technical differences between the two situations, including the lack of a market and market price to signal indirectly increases in production, but there are sufficient structural similarities to justify proceeding along similar lines. We use this approach in chapter 5 to investigate how arms treaties might be maintained by an equilibrium of this kind in the face of information problems.

These results from oligopoly theory provide a straightforward means of investigating equilibria in the presence of uncertainty about the opponent's utility (chain store example) or in the presence of imperfectly observed actions (trigger-price strategies). When these two problems exist simultaneously, the equilibrium analysis becomes far more difficult and complex. Our approach will be to employ formal equilibrium analysis when considering the impact of information uncertainty or utility uncertainty separately, but to use simulation to explore their joint effect. This characterizes the analysis of strategies to attain arms cooperation in chapter 4 and the analysis of treaty maintenance strategies in chapter 5.

Chapter 4

Tacit Bargaining and the Achievement of Arms Control: Models and Solutions

4.1 Introduction

In this chapter we evaluate the ability of cooperation-based tacit bargaining strategies to stabilize or reduce arms races. Equilibrium analysis and simulation are used to explore the impact of factors that are regularly present in historical (as opposed to simple game-theoretic) formulations of arms races. These factors include uncertainty about the strategy of the rival state, misinterpretation of the opponent's behavior, multiple-response options, and variations in the time preference or discount rate of decision makers. Despite the complexity of the decision environment created by the simultaneous operation of these different factors, certain rules of thumb emerge. These can aid a state in deciding whether tacit bargaining is feasible and how it should be conducted. Of particular note are the findings (1) that no single strategy such as Tit-for-Tat performs well across a broad range of plausible decision environments, and (2) that the utility and information uncertainty that are likely to plague real-world arms races generate a fundamental paradox of tacit bargaining that must be recognized if cooperation is to emerge; that is, a state will rarely be certain enough about an opponent's response to make a large cooperative gesture, and the opponent will rarely be trusting enough to respond enthusiastically to a small gesture. The chapter concludes with a discussion of how these prescriptions and other aspects of the model permit a better understanding of the past and future role of tacit bargaining in the arms control area.

This chapter begins with an equilibrium analysis designed to cope with the problem of utility uncertainty. We then use more decision-oriented simulation models to investigate the complications posed by observational error, variations in time preference, continuous strategy spaces, and a wide variety of strategic choices. In this way, we hope to take advantage of the rigor of the equilibrium approach and the flexibility of the simulation method. This methodological eclecticism is also a necessary product of the number of factors examined. While it would obviously be more rigorous to incorporate all of the relevant dimensions into a formal equilibrium, the state of the mathematical modeler's art necessitates a trade-off between rigor and realism: equilibrium analysis does not easily cope with the simultaneous operation of a large number of variables. In this case, the fact that the two sets of conclusions support each other gives us greater confidence in the generality of the analysis.

The tacit bargaining strategies dealt with in this chapter are all based on cooperation, in the sense that they require the state that implements them to limit its rate of arms growth below that which would otherwise be optimal. The extent of this reduction, its duration, and how it is adjusted as a result of the rival state's response are what distinguishes one strategy from another. In each case, the goal of the strategy is to convince the rival that both states would fare better if the current arms race were slowed, and that the initiating state (i.e., the one employing the strategy) is willing to engage in the self-controlled behavior necessary to establish this more mutually satisfying state of affairs.

A tacit bargaining strategy designed to slow an arms race need not, of course, be based on cooperation. It might rely instead on the selective use of negative reinforcement in the form of escalations in arms growth to convince the rival that the absence of restraint would be extremely costly. This was the approach periodically adopted by Britain in its naval races with France in the nineteenth century and with Germany before World War I. From a historical standpoint, examples of such punishment-based tacit bargaining strategies are far more common than cooperation-based ones, and their logic is embedded in the rhetoric justifying countless military appropriations requests. The focus on cooperation-based strategies in this chapter is justified not by the frequency with which they are employed, but by their potential ability to reduce the intensity of an arms race without the dangers and costs of requiring that it first be escalated. Despite the popularity of punishment-based strategies, they have not been notably successful. It has proved to be no simple matter to convince a rival state tacitly that an escalation in arms growth is aimed at stabilizing the race rather than at obtaining increased policy leverage. Because the behavior is likely to appear indistinguishable from previous escalations that were motivated by more aggressive aspirations, it can easily be given a provocative interpretation and result in a still more intensive arms race.

4.2 An Equilibrium Model of Achieving Cooperation

Chapters 1 and 2 both emphasized that arms races are characterized by different underlying games and that various tacit bargaining strategies are likely to be more effective in the context of one game than in another. If intelligence regarding another nation's objectives (i.e., utility) is perfect, this may not present any great strategic dilemma. Decision makers can use whatever strategy is optimal. The problem is that most of the time no amount of intelligence will unequivocally settle the question of objectives. Even an action as provocative as Hitler's Austrian *Anschluß* did not provide incontestible information about his intentions for France or Britain. How much less does the construction of the SS-25 tell us about Soviet willingness to control the arms race?

It is easy to appreciate that uncertainty will play a central role in the creation and initiation of tacit bargaining strategies designed to promote cooperation. The more a nation is persuaded that the intentions of its rival are benign and that the arms race is simply a consequence of mutual misperception, the more gen-

erous a tacit bargaining strategy it can employ. It is not so easy
to go from this obvious homily to a real-world policy prescription.
This requires a more quantitative statement. Below we attempt
to characterize precisely when a nation should employ one tacit
bargaining strategy rather than another. What makes this a particular challenge is that an aggressive and intelligent rival may
attempt to appear to be cooperative for purposes of exploitation.
It is this problem that requires an equilibrium analysis.

Given the centrality of utility uncertainty in the problem of
achieving arms cooperation, we have chosen to begin with a model
in which this uncertainty is a key feature. For the sake of clarity, this model reduces the tacit bargaining problem to a very
schematic representation. The key uncertainty in this problem is
the utility of the other side. For the tacit bargain to be reached,
one side must make a gesture, at some cost, and the other must
accept, at some risk. This initial equilibrium analysis assumes
perfect observation of the opponent's actions, a finite strategy
space, a two-period time frame, and a simplified utility function
that does not take into account the accumulation of arms stocks.
All of these assumptions are made more realistic in the simulation
analysis that follows.

This model assumes two nations A and B to be in an arms race.
Nation A contemplates one of two cooperative gestures designed
to appeal to B under two alternative ideas that A may have about
B's utility. In the "game" that models this situation, A makes a
small cooperative gesture (or not); if B does not respond with
agreement, A may make a larger gesture (or not). The outcome
may be an agreement to lessen the arms race or the attempt may
end in failure. Those who are uninterested in the technicalities of
the equilibrium analysis may skip to the end of this section, where
the conclusions drawn from the analysis are laid out.

Suppose that A and B are in an arms race in which A produces
an amount of arms M_A and B produces M_B each period. Assume
that each period A may choose from a production set $[0, M_A]$,
and similarly for B. Assume that A's utility in any given period
when the actual production levels are (P_A, P_B) is $U_A(P_A, P_B) =
a_A P_A - b_A P_B$ and that B's utility is $U_B(P_A, P_B) = a_B P_B - b_B P_A$.
Thus, a is the benefit of a unit of arms, and b is the cost of the
opponent having a unit of arms. The utility of a time stream of

such production decisions is assumed to be the discounted sum of the utilities for each period separately, using discount rates δ_A and δ_B.

Assume that nation B might be one of three types. First, B might be "weak," implying that it strongly prefers a treaty to an arms race. Second, B might be "strong," meaning that it prefers only an advantageous treaty to an arms race. Finally, it may have Deadlock preferences, so that it prefers a continued arms race to any treaty. In short, as we move from weak to strong to Deadlock, an arms race is relatively more attractive compared to a tacit treaty. We denote the utility parameters for these three types by subscripts of W, S, and D (or BW, BS, and BD, if required to avoid ambiguity). Similarly, we suppose that A may be of two types, weak and strong.[1]

Suppose some level Δ^B is given and that an attempt will be made by A to negotiate tacitly a treaty in which B builds Δ^B and A builds an amount to be determined, with the alternative being the continuation of the current arms race. The first point is that the proposed treaty (Δ^A, Δ^B) must be preferred by both sides to the status quo (M_A, M_B). For B to prefer the offer requires that

$$a_B M_B - b_B M_A \ \leq \ a_B \Delta^B - b_B \Delta^A$$

$$\Delta^A \ \leq \ M_A - \frac{a_B}{b_B}(M_B - \Delta^B) \qquad (4.1)$$

$$M_A - \Delta^A \ \geq \ \frac{a_B}{b_B}(M_B - \Delta^B).$$

M = t−1 level
Δ = t level

This means nothing more than that A must offer to reduce its arms more than B, adjusted by the arms cost-benefit ratio of B. For simplicity, suppose A can choose between two levels of arms reduction Δ_{BW}^A and Δ_{BS}^A appropriate to weak and strong B, so that

$$\Delta_{BW}^A \ < \ M_A - \frac{a_B^W}{b_B^W}(M_B - \Delta^B) \qquad (4.2)$$

---

1. Deadlock A is excluded from consideration, since this type would never initiate a cooperative gesture, which is the object of study in this section.

$$\Delta_{BS}^A \;\; < \;\; M_A - \frac{a_B^S}{b_B^S}(M_B - \Delta^B) \qquad (4.3)$$

and suppose that these levels are common knowledge. Of course, for a B possessing Deadlock preferences, no concession on A's part will be sufficient, so that

$$a_B^D M_B - b_B^D M_A > a_B \Delta^B$$

(even if A offers to produce zero, B will still prefer the arms race).

Naturally, it is also necessary that A should prefer the offered deal to the status quo, which requires that

$$a_A M_A - b_A M_B \le a_A \Delta^A - b_A \Delta^B \qquad (4.4)$$

or

$$\frac{a_A}{b_A} \le \frac{M_B - \Delta^B}{M_A - \Delta^A}. \qquad (4.5)$$

A weak A will prefer either deal to the status quo, but a strong A will prefer the status quo to the greater concession required to please a strong B. That is, assume that

$$\frac{a_A^W}{b_A^W} \le \frac{M_B - \Delta^B}{M_A - \Delta_{BS}^A} \le \frac{M_B - \Delta^B}{M_A - \Delta_{BW}^A}$$

and

$$\frac{M_B - \Delta^B}{M_A - \Delta_{BS}^A} \le \frac{a_A^S}{b_A^S} \le \frac{M_B - \Delta^B}{M_A - \Delta_{BW}^A}.$$

In this formulation, all of this is common knowledge, except that A does not know which type B is. A only has prior probability estimates $(p_0^{BW}, p_0^{BS}, p_0^{BD})$ and B similarly has estimates (p_0^{AW}, p_0^{AS})—both sets of prior probabilities are common knowledge. This uncertainty about the other sides' preferences is the key feature of this model.

The game that models a cooperative gesture to initiate a tacit treaty is depicted in figure 4.1. A begins (Stage I) by choosing either to continue the arms race at (M_A, M_B) or to make a gesture by reducing production to Δ_{BW}^A. Next, (Stage II) B may respond

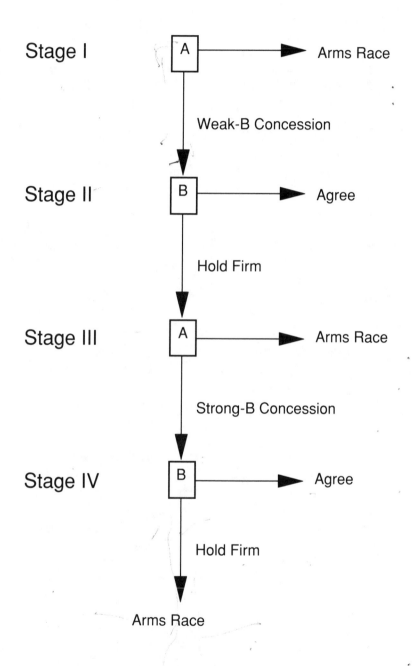

Fig. 4.1. Cooperative gesture game

to the gesture by producing Δ^B, thus tacitly ratifying the agreement, and terminating the game. This act would be attractive to a weak B but not a strong or Deadlock B—both of which would choose to continue producing M_B. This would be the optimal act of a Deadlock B who does not prefer cooperation in any case. If B is strong, this should be interpreted as "holding out" for a better offer—one which (strong) B would actually prefer to the status quo ante. A complication is that a weak B may choose to bluff by making this move, in order to prompt A to make a better offer. This could result in a treaty that is more desirable from B's point of view, but it is a strategy that carries a certain risk, as will be clear in the discussion of the next move.

At Stage III, A must choose what to do if B holds out. If A is strong, we assume that reversion to an arms race will occur, since no agreement has been reached at the only contract point that A prefers to the status quo. If A is weak, then there is still a choice between reversion to the arms race (optimal if B has Deadlock preferences) or making a greater gesture by producing only Δ^A_{BS} (optimal if B is strong).

In Stage IV, B will accept if weak or strong by producing Δ^B, but will continue to produce M_B under Deadlock preferences. Note that the weak B who does not respond to the original gesture risks losing the benefits of the tacit agreement if A is strong, or if A is weak but suspects B of having Deadlock, rather than strong, preferences.

Given this game, we will now determine the equilibrium strategies for A and B, assuming Bayesian updating. These strategies and beliefs will form a subgame perfect equilibrium in the sense of Selten (1975) as well as a sequential equilibrium (Kreps and Wilson 1982b). The main point will be to discover a pair of strategies so that each forms a good reply against the other, when considered at any point of the game tree.

As usual with sequential equilibrium analysis, we proceed by reverse induction. For Stage IV, B's strategy is apparent—if B has Deadlock preferences, the production level chosen is M_B, otherwise it is Δ^B. For Stage III, A will choose to revert to an arms race if strong, otherwise A will consider the possibility of a further concession to Δ^A_{BS}, if it seems profitable to do so. If A tries this concession and B refuses, A's payoff is

$$U_A(\Delta_{BS}^A, M_B) + \left(\frac{\delta_A}{1 - \delta_A}\right) U_A(M_A, M_B)$$

$$= a_A \Delta_{BS}^A - b_A M_B + \left(\frac{\delta_A}{1 - \delta_A}\right)(a_A M_A - b_A M_B)$$

while if B responds, A's payoff is

$$U_A(\Delta_{BS}^A, \Delta^B)/(1 - \delta_A) = (a_A \Delta_{BS}^A - b_A \Delta^B)/(1 - \delta_A).$$

Thus the necessary condition for A to prefer to make the cooperative gesture is

$$a_A M_A - b_A M_B$$

$$\leq (1 - p_1^{BD})(a_A \Delta_{BS}^A - b_A \Delta^B)$$

$$+ p_1^{BD}\left[(1 - \delta_A)(a_A \Delta_{BS}^A - b_A M_B)\delta_A(a_A M_A - b_A M_B)\right]$$

$$= p_1^{BD}\left\{a_A\left[(1 - \delta_A)\Delta_{BS}^A + \delta_A M_A - \Delta_{BS}^A\right]\right.$$

$$\left. - b_A\left[(1 - \delta_A)M_B + \delta_A M_B - \Delta^B\right]\right\}$$

$$+ (a_A \Delta_{BS}^A - b_A \Delta^B)$$

where p_1^{BD} represents A's probability at Stage III that B is Deadlock, updated in a Bayesian fashion from the initial probability vector $(p_0^{BW}\ p_0^{BS}\ p_0^{BD})$ Thus the condition is

$$p_1^{BD}\left[\delta_A a_A(M_A - \Delta_{BS}^A) - b_A(M_B - \Delta^B)\right]$$

$$\geq a_A(M_A - \Delta_{BS}^A) - b_A(M_B - \Delta^B)$$

or

$$p_1^{BD} \leq \frac{a_A(M_A - \Delta_{BS}^A) - b_A(M_B - \Delta^B)}{\delta_A a_A(M_A - \Delta_{BS}^A) - b_A(M_B - \Delta^B)} \qquad (4.6)$$

Thus A will not make the second gesture if the probability that B has Deadlock preferences is too high. That there is some such point is obvious. What is not so obvious is that this constraint can be quite severe if A only slightly prefers the treaty at $(\Delta^A_{BS}, \Delta^B)$ to an arms race. This is so since the numerator of Equation (4.6) is the number that must be positive for A to prefer the treaty. For example, if the numerator were $50 - 45$, then the denominator would be $50\delta_A - 49$, which could easily be small, even negative, and this ratio would give a low threshold for p_1^{BD}.

Now consider B's decision problem at Stage II. A has just made the gesture of reducing production to Δ^A_{BW}. If B is strong or Deadlock, then M_B is the indicated choice. If B is weak, B must decide whether to respond or bluff. Note that, if a weak B will (optimally) respond cooperatively, then, conditional on B playing M_B at Stage II we have

$$p_1^{BD} = \frac{p_0^{BD}}{p_0^{BD} + p_0^{BS}} \tag{4.7}$$

and if B will optimally bluff, then B will play M_B at Stage II regardless, so

$$p_1^{BD} = p_0^{BD} \tag{4.8}$$

so that bluffing reduces p_1^{BD}. A weak B will need to take account of whether a weak A will make the second gesture before deciding to bluff and also has to endure the risk that a bluff will cause a strong A to revert to an arms race, thus losing the opportunity for a tacit agreement.

At Stage II, if A is strong, then reversion to an arms race will be the result if B bluffs, so the payoff to bluffing is

$$(a_B M_B - b_B \Delta^A_{BW}) + \left(\frac{\delta_B}{1 - \delta_B}\right)(a_B M_B - b_B M_A).$$

This is also the payoff to B if A is weak, but declines to make the further concession and reverts to the arms race. On the other hand, if A is weak and will offer the second round concession, then the payoff to B is

$$(a_B M_B - b_B \Delta^A_{BW}) + \left(\frac{\delta_B}{1 - \delta_B}\right)(a_B \Delta^B - b_B \Delta^A_{BS}).$$

The payoff if B agrees immediately is

$$\frac{(a_B \Delta^B - b_B \Delta_{BW}^A)}{(1 - \delta_B)}$$

Thus, under the assumption that a weak A will make the second cooperative gesture, a weak B will prefer to bluff when

$$(a_B \Delta^B - b_B \Delta_{BW}^A)$$

$$\leq p_0^{AS} \Big[(1 - \delta_B)(a_B M_B - b_B \Delta_{BW}^A)$$

$$+ \delta_B(a_B M_B - b_B M_A)\Big]$$

$$+ (1 - p_0^{AS}) \Big[(1 - \delta_B)(a_B M_B - b_B \Delta_{BW}^A)$$

$$+ \delta_B(a_B \Delta^B - b_B \Delta_{BS}^A)\Big] \qquad (4.9)$$

or

$$a_B(1 - \delta_B)(\Delta^B - M_B) - b_B \delta_B(\Delta_{BW}^A - \Delta_{BS}^A)$$

$$\leq p_0^{AS} \delta_B \Big[a_B(M_B - \Delta^B) - b_B(M_A - \Delta_{BS}^A)\Big]. \qquad (4.10)$$

Now the sign of the right-hand side of Equation (4.10) is negative since B prefers the treaty to an arms race, so the condition on p_0^{AS} for B to bluff is

$$p_0^{AS} \leq \frac{a_B(1 - \delta_B)(\Delta^B - M_B) - b_B \delta_B(\Delta_{BW}^A - \Delta_{BS}^A)}{\delta_B \left[a_B(M_B - \Delta^B) - b_B(M_A - \Delta_{BS}^A)\right]}. \qquad (4.11)$$

If B's prior probability that A is strong is larger than this limit, then the cost attendant to a strong A reverting to an arms race is greater than the benefit attendant on a weak A being forced to a greater concession.

On the other hand, if a weak A will not make the second concession, because Equation (4.6) is not satisfied, then B must accept, for an arms race is the only alternative.[2] This might be

---

2. Only if the payoff to cheating on the next move were higher than the accumulated payoff to an arms agreement would B still bluff. With realistic parameters, this seems unlikely.

brought about if A has too high a probability that B has Deadlock preference or if A only slightly prefers the treaty to an arms race.

Finally, we need to compute whether A will make the cooperative gesture to begin with. This analysis is much more complex than the preceding because the number of possibilities multiplies as we go backward in the game tree. By continuing the arms race A can guarantee a payoff of $(a_A M_A - b_A M_B)/(1 - \delta_A)$. To decide if making the initial cooperative gesture yields a higher payoff A must consider several cases, depending on its own preferences and on the satisfaction of several conditions that determine the future course of the game.

The easier analysis is when A is strong. If a weak B would be inclined to bluff (determined by conditions (4.11) and (4.6)) then A will not initiate a cooperative gesture because no acceptable agreement can occur. Note that this undesirable condition would occur if B did not take seriously enough the possibility that A was strong. If a weak B would cooperate, then A will decide to make the gesture based on the probabilities of the two possible outcomes. If B is, in fact, weak, then A's gesture will be accepted. If B is strong or Deadlock, then B will hold firm, and A will revert to the arms race.

If B is weak, an event of probability p_0^{BW}, then the offer is accepted and A's payoff is

$$(a_A \Delta_{BW}^A - b_A \Delta^B)/(1 - \delta_A).$$

If B is strong or Deadlock, an event of probability $p_0^{BS} + p_0^{BD}$, then the outcome will be

$$(a_A \Delta_{BW}^A - b_A M_B) + \delta_A(a_A M_A - b_A M_B)/(1 - \delta_A).$$

Thus A's expected payoff is

$$p_0^{BW}\Big[(a_A \Delta_{BW}^A - b_A \Delta^B)/(1 - \delta_A)\Big]$$

$$+ (p_0^{BS} + p_0^{BD})\Big[(a_A \Delta_{BW}^A - b_A M_B)$$

$$+ \delta_A(a_A M_A - b_A M_B)/(1 - \delta_A)\Big]$$

$$= \Big[(a_A \Delta_{BW}^A - b_A M_B) + \delta_A(a_A M_A - b_A M_B)/(1 - \delta_A)\Big]$$

$$- p_0^{BW} \left[a_A \delta_A (M_A - \Delta_{BW}^A) - b_A (M_B - \Delta^B) \right] / (1 - \delta_A)$$

$$(4.12)$$

and A will initiate a cooperative gesture if this payoff is larger than the payoff to an arms race. Thus there is a critical value for p_0^{BW}, the initial probability that B is weak, below which A will not initiate the cooperative gesture.

The analysis for a weak A is slightly more complex, since there are three possible outcomes rather than two. First consider the case where a weak B will bluff (which implies also that a weak A will make the second gesture). Here, the first offer is never accepted, so the only possible outcomes are agreement at $(\Delta_{BS}^A, \Delta^B)$ and reversion to an arms race after two futile gestures.

If B is weak or strong, an event of probability $p_0^{BW} + p_0^{BS} = 1 - p_0^{BD}$, then the outcome will be

$$(a_A \Delta_{BW}^A - b_A M_B) + \delta_A (a_A \Delta_{BS}^A - b_A \Delta^B) / (1 - \delta_A)$$

and if B is Deadlock (p_0^{BD}), the outcome is

$$(a_A \Delta_{BW}^A - b_A M_B) + \delta_A (a_A \Delta_{BS}^A - b_A M_B)$$

$$+ \delta_A^2 (a_A M_A - b - A M_B) / (1 - \delta_A).$$

Thus A's expected payoff is

$$(1 - p_0^{BD}) \left[(a_A \Delta_{BW}^A - b_A M_B) \right.$$

$$\left. + \delta_A (a_A \Delta_{BS}^A - b_A \Delta^B) / (1 - \delta_A) \right]$$

$$+ p_0^{BD} \left[(a_A \Delta_{BW}^A - b_A M_B) + \delta_A (a_A \Delta_{BS}^A - b_A M_B) \right.$$

$$\left. + \delta_A^2 (a_A M_A - b_A M_B) / (1 - \delta_A) \right]$$

$$= \left[(a_A \Delta_{BW}^A - b_A M_B) + \delta_A (a_A \Delta_{BS}^A - b_A \Delta^B) / (1 - \delta_A) \right]$$

$$+ p_0^{BD} \delta_A^2 \left[a_A (M_A - \Delta^A BS) - b_A (M_B - \Delta^B) \right] / (1 - \delta_A)$$

and A will initiate a cooperative gesture if this payoff is larger than the payoff to an arms race. This depends only on a threshold value for p_0^{BD}. If A's assessment of the chance that B is of Deadlock type is large enough, no initial gesture will ensue. Note, however, that this conclusion is somewhat simplified, since the chance that B decides to bluff is also a function of the various probability values.

Now suppose that A is weak and that B will not bluff if weak. There are still two cases to consider depending on whether A (who is weak) will extend the second gesture or not, which depends on p_1^{BD}, which is A's assessment at the time the decision must be made that B is in Deadlock. If A is sufficiently confident to make the second gesture, then there will be three possible outcomes, depending on whether B is weak, strong, or Deadlock.

If B is weak, an event of probability p_0^{BW}, then the offer is accepted and A's payoff is

$$(a_A \Delta_{BW}^A - b_A \Delta^B)/(1 - \delta_A).$$

If B is strong, an event of probability p_0^{BS}, then the outcome will be

$$(a_A \Delta_{BW}^A - b_A M_B) + \delta_A(a_A \Delta_{BS}^A - b_A \Delta^B)/(1 - \delta_A)$$

and if B is Deadlock (p_0^{BD}), the outcome is

$$(a_A \Delta_{BW}^A - b_A M_B) + \delta_A(a_A \Delta_{BS}^A - b_A M_B)$$

$$+ \delta_A^2(a_A M_A - b - A M_B)/(1 - \delta_A).$$

Thus A's expected payoff is

$$p_0^{BW} \left[(a_A \Delta_{BW}^A - b_A \Delta^B)/(1 - \delta_A) \right]$$

$$+ p_0^{BS} \left[(a_A \Delta_{BW}^A - b_A M_B) + \delta_A(a_A \Delta_{BS}^A - b_A \Delta^B)/(1 - \delta_A) \right]$$

$$+ p_0^{BD} \left[(a_A \Delta_{BW}^A - b_A M_B) + \delta_A(a_A \Delta_{BS}^A - b_A M_B) \right.$$

$$\left. + \delta_A^2(a_A M_A - b_A M_B)/(1 - \delta_A) \right]$$

and A will initiate a cooperative gesture if this payoff is larger than the payoff to an arms race. Unlike the previous cases, this result depends on all the probability assessment parameters. In general, if p_0^{BW} is large enough, A will make the first gesture, while if it is sufficiently small, A will not do so. For intermediate values, the outcome will depend on how the remaining probability is divided between p_0^{BS} and p_0^{BD}.

If A is not sufficiently confident to make the second gesture, then the outcomes will look very much like the case when A is strong. The payoff to A will be

$$\left[(a_A \Delta_{BW}^A - b_A M_B) + \delta_A(a_A M_A - b_A M_B)/(1 - \delta_A)\right]$$

$$- p_0^{BW}\left[a_A \delta_A(M_A - \Delta_{BW}^A) - b_A(M_B - \Delta^B)\right]/(1 - \delta_A)$$

and A will cooperate or not depending on a comparison of this value with the value of continuing the arms race.

This complicated analysis has a number of fairly straightforward implications. First, and perhaps least remarkable, is that uncertainty about opponent preferences can lead to less than optimal results. It is not difficult to see how a weak nation A may yield too much to a weak nation B because it thinks that B is strong. So much is obvious. Some other, more paradoxical outcomes are not so obvious and are better revealed by formal modeling than by intuition. It turns out, for example, that an increase in the certainty of one of the nations in a bilateral arms race may actually make things worse. Suppose that A is strong and B is weak but each side is quite uncertain about the other side's utilities. If A is known to give a fairly high probability to B being in Deadlock, then B will not bluff on the second round, since even a weak A would not respond under these conditions. It is easy to find parameter values that will lead to agreement at $(\Delta_{BW}^A, \Delta^B)$. Now suppose that B's true utilities are revealed, so that A discovers with a high degree of certainty that B is weak. This would seem to make an agreement at $(\Delta_{BW}^A, \Delta^B)$ even more achievable. However, one of the key disincentives for B to bluff has now been removed. If B still thinks that there is at least a modest chance that A is weak, then B will always bluff. This in turn will prevent A from making an offer that B would accept, and that would make them each better off. Unlike some other areas, improved intelligence by one side is often not enough to guarantee success. *A* must not only do everything it can to secure the best intelligence, it must also often ensure that *B*'s intelligence is also good.

In the same vein, it is not necessarily to a nation's advantage to be thought tougher than it actually is. It is true that this can lead an opponent to be bluffed into making a more generous treaty offer, but it is also true that it can frighten an opponent away from making a cooperative gesture. If nation *B* is certain that nation *A* has Deadlock preferences and believes that it will exploit a gesture of cooperation, why bother making a gesture at all?

The main lesson that can be drawn from the analysis of this simple model is the complicated interactive nature of arms cooperation. In order to predict whether arms cooperation will be achieved, we need to know not only what the utilities of the players are, but how the other side assesses them. There is a complex interplay between the various parameters of the model in determining when cooperation will be achieved. Although the specific predictions of this model cannot be expected to hold in practice, the same principles clearly apply in ending real arms races.

4.3   The Structure of the Simulation

The results of the equilibrium analysis reinforce our initial contention that utility uncertainty must play a critical role in determining the choice of tacit bargaining strategies, but there are other factors with a claim to almost equal importance. The chief rival is information uncertainty, which has been discussed at considerable length in the first two chapters. Intelligence problems have been associated with every arms race that has ever taken place and it is not difficult to appreciate how these problems might interfere with the attempt of states to "signal" their rival. A modest gesture of cooperation might be ignored; an attempt at reciprocity might be seen as a strong move toward escalation.

The potential significance of information uncertainty need not be elaborated on here, but two other factors that play a major role in the simulation that follows require a brief introduction. The first is variable response. In the equilibrium analysis, as in the familiar 2 × 2 characterizations of the Prisoner's Dilemma or Deadlock, each side must select one of two choices—defect or cooperate. In a real-world arms race, the alternatives are not as limited. They range from deactivating weapons systems and releasing troops from active duty to committing every available resource to increasing weapons stockpiles. The fact that modern superpowers possess a vast array of weapons systems and are developing new ones at a rapid rate simply expands the menu of alternative defection and cooperation behaviors to an unprecedented degree. One implication of this large number of options for tacit bargaining is that it opens the possibility of increasing the effectiveness of signaling behavior and minimizing its associated risks. For example, a state might attempt to overcome the atmosphere of suspicion created by a protracted arms race and simultaneously minimize its own vulnerability by engaging in a number of modest unilateral concessions over a substantial period of time. Alternatively, a state concerned with the potential for misinterpretation might choose to make a single, dramatic gesture that it considered to be impossible to misinterpret, and then in the clearest possible terms demand an equivalent action from its rival as a prelude to further cooperation. These two strategies do not, of course, begin to exhaust the possibilities created by the availability of continuous, as opposed to dichotomous, alternatives. A state could begin with a modest gesture and then gradually increase it, or begin with a dramatic cooperative move and then reduce it in such a way as to signal both a continued willingness to cooperate and a refusal to be exploited. The real questions are which strategy is best under the sort of conditions that are believed to characterize a particular arms race, and how robust any given strategy might be if decision makers miscalculated.

The second factor that requires a few words of introduction is what Axelrod has referred to as the "shadow of the future." As noted in chapter 2, this represents the relative value that the players place on the future as compared with the present, and it is the key to success in an iterated Prisoner's Dilemma. If the benefits that accrue through long-term cooperation ("the shadow of the future") are large, players will not be seduced by the prospect of the modest gains that can be had by defecting in the present. This simple principle can provide the basis for a variety of strategies designed to promote cooperation; Axelrod discusses a number of them—such as increasing the frequency and the length of time that two players interact.

In Axelrod's simulation experiments, the shadow of the future affects both players in the same way. That is often a reasonable assumption. If Player A can look forward to twenty meetings with Player B, it is likely that Player B will share the same expectation. If they then employ the same discount rate to translate future benefits into current benefits, they will place the same value on their interactions. In the case of arms races (and other classes of international interactions), however, symmetry may be absent. It is true that the United States can expect to have to deal with the Soviet Union as often as the Soviet Union with the United States. However, key decision makers in these countries may have quite different expectations about the length of time they are likely to be in office (and therefore directly responsible for the future relations between their countries), and very different views about the relative importance of present exigencies vis-à-vis future benefits. It is not enough to specify that the administration assuming power in State A hold Prisoner's Dilemma preferences, or even to define a specific payoff matrix. The discount rate that will be used by the new administration must be estimated. It is one thing to believe in the superiority of mutual cooperation over mutual defection, and another to be willing to make the short-term sacrifice that will communicate the desire for cooperation. Only the latter will make the long-term benefits associated with a less intensive arms race achievable.

Although substantially more complicated than any past representation of tacit bargaining and the equilibrium model presented earlier in this chapter, the simulation that will be described here contains its own set of simplifying assumptions. In part, the simplifications represent the inevitable sacrifices of complexity that characterize any effort at model building; another constraint is generated, however, by the need to make the presentation as accessible as possible. Long lists of output, showing how a large number of strategies vary in attractiveness as an equally large number of parameters changes, are virtually incomprehensible without extraordinary effort on the part of a reader. A small number of summary statistics with no clear reference to policy options, supplemented by ten qualifying footnotes, is no better. With these difficulties in mind, we decided to depict graphically the results of a small number of simulation experiments in which the most critical parameters are varied. We have used only two values of each parameter instead of a large number—this is sufficient to depict the range over which the parameters might vary without overcomplicating the presentation. In the simulation, we examine the effects of three parameters, using a base case and three sensitivity analysis cases that vary one parameter at a time. Two widely separated values allow the detection of the major effects; intermediate results can be inferred approximately by interpolation. Thus, we examine the impact of two dramatically different discount rates rather than all possible ones, and a set of three possible arms strategies instead of twenty or thirty that a rival state may plausibly employ. In the sections on Simulation Results and on Implications, we summarize what we consider to be the major descriptive and prescriptive policy findings, leaving the reader to employ the charts for answers to more specific and/or complicated questions.

The simulation is designed to model a situation in which a new administration assumes power in one of two states (subsequently referred to as State A) currently engaged in a bipolar arms race. This administration sees substantial economic and security advantages to be gained by slowing the arms race, but appreciates both the dangers of losing ground relative to the rival (State B) and the policy leverage that arms superiority occasionally permits. In short, its preferences can be represented by one side of the classic Prisoner's Dilemma. This sort of preference ordering is probably common to many nineteenth- and twentieth-century regimes that were interested in, but not dedicated to, arms control. The preference for mutual cooperation (i.e., arms reduction) over mutual defection (i.e., arms increases) is obviously a prerequisite for any tacit bargaining initiative. A distaste for permitting the enemy to gain a noticeable advantage in an ongoing arms race seems almost universal; an appreciation of the benefits of arms superiority seems common (if possibly misplaced). To capture the effect of variations in the perceived benefits and costs of arms superiority simultaneously, we will look at two different sets of payoffs. What we refer to as the Base Case is typical of Prisoner's Dilemma stud-

ies; the Low-Benefit Case represents a situation where less value
is placed on arms superiority.

We have adopted a much broader definition of the game than
is usually employed in Prisoner's Dilemma studies. In our game,
the status of each side is a level of armaments. On each move,
each side may increase or decrease its arms level by any amount.
After both sides have moved, each side attains a benefit that is
proportional to the difference in arms, minus a maintenance cost
associated with its own arms stock. (The cost-benefit ratio is 1:6
and 1:3 in the two cases.) In addition, a building cost is included to
avoid having an instantaneous, infinite arms buildup as an optimal
move. In the results of this model, a myopically rational actor will
increase arms by 2.5 units per year in the Base Case and by 1 unit
in the Low-Benefit Case. The Prisoner's Dilemma aspect of this
model is that each side is better off if both sides reduce arms, but
it would be still more advantageous to build when the rival does
not.

Formally,[3] we suppose that a state A achieves a net benefit of

$$U_A(S_t^A, S_t^B, P_t^A) = a_A(S_t^A - S_t^B) - b_A S_t^A - c_A(P_t^A)^2 \quad (4.13)$$

when arms are increased, and

$$U_A(S_t^A, S_t^B, P_t^A) = a_A(S_t^A - S_t^B) - b_A S_t^A - d_A(P_t^A) \quad (4.14)$$

when arms are decreased, where S_t^A and S_t^B are the arms stocks
for the two sides, and P_t^A is the arms production for side A. The
cost function is quadratic for arms increases, to represent the difficulties that the industrial infrastructure and the political system
have with arbitrarily large increases. Values used in the simulation are $b = 1.0$, $c = 1.0$, and $d = 0.5$ in all cases, with $a = 6$ in
the Base Case and $a = 3$ in the Low-Benefit Case. It is easily seen
that the "optimal" one-period increase of arms for side A is given
by

$$\Delta^A = (a_A - b_A)/(2c_A) \quad (4.15)$$

---

3. This formulation is slightly different from that described in chapter 3 and
used in chapter 5 in that there is an asymmetry between arms increases and
arms decreases. Because we are using simulation here instead of equilibrium
theory, we can adopt this more realistic feature.

regardless of the level chosen by side B. Thus, the simulation is begun by assuming that the arms race has been proceeding at this "optimal" level for some time.[4]

For reasons described in the previous section, State A is likely to be uncertain about the intentions and strategies of its rival, State B. While in theory the range of possibilities is infinite, we will begin by assuming that State B's utility function and expectations are such that it has adopted one of three possible arms strategies. In the first, its preferences are identical to those of the new administration of State A, and it has adopted a strategy of reciprocity. State B has not, however, made any recent cooperative gestures. An explanation for this lack of cooperative initiative is not difficult to imagine. B prefers mutual arms reduction to a continued arms race, but it possesses no confidence that a unilateral arms reduction will inspire reciprocity on the part of A, and fears the cost of losing ground. If B has adopted a strategy of reciprocity, a cooperative gesture on the part of the new administration will yield large benefits; the larger the gesture, the better.

A second possibility is that State B is prepared to continue its arms buildup regardless of any action taken by State A. The reasons are countless: the pace of its buildup may be determined by internal constituencies whose economic and internal political motives are insulated from the effect of cooperative gestures; it may fear that it is being duped when it is urged to make a significant sacrifice in response to what it views as a trivial cooperative move; its economy may recently have improved to a point where it can afford substantially greater arms expenditures; its political goals may have become more aggressive; and so forth. Historical precedents for each of these motives are easy to find; collectively, they help us understand the relative infrequency with which arms races have been resolved through either formal negotiation or tacit

---

4. As a detailed analysis in chapter 5 shows, the optimal increase when the entire discounted stream of benefits is accounted for is larger by a factor of $(1 - \alpha\delta_A)^{-1}$, where δ_A is the discount rate and α is the depreciation rate. This represents a true all-out arms race. The level of production chosen for this chapter seems a plausible choice to represent an existing arms race that is proceeding at less than the maximum value (so there is something to lose) but at a greater rate than the participants would prefer.

bargaining (Downs et al. 1985). From the standpoint of A, the suspicion that B holds such Deadlock preferences and/or is committed to a strategy of continual defection obviously discourages a cooperative gesture.

The third possibility considered is that State B prefers mutual cooperation to mutual defection, but will respond only partially to a cooperative gesture. This less-than-reciprocal response represents the caution experienced by an opponent in an extended arms race about the sincerity of the cooperative gesture that has been extended. Is the gesture a trick? Does it signify nothing more than a momentary lull in arms development caused by economic strain or indecisiveness about which weapon system to invest in? The atmosphere of distrust that builds up in an arms race is not dissipated overnight; it may require the adoption of a patient strategy that calls for making a number of cooperative gestures without expectation of an immediately cooperative response. In the simulation, this model is operationalized by the opponent basically playing Tit-for-Tat, but returning a cooperative gesture with one that is only half as strong.

In the first case, when B employs a reciprocal strategy, the increase will be $P_t^B = P_{t-1}^A$, matching A's increase (or decrease) from last time. In the second case, B will continue its past buildup no matter what, so the increase will be some fixed value Δ^B, independent of A's gesture. Thus, the current increase is exactly the same as the last turn's increase. In modeling cautious reciprocity, we imagine that B examines A's last change compared to B's own change two turns ago. If A were playing a reciprocal strategy, these two quantities would be identical. If they are, or if A's move is larger, then B plays reciprocally, subject to staying below the optimal increase; otherwise, B makes an increase midway between A's last move and B's own last move. Thus

$$P_t^B = \begin{cases} P_{t-1}^A, & \text{if } P_{t-1}^A \geq P_{t-2}^B; \\ 0.5(P_{t-1}^A + P_{t-1}^B), & \text{otherwise.} \end{cases} \qquad (4.16)$$

Although this strategy seems complex, it only amounts to following up a cooperative gesture with a smaller cooperative gesture, while preserving a full ability to punish defection.

It should be clear from the previous section that, whatever strategy our cooperatively minded state chooses to play, it will have to be carried out in a less-than-perfect information environment. For the sake of simplicity, we assume that each side has an accurate picture of what it has done itself, but that perceptions of what the opponent has done are subject to bias and error. The bias component represents the psychological tendency of individuals (and the historical inclination of states) to underestimate the magnitude of an opponent's cooperation and to overestimate the extent of its defection or continued weapons buildup. The value we chose is relatively small, 0.05 units. In addition to bias, we assume the existence of a normally distributed noise component that summarizes the impact of all of the other factors that essentially operate at random to degrade the information environment. These might include delays in updating force structures and weapons assessments, or inaccurate intelligence estimates, but could also arise as a function of the complexity and variation of weapons inventories. Tacit bargaining across disparate weapons systems made up of equipment that is far less homogeneous than battleships and that is valued differently by different states is an uncertain, "noisy" process. We employ a noise distribution with a standard deviation of 0.1 for the Base Case and go on to describe the implications of a high-noise scenario where the standard deviation is 0.5. An even higher amount of noise is used for examples in the next chapter, with a standard deviation of 1.0 units. Maintenance of treaties may be possible with a higher amount of noise than will permit the arrival at the treaty in the first place, at least by tacit bargaining.

To capture the implications of the administration of State A taking a long- or short-term view of the benefits of cooperation vis-à-vis continued defection, we work with discount rates of 0.05 and 0.10, which represent the long- and short-term perspectives. While one might argue that the 0.10 rate, which depreciates future benefits at the rate of 10 percent, is actually not as high as that employed by many short-term-oriented politicians, it hardly matters. As the next section will reveal, if the discount rate approaches this value, an uncertain State A will be driven away from making any cooperative gesture.

Table 4.1 summarizes the four decision environments that are utilized in the analysis and that provide the context in which State A will attempt to cope with the three possible strategies of State

TABLE 4.1. Parameters for the Four Cases in the Simulation

	Discount Rate	Benefit of Arms Superiority	Noise Level
Base	.05	6	.1
High-Discount	.10	6	.1
Low-Benefit	.05	3	.1
High-Noise	.05	6	.5

B. The simulation is designed to tell us how sensitive A's choice of strategy is to these changes in context.

The strategic alternatives that are available to the new administration of State A involve maintaining parity with the rival state by continuing the arms race at its present level or making some cooperative gesture (G), which will be continued for some duration (d) before it is reduced at some rate (c). To eliminate ambiguity about what G actually represents, we will define it in terms of the parity strategy. That is, a cooperative gesture of size G means G units less than what would be required to maintain parity. If G is 2 units of armaments and the opponent's last move was 7, State A will build 5. Because both states act simultaneously, the duration parameter (d) will be at least 2 in order to allow time for the other to react.

4.4   Simulation Results

The first stage of the simulation was designed to reduce the limitless set of strategies from which the new administration of State A might choose to a number that is realistic in a policy sense and also permits coherent discussion. One way to do this is to examine some simple but fundamental relationships among the variables central to the analysis, and to see whether they suggest any strategic alternatives that are dominant over a wide range of conditions. A sensible place to begin is with the effect of utility uncertainty on the magnitude of the initial cooperative gesture. Obviously, if State A is convinced that its rival is pursuing a strategy of reciprocity and will respond in kind to any cooperative

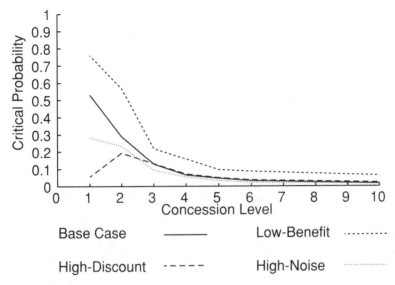

Fig. 4.2. Critical probabilities of Deadlock for various concession levels and four conditions

gesture, the optimal strategy is to make a very large gesture as quickly as possible. Such an action would lead to mutual disarmament within a few moves. The question is whether such large gestures are still a viable strategic possibility when State A is uncertain about the nature of B's response. That is, to what extent does the possibility that the rival may not respond positively lead a rational actor to make more modest and tentative unilateral gestures?

Figure 4.2 depicts the optimal concession level against an opponent who has a probability p of playing Deadlock (i.e., of ignoring a cooperative gesture and continuing to expand its arms at the previous rate) and a probability of $1 - p$ of responding with an equivalent gesture. For each environment and each potential level of concession, the figure shows what probability of response is required to make that gesture.[5] What is interesting here is that, once the probability of unresponsiveness is believed to be

---

5. The numbers were calculated from simulations run separately for the case in which the opponent is playing Deadlock and the case in which the opponent is employing the reciprocal strategy.

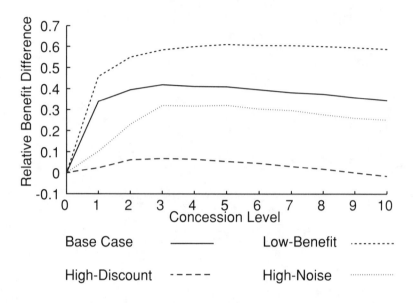

Fig. 4.3. Relative benefit of various concessions against cautious reciprocity

greater than about 23 percent—a relatively low figure—the optimal concession level is less than three. That is true for each of the decision environments described in table 4.1: the Base Case with standard Prisoner's Dilemma payoffs, low discount rate, and low noise, as well as the three alternative decision environments with lower benefits for arms superiority, a higher discount rate of 10 percent, and high noise. In terms of policy, this means that if there is even a modest suspicion that the rival may not be receptive to a cooperative gesture, State A will limit its cooperative gesture to what amounts to a one-year moratorium on weapon increases rather than offer something more substantial; this decision is not significantly affected by varying the decision environment.

Figure 4.3 depicts the relative benefit that accrues to State A from making gestures of various sizes against an opponent employing a strategy of cautious reciprocity.[6] It might at first appear

---

6. If the payoff for making no cooperative gesture is P_0 and the payoff for making a cooperative gesture of size G is P_G, then the quantity graphed against G is $(P_G - P_0)/P_0$. The required numbers were estimated by simulation.

that if one could be certain that the other side was engaged in a strategy of cautious reciprocity, the optimal move would be to make a dramatically large initial gesture, just as one would do if one could be certain that the opponent was pursuing a normal reciprocal strategy. This, however, is not the case. Although it is true that certainty insures a favorable response, a basic attribute of the cautious reciprocity strategy is that the response will be proportionately smaller than the initial cooperative gesture. The difference between the gesture that State A makes and the response that it gets is a cost because it constitutes an arms advantage for a potential adversary, and there is a limit on how large a cost the new administration in State A is willing to incur. Figure 4.3 shows substantial differences in the relative benefit (depending on the assumptions we make about noise, etc.); remarkably, it also reveals that the largest relative benefit always takes place in the 3–4 range. As in the case of figure 4.2, this tells us that the optimal concession will be no greater than a 12–18 month moratorium on increases.

The results described above simplify our subsequent simulation and presentation task significantly because they establish an upper bound on the initial concession level of about three units. For State A rationally to offer more, it would have to be at least 80 percent certain that state B would neither ignore the gesture nor respond to it cautiously—a level of confidence that is rarely found in the real world. The upper bound on the initial gesture allows us to conduct the subsequent simulation using a relatively narrow range of strategies. We have chosen seven: pure reciprocity by which State A increases its arms at precisely the same rate as B with no cooperative gesture, and six cooperative strategies with two levels of initial gesture and three levels of patience. These are described in table 4.2. The six cooperative strategies were chosen to reflect two concession levels, a near maximum level of three and a smaller level of one. This was combined with three forms of patience upon nonresponse. State A might immediately abandon the cooperative gesture if it was not returned—corresponding to a decay parameter of 1.0—or reduce it in size by a factor of 0.5 or 0.25.

The second portion of the simulation consists of evaluating the merits of each of State A's seven possible strategies against each

TABLE 4.2. Parameters for the Seven Strategies Used in the Simulation

Strategy Number	Initial Concession	Decay of Cooperation upon Nonresponse
1	0	—
2	1	1.0
3	3	1.0
4	1	0.5
5	3	0.5
6	1	0.25
7	3	0.25

of State B's strategies in the four different environments. The results are presented in figures 4.4 to 4.7. For each triangle, the vertices represent certainty that the rival will employ the labeled strategy. Any degree of uncertainty about what strategy the rival will employ is represented by a point along the edge or inside the triangle. The numbers indicate which of State A's strategies is optimal at that level of uncertainty. Payoffs were calculated by simulation for each of the seven strategies against each of the opponent's strategies for each environment. A typical point (p_1, p_2, p_3) in the triangle represents an estimated probability of p_1 that State B is playing its first strategy, etc. The expected payoff to a given strategy is a weighted average, by p_1, p_2, and p_3, of the outcomes against the three possible strategies of State B. From the payoff formula for each strategy at each point, the areas of optimality for each strategy were computed.

For example, in the Base Case in figure 4.4, suppose the new administration believed that there was a 50 percent chance that the rival was playing a reciprocity strategy, a 50 percent chance that it was playing a cautious reciprocity strategy, and a 0 percent chance that it was playing Deadlock. In that case, the unlikelihood of the rival's constant defection focuses our attention as far from the left vertex as possible and places it on the right side of the triangle. Because we know that there is a 50 percent chance that the rival has adopted a strategy of reciprocity and a 50 per-

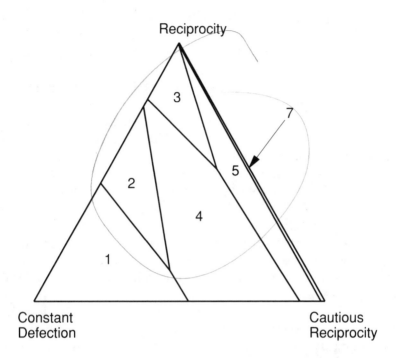

Fig. 4.4. Optimal strategies for the Base Case

cent chance that it has selected cautious reciprocity, we locate a
point halfway between the top and the right-hand vertices on the
right edge and see which strategy is prescribed. In this case, the
probability of reciprocity versus cautious reciprocity is irrelevant
since Strategy 7 (the most generous and trusting strategy) is prescribed at every point along the right side; that is, Strategy 7 is
best whenever there is no chance that the rival will constantly defect. Note that this is the only situation in which the knowledge
of one probability provides sufficient information for choosing the
optimal strategy. Had we been told that there was a 0 percent
chance of the rival employing cautious reciprocity, we would have
to know the relative probabilities that it would constantly defect
or behave reciprocally before we would know whether Strategy 1,
2, 3, 4, or 7 was superior. To take another example, suppose the
new administration believed that there is an equal probability that
the rival will play any of the three strategies (i.e., the probability
of each is 33.33 percent). Attention would then shift to the center

of the triangle where we see that the optimal course of action is Strategy 4, which involves a small initial concession of 1 that is diminished by a factor of 0.5 per round if there is no response.

Let us consider the Base Case in greater detail. One striking feature is that if the estimated probability that the rival will employ a strategy of Deadlock or ignore a cooperative gesture is greater than about 55 percent, the optimal strategy is to make no gesture at all, not even a small one. This suggests that it would not be difficult for a rational but uncertain administration to talk itself out of initiating any serious tacit bargaining. Moreover, the prevalence of 2's and 4's suggests that even when the estimated probability of Deadlock falls to about 20 percent, the size of the initial overture is likely to be modest. The initial gesture of 1 that is basic to both strategies represents a moratorium of less than one-half of one year's weapons growth. The large initial gesture of Strategies 3, 5, and 7 is rarely optimal and requires a great deal of assurance—an impossibly great deal of assurance in the case of Strategy 7—that the opponent will not simply ignore it. The optimal strategy is also often conservative from the standpoint of how quickly the initial gesture is decreased in light of nonresponse. Of the strategies that are the most generous in the face of nonresponse (i.e., 6 and 7), one is never optimal and the other is optimal only under very unusual conditions. Strategy 5, which prescribes a proportional decay rate that is twice as great as these, is still relatively rare; Strategy 4, which has a similar decay rate, is more popular only because the size of its initial gesture is so modest that subsequent gestures are relatively costless.

Figure 4.5 depicts the same situation except that State A has a short-term perspective (that is, it discounts future benefits at a fairly high rate of 10 percent per year). As Axelrod suggests in his discussion of the shadow of the future, a prerequisite for the cooperative resolution of Prisoner's Dilemmas is that future benefits be valued highly. What is notable about the figure is just how little uncertainty can be tolerated in an environment with a short-term perspective before the optimal strategy will be to continue with the arms race and make no move toward tacit bargaining. If there is even a 10 percent chance that State B will ignore the cooperative gesture, the cooperatively minded state will do nothing.

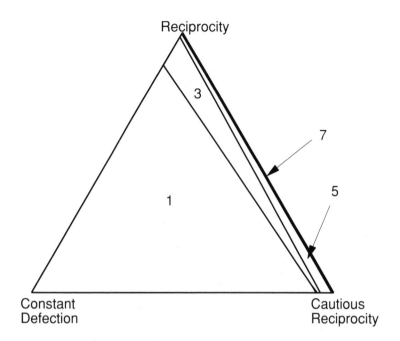

Fig. 4.5. Optimal strategies for the High-Discount Case

Figure 4.6 deals with the case where the advantage of arms superiority—or the temporary disadvantage of falling behind—is thought to be modest. As one would expect, such a decision environment promotes tacit bargaining. The probability of a nonresponse that is needed to discourage any bargaining overture climbs to about 80 percent; Strategy 3 (which involves a large initial concession but a steep withdrawal rate) and Strategy 4 (which consists of a small initial gesture but only a moderate withdrawal rate) both become optimal in many situations. Note, however, that even in this relatively benign environment there is a limit to the degree of generosity that is prescribed. Strategies 5, 6, and 7, which involve either slow decay rates or slow decay rates and large initial gestures, are still optimal in only a small proportion of possible situations. This means that the declining marginal utility of weapons or "overkill" environments would tend to promote tacit bargaining, but would not lead states to embrace it with the fervor that more aggressive partisans of arms control might desire.

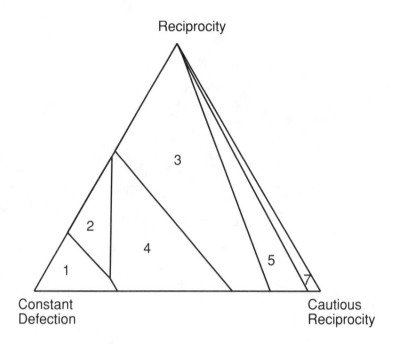

Fig. 4.6. Optimal strategies for the Low-Benefit Case

Finally, figure 4.7 depicts the case in which there is a high level of noise and misperception in the system. Whether this is brought about by problems of weapons incomparability, poor intelligence, or the difficulties of trying to bargain tacitly across different categories of weapons systems, it greatly suppresses the tendency of the cooperatively minded state to make an initial cooperative gesture. To be specific, if misinterpretation is a strong possibility and there is more than a 20 percent chance that the other state is pursuing a Deadlock strategy, it would be optimal to make no cooperative gesture. If the chance of a Deadlock strategy on the part of the rival is less than 20 percent, Strategies 5 and 6 are often prescribed. These strategies meet the problem of noise head-on because they contain a decay rate that is small relative to the size of the initial gesture. That is, they cope with the problem of noise by assuming the need to repeat the message (i.e., the cooperative gesture) a number of times. Note, however, that the advantages

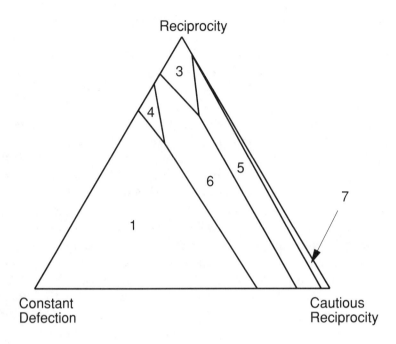

Fig. 4.7. Optimal strategies for the High-Noise Case

of repetition do not extend to expanding the role of Strategy 7. Unless the decision maker is virtually certain that Deadlock is an impossibility, the large initial gesture and slow decay rate prescribed by that strategy continue to make it irrationally generous.

The foregoing results have a number of implications for the conduct of tacit bargaining by foreign policy decision makers in a cooperatively minded state. Perhaps the most important lesson is that there is no specific strategy that is always dominant and upon which a state can always rely. The simulation shows how the optimal strategy changes as the nature of the decision environment changes; and the history of arms races leaves little doubt that the decision environment does vary. Decision makers therefore have no alternative but to estimate certain values and probabilities before they select a strategy. They need to estimate, first, the extent to which they value the benefits of security and budgetary savings that may not be realized for some time (i.e., the discount rate), the amount of noise in the system and the likelihood of misinterpretation, and the strategic cost associated with their cooperative gesture being ignored by the other side. Then they need to make some judgment about the strategy the rival nation is employing as it conducts its arms race. Since it is highly doubtful that decision makers can make this judgment with absolute certainty, it will inevitably take the form of an estimate of how likely it is that the rival has chosen each of the various possible alternative strategies. Only after this information has been gathered is it possible to recommend an appropriate tacit bargaining strategy. Although it would be conceptually neater and also more reassuring if someone could formulate a tacit bargaining strategy that was robust across all decision environments and made fewer information demands on policymakers, it is extremely unlikely that such a strategy exists.

Although it is impossible to summarize the implications of the simulation by prescribing a single strategy that can always be confidently employed to reduce the intensity of arms races, certain guidelines do emerge. One of the clearest holds the most disheartening implication: if the chances that the rival state will ignore a conciliatory gesture are estimated to be greater than 55 percent, then the cooperatively minded state should continue to increase its arms strength at the same rate as the other state until it receives a conciliatory gesture. It is true that if the cost of falling behind in the arms race is particularly small, this figure rises, but it is also true that it falls dramatically in the presence of high noise or a high discount rate. Since one suspects that the presence of noise and misinterpretation problems is at least as likely as a conviction that falling behind in the arms race is relatively costless, the optimal strategy may all too often be to make no cooperative gesture.

The analysis suggests that, even when the likelihood of constant defection on the part of the rival is relatively low, the magnitude of the conciliatory gesture should be modest. Although its precise size varies with the basic assumptions and probability estimates, it would rarely represent more than the equivalent of a six-month moratorium on arms increases and almost never more than an eighteen-month moratorium. It is surprising that this is true even when the conditions for tacit bargaining are almost ideal (i.e., when there is only a small benefit associated with an arms advantage and a strong possibility that the rival is engaging in a strategy of pure or cautious reciprocity). Regardless of the other factors that comprise the decision environment, a small amount of uncertainty has a pervasive effect on the character of the opening move.

Decision makers in the cooperatively minded state must also decide how patient they will be in dealing with responses that do not immediately match their initial gestures. To some extent the answer is contingent on the character of the first move. The fact that Strategies 2 and 7 seldom dominate the other strategies indicates that it is unwise to be extremely impatient if the initial gesture has been small, or extremely patient if it has been large. Strategy 2 is problematic because it is difficult to interpret in a noisy and uncertain environment; Strategy 7 is usually a poor choice because it permits exploitation. The message of moderation is reinforced in the Base and Low-Benefit environments generally. Note that uncertainty about the strategy of the opponent leads to the domination of Strategies 3 and 4, which call for the moderate decay rate of 0.5. One might expect that the optimal amount of patience would always depend on the magnitude of the opening gesture, as it did in the case of Strategies 2 and 7. Yet it does not; as uncertainty about the opponent's strategy increases, the level of patience that is optimal stabilizes and ceases to depend on the initial concession. "Reduce your offer—whatever it is—by half in the face of nonresponse" is a robust tactic when dealing with an enigmatic rival.

It is also wise to avoid tacit bargaining across weapon systems and in areas where estimates of weapon effectiveness are far apart. Either situation creates an environment analogous to the High-Noise Case. The rival state may well miss the significance of the initial concession; even if it does not, there is a real possibility that its cooperative response will be misinterpreted. The history of U.S.-Soviet negotiations has taught us that either side's initial calculations about the value the other side places on a given system are often wildly incorrect, and that one of the virtues of formal negotiation is that it provides a context in which these estimates can be revised. Tacit bargaining presents a rival with little opportunity to inspire such a revision and raises the possibility that misinterpretation or misintelligence will lead to further escalation of the arms race.

Another prescription concerns the periodic reevaluation of arms policy in light of changing conditions. The absence of a broadly dominant tacit bargaining strategy and the ever-changing character of some of the factors that determine the "best" strategy make it unwise to pursue a single strategy over a long period. For example, the probability of misinterpretation can change with the development of new weapons systems. The country that develops the system may view it as consistent with the current equilibrium, but the rival may believe that it represents an escalation of the arms race. Different administrations are also likely to have at least marginally different views of the benefits associated with being slightly ahead or behind in the arms race; depending on their political security, they could be using different discount rates as well. Any of these changes might well favor the choice of a new tacit bargaining strategy. The most frequent and significant changes, however, may be prompted by uncertainty about the arms strategy the rival state is pursuing. Each of the figures illustrates that, as assurance mounts that the rival has committed itself to a specific strategy, the prescribed tacit bargaining strategy of the cooperatively minded state can change dramatically.

Finally, if cooperation-based tacit bargaining is to be successful, decision makers must do everything possible to minimize the bias with which they view a rival state's actions as well as their own natural inclination to avoid risk. That is equally true whether they are sending a cooperative message to their opponent or trying to determine whether they have been sent such a message. The simulation results reveal what might be called the basic paradox of tacit bargaining. The key is uncertainty. *A state will rarely be certain enough about an opponent's response to make a large cooperative gesture, and the opponent will rarely be trusting enough to respond enthusiastically to a small one.* We believe that this is one of the reasons why Gorbachev's gestures struck observers as so unusual. It also provides a partial test of the theory. That theory would lead us to believe that a gesture of this magnitude would only be offered when the following conditions hold: the probability that the opponent has Deadlock preferences is low, the noise in transmitting the gesture is low, the leader extending the gesture has a long-term perspective, and the benefits to cooperation greatly exceed the potential cost of the gesture. These conditions all arguably characterize the current situation in the Soviet Union.

Gorbachev's offer does not detract from the main message that tacit bargaining is a fragile, opaque process and tacit bargaining initiatives often end in frustration or further escalation. The only way around the problem is for decision makers to approach tacit bargaining with the expectation that the other side would be acting irrationally if it made a gesture large enough to be unambiguous. If a state chooses to take the initiative, it should prepare itself for a response that is slower in coming and smaller in magnitude than it might desire. If a state chooses to be conservative and wait for a cooperative signal from its rival, it should know that the signal will almost certainly be modest.

Although the goals of this simulation exercise are primarily analytic and prescriptive, our confidence in the results would be strengthened if its descriptive implications were broadly consistent with the historical record and particularly with the U.S.-Soviet experience. The importance of uncertainty about the rival's intentions is corroborated by internal debates about the consequences of making an initial cooperative gesture or of responding to one. If the U.S.-Soviet race—the arms race about which we have the best information—is characteristic, these debates are endless. Should the United States halt deployment of the MX and sea-launched cruise missiles (SLACMs) and wait for a response? Should it extend its unilateral ban on developing an antisatellite weapon (ASAT) while a treaty is being negotiated? Should it discontinue SDI development in hopes of inspiring a spirit of cooperation that will lead to significant disarmament? Each policy has supporters who are convinced that the Soviet Union will be eager to cooperate if its negative expectations are overcome, as well as opponents who argue that it has no intention of exchanging its strategic buildup for U.S. restraint. Debates about the intentions that may have motivated a potentially cooperative gesture initiated by the Soviet Union are no less frequent or controversial. Certainly there is no greater consensus on the meaning of the Soviet moratorium on nuclear testing in 1986 than there was on Soviet troop reductions in Eastern Europe in 1956.

The sensitivity of tacit bargaining to noise and misinterpretation has implications both for the simplicity and decomposability of the agreements that are achieved and for the time they are likely to last. Because problems of noise and interpretation work against the construction of complex agreements, we would generally expect successful tacit bargaining to involve only one type of weaponry or weapon system. Historically, this always seems to have been the case. Tacit bargaining in the Anglo-German and Anglo-French naval races each involved a single type of ship, and U.S.-Soviet gestures have been similarly focused. The American unilateral renunciation of nuclear weapons in space (1962) and renunciation of biological and toxin weapons (1969) can be viewed as gestures that are characteristic in this regard.

4.5   Conclusion

The small number of instances in which cooperation-based tacit bargaining has led to progress in arms control, coupled with the limitations that emerge from the simulation, might easily lead one to underestimate the potential contribution of the process. It is true that its inability to deal with complex trade-offs means that it is unlikely to lead to comprehensive arms reduction. It is also true that the belief in a single strategy that can reliably serve policymakers in every situation is chimerical; nonetheless, it can play an important role. If skillfully applied to specific categories of weapons, it can stabilize an arms race by limiting the deployment of such weapons or restricting the conduct of tests necessary to their development; in some cases, it can lead to their dismantling.

Despite its limitations, tacit bargaining enjoys a number of advantages over formal negotiations. Its iterative character permits progress to occur in small increments with low transaction costs. No summit conference need be convened; no broad treaty need be accepted or rejected whole sale; no elaborate ratification process need be overcome. True, a tacitly bargained agreement is less "institutionalized" than a formal treaty, and therefore more vulnerable to violation from both sides. But this permits states to experiment with cooperation at a lower cost than a formal treaty would demand. If the tacit bargain does not produce the desired results, it can be allowed to dissolve.

The natural affinity of tacit bargaining for decomposable problems, which bounds its ability to produce comprehensive disarmament, can inspire decision makers to cooperate in specific areas even while most of their interactions continue to be uncooperative. Just as tacit bargaining led to unrestricted travel within the city of Berlin even during the height of the Blockade, so it can lead to the control of nuclear weapons in space or the development of an antiballistic missile system during a period when a new generation of long-range strategic missiles is being deployed. Moreover, the fact that the weapons systems most likely to yield to tacit bargaining must be decomposable from other weapons systems for negotiation purposes does not mean that they are decomposable in a historical sense. By slightly altering a state's expectations about the strategy and motivations of its opponent, every successful tacit bargain increases the likelihood that another will take place. Eventually, they can accumulate to the point where the arms race is significantly slowed and where the climate is improved for the formal negotiations that are necessary to handle the difficult and complex trade-offs that a major disarmament effort requires.

The catch is that skillful tacit bargaining, like skillful negotiation, is more difficult than one might at first imagine. Its successful application is dependent on information that is likely to come from a number of different sources, a thorough understanding of the probabilistic effect of several key parameters, and a willingness to switch strategies when conditions change. Perhaps it depends above all on an ability to cope with the inevitable ambiguity caused by the fundamental paradox of tacit bargaining.

Chapter 5

Maintaining Arms Treaties

5.1 Introduction

There is a marked tendency on the part of both politicians and the general public to treat arms treaties as documents that will endure forever. Proponents speak of unprecedented achievements that will give birth to a new political order and opponents speak in terms of tragic mistakes that will cede strategic superiority until the end of time. Some of this is hyperbole designed to attract supporters to a particular point of view but there is clearly something more going on. For whatever reason, nations approach treaties in the same way that people approach marriage. They consider them as the terminal point of a process and something perpetual in the face of every evidence that they are all too often transient. A principal consequence of this is that neither proponents nor opponents give much thought to what it will take to keep the treaty alive or the consequences of its demise. True, there is often considerable interest in verification procedures to prevent cheating, but these provide little guidance about what pattern of sanctions should be employed in the event that cheating takes place, or what expectations about sanctions will prevent cheating from occurring.

The scholarly community seems prone to much the same bias. There is a general recognition that verification should be as thorough and as creative as possible, that a well-defined dispute settlement mechanism should be established as part of the treaty, and that self-restraint in innovation is desirable to avoid simply displacing the locus of the arms race from one weapon system to another, but apart from verification, these primarily constitute a plea for mutual restraint and cooperative problem solving. There almost appears to be a psychological block to generating theories about the most effective treaty maintenance strategy that recognizes the competitive forces that persist after a treaty is signed. When scholars think about the dissolution of treaties, they variously emphasize changes in leadership and domestic politics, the development of new technologies, changing relations with other nations, alliance problems, and economic conditions. That these are clearly important and are the genesis of the majority of treaty problems is undeniable. The fact that this is true, however, does not negate the role of the pattern of incentives and disincentives that have been used to establish expectations about what the cost of treaty violations will be.

Although more robust than their more strident critics contend, it would be difficult to review the history of arms control agreements in the twentieth century without concluding that they are fragile structures. All too often, significant violations occur soon after treaties are ratified or they are undermined by technological advances and increased acquisition of other weaponry. In 1902, Chile and Argentina agreed to restrict the rate of growth of naval forces, but within three years there were notable violations on both sides and, by 1906, Argentina took steps to dissolve the agreement completely (Livermore 1944). The Washington Naval Treaty of 1923, the most pathbreaking attempt to regulate a great power arms race, fared little better. Even prior to formal Japanese abrogation in 1934, the treaty was undermined from every quarter: by cheating, technological innovation, force structure change, the exploitation of loopholes and ambiguities, and innovations in strategy and tactics (Goldman 1989, 8). For example, the treaty permitted the conversion of battle cruisers into aircraft carriers up to a maximum of 33,000 tons, yet both the USS *Lexington* and *Saratoga* were closer to 36,000 tons. The British and French engaged in similar tactics and the Japanese and Italians were still more flagrant. Japan's *Atago* was 45 percent larger than announced, Italy's *Glorizia* exceeded its announced size by 20 percent, and Japan's *Yamato* was 95 percent heavier than announced and carried 18-inch rather than 16-inch guns.

Technological innovation and force structure changes combined to create a "displacement effect" of the kind noted in chapter 1 that had even more profound implications. The French and Italians simply shifted their resources to the stepped-up building of submarines. The French had built or authorized fifty-nine new submarines between 1922 and 1929; the Italians twenty-eight. The Japanese stepped up the pace of shipbuilding in every auxiliary category. During the same period, they had either built or authorized three aircraft carriers, twenty-one cruisers, fifty-two destroyers, and fifty-two submarines (Hoover 1980, 69).

This is not the sort of building program that stabilizes an arms race. In fact, with the advantage of hindsight, those disposed to be cynical about the legacy of arms control agreements could even argue that the uncertainty associated with the new weaponry and the strategic doctrine that was shaped by these weapons made the arms race more unstable in the wake of the treaty than if it had never existed. The accelerated production of submarines threatened great-fleet communication and supply lines. The switch in emphasis from the battleship to the aircraft carrier that was in some measure inspired by the Washington Naval Treaty of 1923 placed a premium on preemptive and offensive strategies. Although the real utility of aircraft carriers would not become apparent until the first months of World War II, the vulnerability of carriers had already begun to create an incentive to attack first and to surprise rather than be surprised (Goldman 1989, 19).

Contemporary arms control agreements have also run into problems. Both the United States and the Soviet Union have contended that the other country has violated major provisions of SALT I, SALT II, the ABM Treaty, the test ban treaty, the Helsinki Accord, and agreements on chemical and biological weapons (Duffy 1988, 271). The majority of such charges were initiated by the Reagan administration and some have been heavily discounted by experts outside the administration. This is especially true of violations of SALT I. The Reagan administration's case for violations of other agreements was stronger, if still open to dispute.

It charged that the Soviet Union employed chemical weapons in Afghanistan, constructed a large, phased-array radar near the city of Krasnoyarsk in violation of the ABM Treaty, encrypted test data in violation of the verification provisions of SALT II, and violated that treaty again by flight-testing a new type of missile (the SS-25) (Schear 1985). For its part, the United States announced its intention to cease abiding by the constraints of SALT I and II in November, 1986, and soon violated SALT II ceilings on the number of bombers armed with cruise missiles (Farley 1988, 216). In addition, President Reagan's commitment to Star Wars (SDI) has raised serious questions about U.S. intentions to abide by the ABM Treaty.

Our point is not to characterize the level of arms control compliance as invariably weak. Indeed, despite the difficulties and continued arms growth on both sides, the U.S.-Soviet experience gives some reason for optimism. One does not have to take a strong position in the debate about whether or not the historical record of arms control has been mostly good or mostly bad to recognize that substantial violations have occasionally occurred and that displacement and technological progress has frequently rendered some agreements ineffective. The question is how to best reduce violations and how to cope with displacement and innovation. While not denying the importance of voluntary cooperation and institutional mechanisms such as the Standing Consultative Commission (SCC), which effectively handled arms treaty compliance issues between the United States and Soviet Union until 1980, the focus of this chapter is once again on ways that states can exploit the self-interest of their rivals to deter treaty violations.

Given the difficulties that have surrounded arms treaties and those that have plagued treaties in other areas, it is surprising that there is so little theoretical literature on the topic of treaty maintenance. While countless pages have been written about the negotiations that lie behind agreements, the fate of specific treaties (e.g., Yalta, Versailles), and the problems of compliance monitoring and verification, remarkably little attention has been paid to what pattern of sanctions best deters violations and, in the case of arms control, minimizes the problems of displacement and innovation. Fred Ikle was concerned about the same lack of attention to the problem of treaty maintenance when he wrote a 1961 article in *Foreign Affairs* entitled, "After Detection—What?" As the title suggests, he was struck by the attention to verification that suffused the domestic debate about arms control and played a major role in arms negotiations contrasted with the lack of attention to what would be done in the event that the verification process detected a violation. As he notes "detecting violations is not enough. What counts are the political and military consequences of a violation once it has been detected, since these alone will determine whether or not the violator stands to gain in the end" (Ikle 1961, 208). As is usually the case with articles that define problems that have previously received little attention, Ikle's contribution lies less in providing authoritative policy guidance than in outlining the advantages and disadvantages of some possible strategies. After using several historical examples to dismiss the power of world opinion to enforce agreements in areas other than arms control, he focuses on two strategies: (1) returning to the level of arms acquisition that characterized the status quo prior to the agreement and (2) stepping up the arms race to punish the rival nation for violating the agreement. He notes that the first option has attracted the most attention and underlies the expectation that verification will be sufficient to guarantee that a treaty is maintained. Both nations will abide by a treaty because they know that if they don't, they will be caught and the benefits of the treaty will disappear. Ikle is not insensitive to the disincentive effects that this provides, but notes that it rests on the assumption that a violation would not provide the transgressor with an irrevocable advantage that outweighs the costs associated with returning to the previous level of arms race. He obviously believes that this assumption will frequently not hold. An aggressive nation will often calculate that it can gain more through the violation of an agreement—either because the detection of violations will always be imperfect or because it will gain a significant arms advantage when political difficulties delay its rival from returning to the previous level of arms competition quickly enough. "The violator, in fact, would be playing a profitable game. 'Heads you lose, tails we're even' " (216). Ikle finds this prospect so seductive that he can easily envision a potential violator entering into agreements solely because of the advantages that cheating provides.

For Ikle, the way around this problem is to raise the cost of violation to the point that it no longer has a positive expected value. This is most effectively done by convincing the potential violator that the arms race that ensues after its violation will be at a level far greater than the previous status quo. If the aggrieved nation increases its defense budget $20 billion beyond the previous level, it will have effectively fined the transgressor nation $20 billion—since that is the sum that the transgressor must now pay to maintain parity (217). Ikle is well aware that this stratagem forces the aggrieved nation to commit itself to a level of spending that it may find unappealing, but he argues that this cost is less than that of the aggression that might take place if the other nation exploited the superiority that it gained through violations.

Although this is a provocative beginning, the nature of arms advantage and the treaty maintenance problem are more complicated than Ikle acknowledges and critical questions are left unanswered. The biggest problem with his analysis is that he ignores the probability that the verification process or intelligence sources will *overestimate* the rival nation's arms activity, which could produce a needless and costly new arms race. This is why Ikle gives such short shrift to the use of treaty abrogation or more modest strategies such as Tit-for-Tat to limit violations. If there is no possibility of making a mistake, it will always be wisest to make the largest credible threat. But what if there is such a possibility?

As indicated in chapter 1, the arms race literature is filled with examples of nineteenth- and twentieth-century arms spirals that have been provoked by such overestimates. Detection uncertainty has also characterized the debate over alleged Soviet violations of the Threshold Test Ban Treaty (TTBT) and the SALT treaties. Charges that Soviet underground nuclear test yields are too large hinge on comparisons between the Soviet tests and those produced by U.S. tests in Nevada. What complicates this comparison is that U.S and Soviet test site geological structures differ in such a way that a Soviet test of equivalent size is "broadcast" more clearly than those from the United States. This means that the magnitude of Soviet tests will be overestimated unless the appropriate discounting factor is applied. The problem is that experts disagree about precisely what the discount factor should be. In 1984–85 many people both inside and outside government began to charge that the Reagan administration was using a discount factor that was too low because it ignored the effect of surface waves that travel through the earth's upper crust. This, they argued, resulted in charges of testing violations where none existed (Smith 1985, 695).

Alleged Soviet violations of SALT I, which prohibits the deployment of mobile radars that can be used in support of ABM systems, are equally controversial. It is true that the Soviets constructed a radar that could be easily placed on a truck, but no one came forth with evidence that one had been moved or placed on wheels (Smith 1985, 696). In short, there is a good chance that the test ban violations do not exist and that the radar is, at most, a technical violation of the spirit, but not necessarily the letter, of SALT I. Doubtless it would be folly for a responsible administration to ignore the possible implications associated with either alleged violation. It is not obvious, however, that either would be best dealt with by Ikle's strategy of immediately abrogating the relevant treaty and punishing the Soviet Union by resuming the arms race at a level of intensity greater than the race that existed prior to the treaty. The tension between the desire to provide the greatest disincentive for treaty violations and the desire to avoid arms spirals provoked by imperfect intelligence and interpretation is the principal focus of this chapter.

One might have expected that in the ensuing thirty years other political scientists and economists would have taken up the gauntlet thrown down by Ikle. Remarkably, this has not occurred. Articles on what might be termed the theory of treaty maintenance are largely absent from the pages of the journals of these disciplines— even those such as the *Journal of Conflict Resolution* that often bring a formal modeling perspective to security issues. As a result, policy discussions about the appropriate strategy to be followed in the event of treaty violations or the rare retrospective analyses of the strategies that were followed in a specific instance tend to be oversimplified and ignore many key questions. For example, in January, 1987, *Science* published a policy forum where verification and violation issues were discussed by Manfred Eimer and Sidney Drell. Both individuals have worked in the arms control area for many years and have held influential government and defense consultant positions. Yet despite their voluminous knowledge of verification problems and their appreciation for the subtleties of U.S.-Soviet interaction, there was no interest on the part of either in the problems posed by uncertainty or about policy decisions that have to be made in the wake of a violation. In fact, despite their differences on a number of important issues, they both found themselves in agreement on what the editors of *Science* referred to as the strategy of "proportionate response" (Koshland 1987, 405). So great was the consensus on this issue that no one felt the need to define the term *proportionate response*, although the reader can infer from the discussion of retaliation for the development of the SS-25 that it is something very close to Tit-for-Tat. No arguments are provided about its relative superiority to more or less severe punishment strategies or whether it should be adapted in the face of uncertainty.

The same tendency to play down the analytic basis that should underlie key policy choices about the appropriate response to treaty violations is even apparent in many of the works included in the recent volume edited by George, Farley, and Dallin, *U.S.-Soviet Security Cooperation* (1988). Although it would be hard to imagine a richer set of articles reflecting on virtually every facet of security cooperation, treaty maintenance is almost never in the foreground. Duffy's history of arms control compliance describes tacit responses to Soviet action or inaction, but does not speculate about whether a different strategy on the part of either the United States or the Soviet Union might have extended the mutual security regime and reduced the compliance crisis of the 1980s. Perhaps because so many of the attempts to regulate military activities in space have been tacitly conducted, the article on that topic by Weber and Drell contains the most elaborate description of the evolution of how the cooperative regime in that area has been supported by different tacit bargaining strategies over time. In the period from 1969 until 1974, U.S. policy was one of contingent restraint: the United States made it clear that it would not engage in unilateral activities and would respond in kind to failures of the Soviet Union to act similarly. This gradually gave way to a "negotiate or else" policy in which contingent threats of escalation were linked to Soviet willingness to negotiate formal agreements (Weber and Drell 1988, 377). Weber and Drell do a fine job explicating the roots of this policy change and how it was manifested. They pay far less attention, however, to its impact and particularly whether or not it was the best strategy to pursue (and how this should be decided).

Uncertainty about whether or not a treaty has been violated and its implications for treaty design and maintenance will be a major topic in this chapter. So, too, will be the relative usefulness of Tit-for-Tat and more extreme strategies, and the opportunities that treaty maintenance strategies present for preventing a treaty from being undermined by technological innovation and displacement. Somewhat less emphasis will be placed on the impact of uncertainty about the motives and capabilities of the rival nation than in the previous chapter. There are three reasons for this concentration on uncertainty about actions (*information uncertainty*) rather than uncertainty about preferences (*utility uncertainty*). First, the possibility of cheating and the necessity of acting on ambiguous intelligence information about a rival's activities have historically played a large role in discussions about treaty maintenance. The political history of SALT I and SALT II are only the most recent evidence of this.

The second reason is more subtle and stems from the robustness of two important categories of treaty maintenance strategies. Both generalized Tit-for-Tat and the trigger strategies introduced in this chapter are reasonably robust to errors in estimating the opponent's preferences. In both cases, exploitation by a secretly aggressive opponent are naturally limited by the defined response to perceived treaty violations. This puts a ceiling on the maximum amount of exploitation (or cost) that can take place at the hands of a manipulative and aggressive opponent.

The third reason has to do with the likelihood of misestimating preferences rather than with the cost of doing so. The very existence of an arms treaty means that a great deal is known about the opponent's preferences. At the very least, and for however short a time, the rival nation has indicated that it prefers an agreement to an all-out arms race. This reassurance is not available to decision makers who are trying to devise a means of attaining an agreement in the midst of an ongoing arms race. The major worry once a treaty has been attained is that these preferences might be replaced by more aggressive ones that will cause the treaty to break down.

Even more than the previous chapter on achieving cooperation, this chapter will depend on a substantial amount of formal modeling. This may seem somewhat paradoxical. While the number of arms agreements that have been achieved through tacit bargaining may be too small to permit much data analysis (or even comparative history), the absence of an international judicial body with coercive powers and the sporadic effectiveness of world public opinion means that tacit strategies and the expectations that they create are the major basis of enforcement of every agreement whether formally *or* tacitly arrived at. It is reasonable to ask why an enlarged data base that contains formal as well as tacit agreements necessitates the use of more axiomatic mathematics.

The answer lies in the fact that a large N does not necessarily convey more information. Regardless of how few cases there are and the incompleteness of the historical record, an arms agreement that has been tacitly arrived at during an arms race leaves a behavioral record behind: prior to the agreement, states increased or decreased weapons stocks of various types and military expenditures at varying rates. There may be biases in the way that these are perceived and differences in the rules by which they are interpreted but a behavior is the basic unit of analysis. The tricky thing about treaty maintenance and the larger problem of deterrence to which it is related is that the empirical trail is not as well marked. Successful treaty maintenance is a nonevent. It is no simple matter to decide how many successes are associated with a treaty that lasts two years. Should the N of successes be measured by the moment, week, month, year? Moreover, the success of a treaty maintenance strategy—again as in deterrence—is obviously a function of the benefits that will be accrued by breaking it as well as the costs that are expected to be incurred. How can these be measured with any reliability? If we simply ignore the problem we run the risk that the rate of maintenance or deterrence success, however measured, is more a function of declining aspirations than of any expectations created by tacit bargaining. Against a fanatical enough opponent, no treaty maintenance or deterrence strategy will work. Against an unambitious or domestically preoccupied nation, virtually any strategy will prove successful. This does not make the concepts of treaty maintenance or deterrence valueless, any more than beauty often lying in the eye of the beholder makes the concept of beauty meaningless. It does mean, however, that accessing the efficacy of tacit maintenance strategies directly from the historical record is not possible without enormously detailed information about the expectations that existed on both sides. Skilled historians have been able to gather this sort of information and persuade us of its correctness in a case or two, but there is not enough information to build a representative set of cases, much less qualify as a reliable data set.

Even if information about expectations and objectives was accurate and plentiful and the data problem could be solved, the other traditional arguments for the use of formal methods would still exist. The range of treaty maintenance strategies that have been actually employed is narrower than the set of possibilities that will be considered here. For example, it is not clear that any nation has attempted to maintain a treaty through the use of a "trigger strategy" (a strategy based on a response to an announced threshold of violations) where the threshold of the trigger is calculated to be responsive to uncertainty. Using induction to estimate the effectiveness of an untried strategy from a set of case studies or an aggregate data set is no easy matter.

This means that much of our understanding of treaty maintenance must come from something that resembles formal modeling with respect to its distance from strict induction, or from a combination of case studies and some very bold assumptions about the way nations "would have" responded. We have chosen to pursue the former course. Because it is impossible to generalize to the historical record without some secure knowledge that the utility functions that are discussed or the degree of uncertainty that is assumed are characteristic of some average treaty, no pretense is made that the conclusions are somehow descriptively typical of historical treaties. That step will have to wait for the slow accumulation of a representative set of historical studies. We can, however, explore the treaty maintenance implications of various patterns of expectations and uncertainty, realizing full well that intelligence and foreign policy experts will be needed to bring the models to life by reporting (or speculating about) the detailed situation that exists at any given time. Even in the absence of specific information about risk and preferences, it is still possible to say something useful about the consequences that are likely to follow and how they might be mitigated. In short, the goal will be to discover what treaty maintenance strategy will be most effective *given various conditions*.

As we have noted, treaty maintenance is closely related to deterrence. In its starkest formulation the problem is that of deterring a rival nation from violating an agreement that has been tacitly or formally achieved. However, there are important differences between the problem of nuclear deterrence and deterrence as it relates to arms control. This necessitates a different conceptual and mathematical approach to the problem. The most important difference lies in the structure of the underlying game. The archetypal game for nuclear deterrence is the game of Chicken, in which mutual defection is the worst possible outcome. Notwithstanding the fact that history supports the argument that no single game can be used to represent every arms race, Chicken does not fall within the class of possibilities. Regardless of whether one assumes aggressive (Deadlock) preferences or defensive (Prisoner's Dilemma) preferences, mutual defection is never the worst possible outcome. This is true even if one were to imagine a situation where an increase in weapons stocks had no strategic value and represented nothing more than a waste of resources. In that case, the worst possible outcome for either nation would be for that nation to build and the other not.

Another difference has to do with the continuous nature of the response variable. In the case of nuclear war, the context in which most deterrence theory has been placed, there is an important discontinuity in the repertoire of responses available to a nation. Even in the case of a limited nuclear conflict, the first use of nuclear weapons represents a large and awesome escalation of the conflict. In arms building, however, a nation has a large variety of options—any of a number of weapons systems may be incremented by large or small amounts. For modeling purposes, this makes the strategy space continuous, as opposed to discontinuous in the nuclear case, and means that there are an essentially infinite number of choices at any time. This requires the use of more complex models than the 2×2 game. Still another difference concerns the information problem. The initiation of nuclear conflict is an unambiguous event; it is often difficult to determine whether another nation has violated an arms treaty. This means that strategies must be formulated that are robust to the problems of imperfect information about the opponent's actions.

The model we use, as introduced in chapter 3, incorporates the central dilemma that both sides would benefit from the observance of the treaty while each would profit individually from violating it. We develop equilibrium strategies for the two sides that are capable of supporting cooperation in the context of an arms agreement. At first this is done in a simplified world in which utilities and actions are common knowledge among the participants. Later these restrictions are relaxed and the equilibrium results are developed for cases in which neither side knows exactly what the other has done, and may not even know about the other side's capabilities and preferences. Throughout, we try to propose strategies that are cognitively achievable as well as intuitively appealing. If these features are absent, the employment of these strategies in actual diplomatic contexts would be unlikely.

The starting place for the analysis is the model introduced in chapter 3 for the utility a nation associates with a given state of arms stock and arms production. This model is general in the sense that it contains a number of parameters that allow different nations to have different preferences. As noted before, arms stocks are treated as unitary goods, rather than the differentiated bundles that they really are. Another assumption is that arms races and arms treaties are examples of a continuum of behavior and that most arms races are usually not conducted at the maximum rate of which the respective states are capable.

We may summarize the discussion in chapter 3 by reiterating the following model.

The Model. *Let the arms production at time t of states A and B be P_t^A and P_t^B and let the arms stocks at time $t = 0$ be S_0^A and S_0^B. Assume that the arms stocks S_t^A and S_t^B are given by*

$$S_t^A = \alpha S_{t-1}^A + P_t^A$$

$$S_t^B = \alpha S_{t-1}^B + P_t^B \qquad (0 < \alpha < 1).$$

Then the utility associated by A with this outcome evaluated at time t = 0 is

$$\sum_{t=1}^{\infty} \delta_A^t U_A(S_t^A, S_t^B, P_t^A)$$

$$= \sum_{t=1}^{\infty} \delta_A^t \left[a_A(S_t^A - S_t^B) - b_A S_t^A - c_A(P_t^A)^2 \right] \quad (5.1)$$

and similarly for nation B.

As previously observed, if the two sides are roughly equivalent and the coefficients a, b, and c have the usual signs, and if $a > b$, this model has certain features in common with the Prisoner's Dilemma often used to model arms races (see Brams 1985; Brams et al. 1979; Brams and Kilgour 1988; Jervis 1976; Majeski 1984; Ordeshook 1986; Snyder 1971; Snyder and Diesing 1977; Wagner 1983); that is, for two levels of production $\Delta^A < \Delta_0^A$ and $\Delta^B < \Delta_0^B$ under consideration, the four outcomes represented by each side choosing Δ or Δ_0 form a payoff matrix of the Prisoner's Dilemma type. In this case, each side prefers to produce more whatever the choice of the other side, but both sides would prefer mutual cooperation to mutual defection. The model we use has, however, several more realistic features. First, it allows cooperative gestures or cheating of any size, so that nations are not presented with dichotomous choices but rather choose from a continuum of production levels. Second, if the two sides are not equal in all respects, the model presents the possibility that one side may prefer mutual defection to equal cooperation. If Δ_0^A was much larger than Δ_0^B, then A might be able to extract a sufficiently large positive utility from the continuing arms advantage to make up for the cost of the arms race. Thus this model can exhibit the Deadlock-like behavior exemplified by the German arms buildup before World War II.[1] Third, and perhaps most notably, the model does not consist of a repetition of the identical game since the payoffs to a choice pair depend on the arms stocks and therefore on the previous choices of the participants. This makes the game and its analysis much more complex.

---

1. See Jervis (1978) and Snyder and Diesing (1977).

5.2   The Value of an Arms Treaty

The first task to is obtain an expression that represents the value of an arms treaty vis-à-vis an arms race. This helps define the underlying game by expressing what is at stake for both parties. The relative sizes of these payoffs, which we expect to vary from one arms race to another, will have a strong effect on the proper strategy to be employed. Formally, the value of an arms treaty is the difference between the utility of the treaty and the utility of an arms race. Alternatives to a treaty obviously differ depending on the particular strategies used by the two sides. A production value that turns out to be of particular importance is the *noncontingent Nash* production level. This is defined to be the level of arms production that would be adopted by a nation that believes that no action on its part, whether cooperative gesture or threat, will influence the arms decisions of the other nation. If both sides adopt this level, the result is obviously a Nash equilibrium, since neither would have an incentive to depart unilaterally from their chosen strategy. Below, we derive conditions under which a nation will prefer the current treaty to the opposing case in which both sides produce at the noncontingent Nash level. Although the satisfaction of this condition does not mean that an arms treaty will necessarily be upheld, it is a necessary condition. If it is not satisfied, the nation involved would always abrogate the treaty. The tension in the situation comes from the fact that both sides have an incentive to produce more than the treaty amount if they could do so without provoking retaliation from the other side.

5.2.1   Single-Period Analysis

Although we have stressed the necessity of representing arms races by multiperiod games, most previous applications of game theory to arms races have been in the form of one-shot models.[2] It is therefore of some interest to contrast the results of the one-period game with those of the more realistic model in the next section.[3]

2. Brams 1985; Brams et al. 1979; Brams and Kilgour 1988; Jervis 1976; Majeski 1984; Snyder 1971; Snyder and Diesing 1977; Wagner 1983.

3. Wittman (1989) presents a two-stage binary choice model in a verification context. The two-stage procedure is, however, carried out only once, so that the indefinite character of a maintained arms treaty is not quite captured.

TABLE 5.1. Approximation to the Single-Period Arms Race Game

	B Chooses 0 (Cooperates)	B Chooses 2.5 (Defects)
A Chooses 0 (Cooperates)	$(0,0)$	$(-22,8)$
A Chooses 2.5 (Defects)	$(8,-22)$	$(-7,-7)$

In the one-period game, side A chooses a production level Δ^A and side B chooses a production level Δ^B. The payoff to side A that results is $a_A(\Delta^A - \Delta^B) - b_A\Delta^A - c_A(\Delta^A)^2$ and correspondingly for side B. Regardless of the choice made by side B, the optimal move by side A is clearly the one satisfying the first-order condition $0 = a_A - b_A - 2c_A\Delta^A$. Since the same is true of side B, the unique Nash equilibrium is $\Delta^A = (a_A - b_A)/(2c_A)$ and $\Delta^B = (a_B - b_B)/(2c_B)$. Like the multiperiod version introduced in the last section, this game is a continuous version of the Prisoner's Dilemma—both sides would benefit if arms increases could be reduced but individual incentives interfere with this cooperative outcome. To make this somewhat less abstract, take a simple example. If the parameter values are $a = 6$ and $b = c = 1$, then the Nash equilibrium production levels would be 2.5. If we restrict choice to the two values 0 and 2.5, the resulting 2×2 game shown in table 5.1 is a form of the Prisoner's Dilemma. Clearly, the prospects for arms control would be dim since the usual Prisoner's Dilemma incentives to defect exist here.

If we accepted this as a representation for arms races, we would be faced with the necessity of resolving the Prisoner's Dilemma within the context of the one-shot game. Although there have been many efforts to accomplish this, particularly by social psychologists, the framework is so simple and the incentives so clear that there seems little scope for a solution to this problem without invoking some form of altruism, a characteristic not usually associated with states defending their national interests. Fortunately, an arms race is inherently a multiperiod phenomenon.

It is important to note that the multiperiod game that we use throughout the remainder of this chapter is not a repeated version of the one-shot game. This is true because arms increases in one period confer a benefit not only for that period, but as long as the weapons are operational. This also means that the Nash equilibrium for the one-period game plays no role in the further analysis.

5.2.2 Multiple-Period Analysis

Before we can evaluate the relative effectiveness of different treaty maintenance strategies, it is first necessary to define the feasible set of treaties that can be sustained by *any* strategy. This requires that we derive a Nash equilibrium for the multiperiod game that is conceptually similar to the Nash equilibrium for the one-period game. This Nash equilibrium is the all-out arms race to which the nations might revert if the treaty fails to be upheld. One necessary (but not sufficient) condition for a treaty to remain in force is that both sides prefer it to the all-out arms race that might ensue if the treaty breaks down. The major result of this section is a series of Propositions about when a treaty will be stable in this limited sense.

Suppose a treaty calls for production levels $P_t^A = P_t^B = 0$. Then the arms stock of nation A at time t will be $S_t^A = \alpha^t S_0^A$ and the payoff to side A will be

$$V_0^A(S_0^A, S_0^B) = \sum_{t=1}^{\infty} \delta_A^t U_A(S_t^A, S_t^B, 0)$$

$$= \sum_{t=1}^{\infty} \alpha^t \delta_A^t \left[a_A(S_0^A - S_0^B) - b_A S_0^A \right]$$

$$= \mathcal{S}_0^A \alpha \delta_A / (1 - \alpha \delta_A) \qquad (5.2)$$

where

$$\mathcal{S}_0^A = a_A(S_0^A - S_0^B) - b_A S_0^A. \qquad (5.3)$$

This expression, then, represents the utility to side A of the zero-level treaty and will form the basis for comparison with other options.[4]

As noted, the value of a treaty is the difference in utility between that treaty and the arms race that would occur in its absence. For the sake of simplicity, we shall begin by assuming this alternative to consist of some constant rate of production at a level greater than zero. Although this case is not perfectly general, it represents an important alternative to a treaty that, as will be seen later, is also a most plausible alternative. If both nations produce at constant rates Δ^A and Δ^B, then the arms stock of A at time $t > 0$ is determined by

$$
\begin{aligned}
S_t^A &= \alpha S_{t-1}^A + \Delta^A \\[2mm]
&= \alpha^t S_0^A + (1 + \alpha + \cdots + \alpha^{t-1})\Delta^A \\[2mm]
&= \alpha^t S_0^A + \Delta^A(1 - \alpha^t)/(1 - \alpha) \qquad (5.4)
\end{aligned}
$$

and, using Equations (5.1) and (5.4) the payoff to A will be

$$
\begin{aligned}
& V_1^A(S_0^A, S_0^B, \Delta^A, \Delta^B) \\[2mm]
&= \sum_{t=1}^{\infty} \delta_A^t U_A(S_t^A, S_t^B, P_t^A) \\[2mm]
&= \sum_{t=1}^{\infty} \delta_A^t \left[a_A(S_t^A - S_t^B) - b_A S_t^A - c_A(\Delta^A)^2 \right] \\[2mm]
&= \sum_{t=1}^{\infty} \left[\alpha^t \delta_A^t S_0^A + \delta_A^t \mathcal{D}^A(1 - \alpha^t)/(1 - \alpha) - \delta_A^t \mathcal{Q}^A \right]
\end{aligned}
$$

---

4. In much of this chapter, a treaty is assumed to consist of the requirement that neither side produce arms. The more general case of restriction to some nonzero level of production is considered from time to time in order to verify that the general nature of the propositions is not thereby changed. Arms treaties also can consist of restrictions on the total arms stock rather than the amount of yearly increase. With the model we are using, the requirements of each kind of treaty can easily be translated into the requirements of the other kind. Restrictions on yearly increases are more consistent with ideas of tacit bargaining and implicit arms treaties, so this is the form that we assume throughout.

$$= V_0^A(S_0^A, S_0^B) + \delta_A \mathcal{D}^A/(1 - \delta_A)(1 - \alpha\delta_A)$$

$$- \mathcal{Q}^A \delta_A/(1 - \delta_A) \tag{5.5}$$

where

$$\mathcal{D}^A = a_A(\Delta^A - \Delta^B) - b_A \Delta^A \tag{5.6}$$

$$\mathcal{Q}^A = c_A(\Delta^A)^2. \tag{5.7}$$

In considering what choices a "rational actor" would make given these utilities, it is important to specify what response is expected from the opponent. The easiest case is when A assumes that B's move is independent of any choice by A. This could occur if A believes that B will defect in any case or will cooperate in any case. The result in this case is given in the following Proposition, which defines the noncontingent Nash level.

Proposition 2. *Suppose A and B have utilities as given above. If A's choices do not affect the choices that B will make, then A's optimal choice is always*

$$P_t^A = \Delta_0^A = \frac{(a_A - b_A)}{2c_A(1 - \alpha\delta_A)}, \tag{5.8}$$

for all t.

Proof. Suppose that there is a contemplated series (P_t^A, P_t^B) of production decisions and that A wishes to decide on the next period's production $\Delta = P_1^A$ under the assumption that none of the other production decisions will change as a result. Let V^A be the resulting utility. Under these circumstances, the optimal move by A can be derived by examining the first-order condition $\partial V^A/\partial\Delta = 0$. First, we have $S_t^A = \alpha^t S_0 + \sum_{s=1}^t \alpha^{t-s} P_s^A$, so that $\partial S_t^A/\partial\Delta = \alpha^{t-1}$. Thus

$$\frac{\partial V^A}{\partial\Delta} = \sum_{t=1}^\infty \delta_A^t \frac{\partial U_A^t}{\partial\Delta}$$

$$= \sum_{t=1}^\infty \delta_A^t(a_A - b_A)\alpha^{t-1} - 2c_A\delta_A\Delta$$

$$= (a_A - b_A)\delta_A/(1 - \alpha\delta_A) - 2c_A\delta_A\Delta \tag{5.9}$$

so the optimal choice is as stated. ∎

If both sides build at this rate, the result is clearly a Nash equilibrium, because neither party has an incentive to depart unilaterally from this level. This is somewhat more interesting than might first appear. In principle, for a given pattern of moves by B that will not be altered in response to A's choices, A's optimal series of moves could be quite complicated—but it isn't. It might seem reasonable if A were informed that B was going to produce 120 missiles this year, 130 the year after, and 150 the following year for A to make a different production decision than if A were to find out that B was going to produce 90 missiles each year. Yet A's best response is the same in both cases. Once A has determined that B's production decisions will not be made conditional on A's decisions, it becomes optimal for A to make production choices that do not depend on B's decisions either.

Note that this production is a multiple of the Nash equilibrium value for the one-period game by a factor $(1 - \alpha\delta_A)^{-1}$. If α and δ are both .9, for example, then this factor is 5.26. This makes the worst potential outcome in the multiperiod game considerably more intense than that of the one-period game. This happens because the continued utility in future periods of arms built in the present increases the incentive to build. For example, with the previously used parameter values, the noncooperative outcome in the one-period game is a production level of 2.5 and the noncooperative outcome in the multiperiod game is a production level of 13.2. Of course, this greater potential for intensive arms races is counterbalanced by a greater scope for cooperation in the multiperiod game.

If Equation (5.5) is compared with Equation (5.2), it is easily seen that they differ by two terms—one is a multiple of $\mathcal{D}^A$, the other is the cost penalty term. In considering the question of whether it might be in A's interest to invite mutual defection rather than to observe the treaty, there are several important cases. If the defection is expected to be of equal magnitude (Δ^A and Δ^B are equal), it is never in the interest of either party to defect. Since arms advantage depends on the relative sizes of the arms stocks, neither side would gain militarily and both would incur higher costs. "Rational" defection would occur, however, if there is an expectation that the difference in the defection levels of the two sides goes beyond some threshold. This could occur if the arms advantage resulting from unequal buildups outweighed the cost of building and maintaining the arms. Thus, if A expects that B will build at a sufficiently lower rate, then defection may be advantageous—the condition is given in the following proposition.

A point that has not been considered up to now is that a surprise defection is worth somewhat more to nation A than the amount given in Equation (5.5) because of the advantage A obtains from increasing arms in the first period when B does not yet know about the defection. As we have seen, this is one of Ikle's chief concerns (1961).[5] Thus, results for surprise defection are also given in the following proposition.

We give the results first in the general case in which the treaty amount is not zero and then specialize to the zero-treaty case. Although the zero-treaty case continues to provide a simple illustration, the more general case describes the majority of twentieth-century treaties.

Proposition 3. *Suppose A and B are in an equal treaty specifying production levels of $\bar{\Delta}^A$ and $\bar{\Delta}^B$ and that A contemplates reversion to an arms race of Δ^A and Δ^B instead. Then*

1. A will prefer the treaty whenever

$$(\Delta^B - \bar{\Delta}^B) > (\Delta^A - \bar{\Delta}^A)[(1 - b_A/a_A)$$

$$- (c_A/a_A)(1 - \alpha\delta_A)(\Delta^A + \bar{\Delta}^A)].$$

$$(5.10)$$

When the treaty amounts are both zero, this becomes

$$\Delta^B > \Delta^A[(1 - b_A/a_A) - (c_A/a_A)(1 - \alpha\delta_A)\Delta^A]. \quad (5.11)$$

---

5. It would be straightforward to provide a similar condition to cover the case when B recognizes the defection at an arbitrary lag, but this would be of little interest in the sequel. Simultaneous defection occurs when both parties recognize that defection is inevitable. Defection at a lag of one turn arises when defection to an all-out arms race is unexpected. In no case is B's information so poor that it requires longer than one turn to detect the difference between observing the treaty and defecting totally.

2. *If the reversion is to an arms race at the noncontingent Nash rates, and if we define $\phi_A = \bar{\Delta}^A/\Delta_0^A$ and $\phi_B = \bar{\Delta}^B/\Delta_0^B$, the treaty amounts represented as fractions of the maximal defection amount, then A will prefer the treaty whenever*

$$\Delta_0^B(1 - \phi_B) > \Delta_0^A(1 - \phi_A)^2(1 - b_A/a_A)/2. \qquad (5.12)$$

When the treaty amounts are both zero, this becomes

$$\Delta_0^B > \Delta_0^A(1 - b_A/a_A)/2. \qquad (5.13)$$

3. *If A considers a surprise defection to an arms race, then the treaty will be preferred whenever*

$$(\Delta^B - \bar{\Delta}^B) > (\Delta^A - \bar{\Delta}^A)\delta_A^{-1}[(1 - b_A/a_A)$$

$$- (c_A/a_A)(1 - \alpha\delta_A)(\Delta^A + \bar{\Delta}^A)].$$

$$(5.14)$$

When the treaty amounts are both zero, this becomes

$$\Delta^B > \Delta^A\delta_A^{-1}[(1 - b_A/a_A) - (c_A/a_A)(1 - \alpha\delta_A)\Delta^A]. \qquad (5.15)$$

4. *If A considers a surprise defection to the noncontingent Nash values, then the treaty will be preferred whenever*

$$\Delta_0^B(1 - \phi_B) > \Delta_0^A\delta_A^{-1}(1 - \phi_A)^2(1 - b_A/a_A)/2. \qquad (5.16)$$

When the treaty amounts are both zero, this becomes

$$\Delta_0^B > \Delta_0^A\delta_A^{-1}(1 - b/a)/2. \qquad (5.17)$$

Proof. The utility to A of the treaty is

$$V_0^A(S_0^A, S_0^B) + \mathcal{D}^A(\bar{\Delta}^A, \bar{\Delta}^B)\delta_A/(1 - \delta_A)(1 - \alpha\delta_A)$$

$$- \mathcal{Q}^A(\bar{\Delta}^A)\delta_A/(1 - \delta_A)$$

and the utility of defection is

$$V_0^A(S_0^A, S_0^B) + \mathcal{D}^A(\Delta^A, \Delta^B)\delta_A/(1 - \delta_A)(1 - \alpha\delta_A)$$

$$- \mathcal{Q}^A(\Delta^A)\delta_A/(1 - \delta_A)$$

so that the difference, which represents the advantage or disadvantage to A of defection, is

$$\mathcal{D}^A(\Delta^A - \bar{\Delta}^A, \Delta^A - \bar{\Delta}^B)\delta_A/(1 - \delta_A)(1 - \alpha\delta_A)$$

$$- (\mathcal{Q}^A(\Delta^A) - \mathcal{Q}^A(\bar{\Delta}^A))\delta_A/(1 - \delta_A). \tag{5.18}$$

The condition (5.10) for A to prefer the treaty then follows. The proof for surprise defection depends on the observation that, compared to Equation (5.5), the only difference that surprise defection makes lies in the terms due to S_t^B. Instead of being given by Equation (5.4), B's arms stock is given by

$$S_t^B = \alpha^t S_0^B \alpha^{t-1} \bar{\Delta}^B + \Delta^B(1 - \alpha^{t-1})/(1 - \alpha) \tag{5.19}$$

and the difference between this and Equation (5.4) is $\alpha^{t-1}(\Delta^B - \bar{\Delta}^B)$. This scenario is worth more to A than immediate defection by both sides as given in Equation (5.5) by the amount $a_A\delta_A(\Delta^B - \bar{\Delta}^B)/(1 - \alpha\delta_A)$. The statement of the proposition then follows.

Cases (2) (4) represent important specializations of (1) and (3). If A contemplates total defection to Δ_0^A, then A should expect that B will also build at the noncontingent Nash rate and Equations (5.12) or (5.16) result. ∎

A first conclusion from this Proposition is that the effect of surprise defection is modest. It only changes the criterion for A to prefer defection by a factor of δ_A^{-1}. With discount rates of plausible sizes, such as .95 or .90, surprise defection is worth only 5 or 10 percent more than simultaneous defection. One implication of this is that, while long-term verification is important, the emphasis on short-term verification is probably overdrawn. It probably makes little difference to overall strategic positions if a treaty violation is detected at a lag of one year rather than six months. This may have relevance for the continued debate over on-site versus more remote verification techniques.

The main implication is that, even if maintenance costs are a negligible fraction of the advantage to be gained by building a unit of arms, Δ_0^A must be over twice Δ_0^B for A to prefer mutual defection to an equal treaty of zero production. Since $\Delta_0^A = (a_A - b_A)/2c_A(1 - \alpha\delta_A)$, defection will only be favored when A values arms advantage much more than B (A is more aggressive) or the costs of arms increases and/or arms maintenance are dramatically smaller than those for B (A is more efficient). Also favoring defection would be a higher discount rate (A values future outcomes more in relation to present outcomes than B). As an example, we may examine the situation using the values $a = 6$, $b = 1$, and $c = 1$. If we let α and δ_A both be 0.9, then $\Delta_0^A = 13.2$ and the requirement for preferring defection to the treaty is that $\Delta_0^B < 0.42\Delta_0^A$. Otherwise put, if B has the utility described by $a = 6$, $b = 1$, and $c = 1$, then for A to prefer defection, one must have either $a_A > 13$ (A obtains something over twice the return from a unit of arms advantage compared to B) or $c_A < 0.42$ (A has a bit less than half the cost of building arms compared to B).

The conclusions for nonzero treaty amounts are quite similar. A comparison of Equations (5.10) and (5.11), for example, shows that the major difference is that the defection levels in (5.11) are replaced by the difference between the defection level and the treaty level. The only other change is that a term in Δ^A is replaced by a term in $\Delta^A + \bar{\Delta}^A$. Since the coefficient of this term is negative, this means that A will be more likely to prefer defection from a nonzero treaty than from a zero-level treaty. This conclusion is quite logical since a higher production level under the treaty reduces the benefit of mutual observance. The implication is that the additional effort required to negotiate or tacitly obtain a more stringent treaty may pay off not only in greater mutual benefit but also in greater stability (in this sense) against changes in technology and leadership.

This provides us with the first modest opportunity to evaluate the realism of the model. One factor often thought to be destabilizing is changes in technology. Suppose two nations are relatively balanced at the time a treaty (tacit or formal) is initiated. Later there may be gradual changes in technology that result in gradual shifts in the cost of producing a given level of arms and that were unanticipated at the time the treaty was formulated.[6] It is striking that differences on the order of 20–30 percent will not affect the stability of the treaty; that is, they will not make mutual defection more attractive to either side than mutual cooperation. In

---

6. The cost here is cost per unit of effectiveness, not cost per tank or airplane.

order for out-and-out defection to be attractive, innovation must lead to cost or effectiveness differences between the two sides of 50 percent or more. This suggests that differential advances in technology sufficiently great to result in an immediate destabilization of a previously quiescent arms race would be quite rare. This result coincides with the conclusions in a recent book by Evangelista (1988). We suspect that many treaty breakdowns attributed to advances in technology occur not because of deliberate violations of treaty provisions but because of displacement and the exploitation of loopholes in formal treaties that apply to a narrow range of weapons. The technological problems associated with the breakdown of the Washington Naval Treaty of 1923, for example, occurred in areas not covered by the treaty such as submarines, heavy cruisers, and aircraft carriers. It did not collapse because the signatories discovered cheaper ways to make battleships, although they did make such discoveries.

Perhaps it would be more likely for changes of such magnitude to be associated with other parameters of the model. Parameter a, which represents the preference for arms advantage, would have an effect on the stability of the treaty similar to the cost parameter, c. A change of leadership can, and probably does, more frequently produce differences of the necessary magnitude. It is probably no coincidence that violations of the Treaty of Versailles, the Washington Naval Treaty 1923, and SALT I and II are all more closely associated with new personalities coming to power than with the discovery of new weapons technology.

In what follows, the focus will be on that set of treaties that can potentially be upheld. Specifically, our interest lies in ways to enforce mutually advantageous treaties that might break down *if left to themselves*. Without the application of the correct treaty maintenance strategy, these potentially advantageous treaties can fail.[7]

---

7. Abreu (1986) has shown that cooperation can, at least in theory, be sustained even when the temptation to defect is very great. This is accomplished through a complex hierarchy of: threats against defection, threats against failure to cooperate in punishment of defection, threats against failure to cooperate in punishment of the failure to cooperate in punishment of defection, etc. The unintelligibility of the previous sentence is no accident. Such a solution is problematic as either a normative prescription for international cooperation, or as a positive description of what really occurs. These sorts of

5.3   Equilibria in the Absence of Uncertainty about Capabilities

In order to investigate the relative merits of abrogation and Tit-for-Tat as treaty maintenance strategies, the place to begin is the simple case in which each side's arms production is perfectly observed. We will show that both strategies can support an equilibrium in which the treaty is perfectly observed by both sides. In this sense, the strategies are equivalent, since they lead to identical payoffs.

The equilibrium concept used in this section is that of a subgame–perfect Nash equilibrium (Nash 1951; Selten 1975). Each side chooses a strategy that specifies the action it will take at each time t, conditional on all previous actions and all information. A pair of such strategies is a Nash equilibrium if A cannot profit by changing its strategy as a whole given that B maintains its strategy, and vice versa. Subgame perfection means that neither strategy prescribes an action that would be considered suboptimal by the player required to perform it at the time it is to be performed. The special significance of this property in the present context is that any threat must be credible; that is, the threatening party must actually be willing to carry out the threat if necessary.

Assume that the treaty requires signatories A and B to produce no more than $\bar{\Delta}^A$ and $\bar{\Delta}^B$, respectively. Assume also that neither side prefers an arms race at the noncontingent Nash level to dual adherence to the treaty, although each side would prefer to break the treaty or cheat if it could do so while the other adhered to the treaty. That is, condition (5.12) and its equivalent for B are both satisfied.

One Nash equilibrium that supports adherence to the treaty involves the use of Ikle's abrogation strategies by both sides—each nation adheres to the treaty unless it detects a violation by the other side, in which case it ceases to abide by the terms of the treaty. This pair of strategies is a Nash equilibrium because the

---

strategies would be politically difficult to carry out since they require actions that may seem irrational, at least in the short term. For example, such a strategy might require a nation to produce more arms than it either needs or wants, simply to punish another nation for a small treaty violation.

cost of having the other side abrogate the treaty is much higher than any potential benefit from cheating on the treaty limits. A possible problem with this strategy is that reversion to an all-out arms race must be credible as a threat. Suppose, for example, that nation B has violated the limits by 1 percent, and A must decide whether to tolerate this or carry out the threat. Since the violation is small, the political will to revert to an indefinite, all-out arms race may not be present. If nation B realizes this, A's threat is not credible. Thus, enforcement of the equilibrium by means of lesser threats or those that permit a return to the treaty might be attractive. The issue hinges on whether the extra disincentive to cheating that the abrogation strategies generate compared to those with smaller levels of punishment is offset by the lesser credibility of the threat.

One potential solution is the reciprocity (Tit-for-Tat) strategy, in which any defection or cheating from the treaty is met by an equal response rather than total defection. If both sides pursue this strategy, does this also lead to a Nash equilibrium? It turns out that the answer is yes, but the reasoning is not as straightforward as in the case of abrogation.

In this analysis, we actually consider a somewhat broader class of strategies that we call *generalized reciprocity strategies*. Proposition 4 shows which generalized reciprocity strategies are able to maintain a given treaty. It describes a particularly simple set of strategies, called proportional reciprocity strategies, in which one responds to a treaty violation by an amount proportional to the size of the violation.

The main tool in deriving an equilibrium is to determine A's optimal sequence of production values $P_1^A, P_2^A, \ldots$ against a known generalized reciprocity strategy r_B. It is useful to note at this point that the advantage or disadvantage of any strategy vis-à-vis a fixed treaty is dependent (in the model used here) only on future production decisions, not on the current arms stocks. This means that, although this is not a repeated game, each nation faces recursively a parallel decision problem at each turn, which therefore is amenable to a parallel solution. This simplifies the analysis greatly since A's correct sequence of choices can be described by the choice of a single value Δ_1^A of a constant production rate. Nation B's response will then be described by $\Delta_1^B = r_B(\Delta_1^A)$ and

A's utility will be given by Equation (5.5) with these values of Δ^A and Δ^B.

Proposition 4. *Suppose that A and B have a treaty specifying production levels $\bar{\Delta}^A$ and $\bar{\Delta}^B$ respectively. Denote the noncontingent Nash levels by Δ_0^A and Δ_0^B. Assume that for each potential production amount P_t^A that A might choose at time t, B will respond by producing an amount $P_{t+1}^B = r_B(P_t^A)$ at time $t + 1$ and suppose that A pursues a similar strategy. Then*

1. *If r_B is continuous, A always has an optimal response.*

2. *The reciprocity function r_B will cause A to observe the treaty by producing $\bar{\Delta}^A$ if*

$$r_B(\Delta^A) - r_B(\bar{\Delta}^A) \;>\; \delta_A^{-1}(\Delta^A - \bar{\Delta}^A)\Big[(1 - b_A/a_A)$$

$$- (c_A/a_A)(1 - \alpha\delta_A)(\Delta^A + \bar{\Delta}^A)\Big]$$

   for all $\Delta^A \in [\bar{\Delta}^A, \Delta_0^A]$.

3. *A sufficient condition for A to observe the treaty is*

$$r_B'(\Delta^A) > \delta_A^{-1}\Big[(1 - b_A/a_A) - (c_A/a_A)(1 - \alpha\delta_A)(\Delta^A + \bar{\Delta}^A)\Big]$$

   for all $\Delta^A \in [\bar{\Delta}^A, \Delta_0^A]$.

4. *Let r_B^* be defined on $[\bar{\Delta}^A, \Delta_0^A]$ by the differential equation*

$$r_B'(\Delta^A) = \delta_A^{-1}\Big[(1 - b_A/a_A) - (c_A/a_A)(1 - \alpha\delta_A)(\Delta^A + \bar{\Delta}^A)\Big]$$

   with boundary condition $r_B(\bar{\Delta}^A) = \bar{\Delta}^B$, so that

$$r_B^*(\Delta^A) \;=\; \delta_A^{-1}\Big[(1 - b_A/a_A) - (c_A/a_A)(1 - \alpha\delta_A)\bar{\Delta}^A)\Big]\Delta^A$$

$$- (c_A/a_A)(1 - \alpha\delta_A)(\Delta^A)^2.$$

Then a sufficient condition for a reciprocity function r_B to enforce the treaty is that $r_B(\Delta^A) > r_B^*(\Delta^A)$, for all $\Delta^A \in [\bar{\Delta}^A, \Delta_0^A]$.

5. *The condition for the treaty to be observed is satisfied by the proportional reciprocity strategy given by*

$$r_B(\Delta^A) = \rho(\Delta^A - \bar{\Delta}^A) + \bar{\Delta}^B, \qquad (5.20)$$

where $\rho = \delta_A^{-1}(1 - b_A/a_A)$.

Proof. Since r_B is a continuous function on a compact set, A's utility is likewise, and therefore attains its maximum, so that (1) is true. To deter departure from the treaty, it is necessary that A prefers adherence to the treaty to surprise defection. A computation similar to that used in Proposition 3-3 yields 2. The remainder is clear. ∎

Formally, A's optimal move does not depend on the treaty limits $\bar{\Delta}^A$ and $\bar{\Delta}^B$; it is the reciprocal strategy of B's that determines what A will do, rather than the conventions of the treaty itself. However, it is assumed that the norms of international diplomacy will allow A to produce at its treaty amount $\bar{\Delta}^A$, and that B will therefore not adopt a strategy that will attempt to force A below that level.[8]

The second step in the determination of an equilibrium is to analyze B's choice of reciprocity function. Under the assumption that B would prefer that the treaty be upheld rather than that A should defect, the problem is to choose $r_B(\cdot)$ so that A will prefer to uphold the treaty rather than defect against B's generalized reciprocity strategy. Because of the lack of noise in this formulation, any function r_B satisfying the previous proposition will do equally well, since all result in eternal observance of the treaty by both sides.

One interpretation of this result is that a reciprocity strategy can enforce an arms treaty if the reaction to an increase of the opponent's arms stock is sufficiently vigorous. Proposition 4-4 provides a threshold of vigorousness that is just sufficient to deter a violation. Again, note that the role of the treaty amounts $\bar{\Delta}^A$ and $\bar{\Delta}^B$ is to constrain the possible solutions to the interval between the treaty amount and the noncontingent Nash amount.

---

8. For tacitly bargained treaties, this allowed level is implicit rather than formally arrived at. For B to attempt to breach this limit by further threats would overturn the current tacit bargain. While this might lead to a superior equilibrium, it could also result in a complete breakdown of the agreement.

Some specific strategies that accomplish this are given in Proposition 4-5. Under this strategy, B responds to any production by A in excess of the treaty by producing ρ times that much over its own treaty amount. Thus if ρ is 0.9, and A exceeds the treaty by 10.0 units, then B will produce 9.0 units over B's treaty amount in the following period. For the parameter values we have been using for illustration, the minimal value of the reciprocity parameter ρ that will enforce a treaty is 0.926.

Thus, we can see that both the abrogation strategy and generalized reciprocity strategy are capable of supporting an equilibrium in which an arms treaty is observed. In this ideal world, the application of either strategy is successful. In equilibrium, the observed outcomes will be identical for the two strategies, as will be the payoffs. Thus adherents to either strategy would be justified in their support. This is not to say that the two strategies are equivalent in every respect. Their strengths and weaknesses are quite different. In the real world, it is also necessary to consider the possibility that the equilibrium will fail. Abrogation minimizes the *chance* of such a failure, by providing a maximal threat. Generalized reciprocity, on the other hand, minimizes the *cost* of such failures. The balance between these is difficult to weigh because it depends on conditions outside the very restricted model that is used.

5.4   Equilibria in the Presence of Uncertainty about Capabilities

To gain a deeper understanding of the relative merits of the abrogation and reciprocity strategies, we need to reduce the restrictiveness of the model by incorporating some mechanism by which the treaty could break down. One candidate mechanism is the uncertainty of each nation about the capabilities of the other. This *capability uncertainty* has a quantitative and a qualitative dimension. The first refers to uncertainty about the physical quantity of weapons produced by the rival. The second refers to uncertainty about the effectiveness of these weapons in time of war.

No student of arms races would deny the prevalence of either type of uncertainty. In the nineteenth century, the British incorrectly estimated the rate of French ship production and the size of the French fleet. On at least one occasion, the size of the French fleet was declining while the British were convinced that they were in an arms race (Cobden 1868; Hirst 1913). Similarly, a minor arms race was on the verge of taking place between France and Germany in 1875 because German intelligence reported heavy French purchases of cavalry horses. It took considerable effort on the part of the French ambassador to reassure the German government that its information was simply wrong (Gooch 1923).

There is no evidence that these problems have diminished in the twentieth century. The United States has had well-publicized difficulties assessing Soviet missile strength, and detection uncertainty has characterized the debate over alleged Soviet violations of the Threshold Test Ban Treaty and the SALT Treaties. Examples of uncertainty about the implications of suspected changes in force strength are no less common. There was no general consensus about the implications of the Soviet reduction in forces of 1.2 million troops in 1956. In more recent times, there has been considerable debate within the United States about the importance of the Krasnoyarsk radar installation and within the Soviet Union about the significance of U.S. research on Star Wars.

Up to this point, we have conducted an entirely deterministic analysis. Now we will add two stochastic factors. A first stochastic term ξ_t^A in the revised model corresponds to information/perception effects, the plague of both arms races and treaties. These refer to intelligence failures and perceptual biases that overestimate or underestimate the military capacities of the rival nation (Jervis 1978; Ross and Anderson 1982). The second (η_t^A) refers to qualitative uncertainty about how effective weapons will be in time of war.

The second factor implies that the effective arms stocks evolve as

$$\tilde{S}_t^A = \alpha \tilde{S}_{t-1}^A + P_t^A + \eta_t^A \qquad (0 < \alpha < 1), \qquad (5.21)$$

rather than Equation (5.1), where η_t^A is assumed to be independent and identically distributed and independent of η_s^B, with mean $\mu(\eta^A)$ and variance $\sigma^2(\eta^A)$.

The strategies that are used in the rest of this chapter assume that the decisions that A and B make are based on the opponent's *apparent* production level

$$\tilde{P}_t^B = \tilde{S}_t^B - \alpha \tilde{S}_{t-1}^B + \xi_t^B = P_t^B + \eta_t^B + \xi_t^B = P_t^B + \epsilon_t^B, \quad (5.22)$$

incorporating both stochastic factors.

We will assume that the arms advantage and maintenance costs depend on the actual arms stocks S_t^A and S_t^B but that the production costs depend on the intended production P_t^A and P_t^B. In this case, any realized sequence of production decisions $\{(P_t^A, P_t^B)\}$ yields a utility to A that differs from the utility in the absence of the stochastic terms by

$$E^A = \sum_{t=1}^{\infty} \frac{\eta_t^A \delta_A (a_A - b_A) - \eta_t^B \delta_A a_A}{1 - \alpha \delta_A} \quad (5.23)$$

a term whose expectation and variance are

$$\mathrm{E}(E^A) = \frac{\mu(\eta^A)\delta_A(a_A - b_A) - \mu(\eta^B)\delta_A a_A}{(1 - \delta_A)(1 - \alpha\delta_A)}$$

$$\mathrm{Var}(E^A) = \frac{\sigma^2(\eta^A)\delta_A^2(a_A - b_A)^2 + \sigma^2(\eta)\delta_A^2 a_A^2}{(1 - \delta_A^2)(1 - \alpha\delta_A)^2}. \quad (5.24)$$

Since these terms are independent of the sequence of production decisions, the difference in expected utility between any two strategies is the same regardless of the realized values of these random variables. This permits us to calculate the expected utilities to compare strategies as if there were no stochastic components. However, since the production decisions are based on the opponent's perceived actions, there is a strong potential effect of the two stochastic components. In this model, these can be expressed in terms of the properties of $\epsilon_t = \eta_t + \xi_t$. We will make such assumptions as are necessary about the distributions F_A and F_B of ϵ^A and ϵ^B.[9]

---

9. We will assume they belong to absolutely continuous location/scale families with continuous, strongly-unimodal density functions f_A and f_B that have tails that decline at least exponentially. In fact, much weaker conditions will suffice, but this is a matter of small importance here.

5.4.1 Ikle's Abrogation Strategy

It is not difficult to see that literal adherence to Ikle's abrogation strategy can be quite damaging when there is uncertainty in the estimated force levels. To see this, suppose that two nations are in a treaty that specifies production levels of $\bar{\Delta}^A$ and $\bar{\Delta}^B$. Suppose that both sides observe the treaty by producing these amounts and that the actual arms production is observed by the other side only with error. If these observational errors have median zero, then there is a 50 percent chance that A will think that B has violated the treaty and a 50 percent chance that B will think the same of A. Thus there is a 75 percent chance that the treaty will end in abrogation after only one period, and virtually no chance that it will endure for a significant length of time.

5.4.2 Reciprocity

Reciprocity has a clear advantage over Ikle's abrogation strategy in an uncertain world because it responds less strongly to treaty violations that may be mere observational errors. However, this strategy can also lead to very unsatisfactory outcomes. Suppose that A and B both begin by observing the treaty but respond after the first move by producing whatever amount the other was perceived to have produced on the previous move (with the modest proviso that no production below zero or above the noncontingent Nash amount will be chosen). Using this fact along with Equations (5.21) and (5.22), we can derive that the apparent choices $\tilde{P}_t$ evolve according to the law[10]

$$\tilde{P}^A_{t+1} = P^A_{t+1} + \epsilon^A_{t+1} = \tilde{P}^B_t + \epsilon^A_{t+1}$$

$$\tilde{P}^B_{t+1} = P^B_{t+1} + \epsilon^B_{t+1} = \tilde{P}^A_t + \epsilon^B_{t+1}$$

Since this bivariate stochastic process is obviously nonstationary, the production levels of the two sides will quickly drift from

---

10. Although the observed production $\tilde{P}^A_t$ and $\tilde{P}^B_t$ may be outside of the interval between zero and the noncontingent Nash level, it is assumed that the choices P^A_t and P^B_t are truncated so as to remain within the given interval. The graph is of actual production rather than observed production, and therefore stays between the limits.

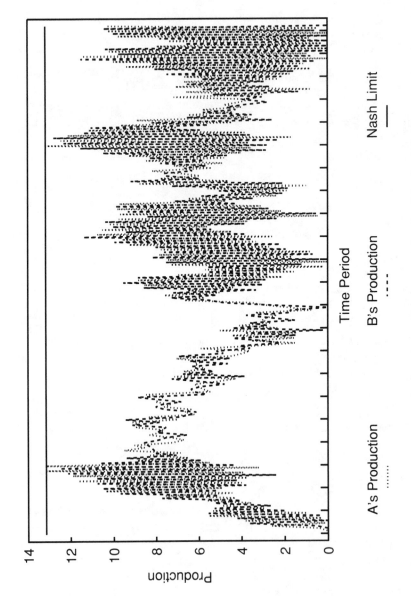

A's Production   B's Production   Nash Limit

Fig. 5.1. Example production paths for Tit-for-Tat

the treaty and, in the long run, the production levels may be found anywhere in the interval $[0, \Delta_0^A]$.[11] Figure 5.1 shows a typical time path of Tit-for-Tat facing Tit-for-Tat, using the same parameters that we have been using in the other illustrations.

Note that the path of the production levels of the two sides wanders back and forth between the constraining levels of the treaty and the noncontingent Nash defection level. This long-run behavior is essentially the same regardless of the size of the errors, as is the case with the simpler 2×2 iterated Prisoner's Dilemma that was analyzed in Downs, Rocke, and Siverson (1985). When viewed from the perspective of discounted expected utility, however, the viability of Tit-for-Tat depends crucially on the size of the errors ϵ_t. If σ_ϵ is very small, then the production levels will stay near the treaty amount for a long time, and the outcome will be almost as good as a costlessly enforced treaty (in discounted expected utility). If σ_ϵ is large, then the departure will be almost immediate, and the outcome will be very poor. Thus, the value (discounted expected utility) of Tit-for-Tat facing Tit-for-Tat will be a continuous function of σ_ϵ. This conclusion is different from the one reached in Bendor (1987) and Downs, Rocke, and Siverson (1985) because of the perspective taken—discounted expected utility versus long-run equilibrium. This point is most easily appreciated by reference to Tit-for-Tat facing Tit-for-Tat in the original 2×2 Prisoner's Dilemma. If there is any chance of misperception, however small, then the long-run frequencies of each of the four cells is identical, and Tit-for-Tat appears to be an ineffective strategy. However, if the chance is small, then the first defection will be (on the average) a long time in the future. If strategies are evaluated on the basis of discounted expected utility, then this long-delayed defection may not matter very much when evaluated at the time the strategies must be chosen.

This recommendation for Tit-for-Tat in low-noise environments must be tempered by the observation that Tit-for-Tat facing Tit-for-Tat is still unlikely to form an equilibrium when there is a significant amount of noise. In the perfect information situation, there is no incentive to change from Tit-for-Tat if the opponent is

---

11. The exact asymptotic frequencies are difficult to determine because of the boundary conditions.

using Tit-for-Tat, since no improvement in the outcome (cooperation forever) is possible. When there is noise, the payoff may be able to be improved by changing Tit-for-Tat to one of the generalized reciprocity strategies or by producing some amount different from the treaty amount. A complete analysis of this situation awaits further research, but we may still conclude that the usefulness of Tit-for-Tat as a strategy is a declining function of the size of the information/perception/control problem.

It is also possible to use a generalized reciprocity strategy in which the retaliation for a violation is less than one-for-one; that is $r_A < 1$ and $r_B < 1$. In this case, the process

$$\tilde{P}^A_{t+1} = P^A_{t+1} + \epsilon^A_{t+1} = \rho_A \tilde{P}^B_t + \epsilon^A_{t+1}$$

$$\tilde{P}^B_{t+1} = P^B_{t+1} + \epsilon^B_{t+1} = \rho_B \tilde{P}^A_t + \epsilon^B_{t+1}$$

will return eventually to $(0,0)$ whenever it departs from this equilibrium. Figure 5.2 shows a typical time track for a generalized reciprocity strategy with $\rho = 0.926$, the minimal level that supports a treaty in a perfect-information environment with our usual example parameter values. The same serious question of equilibrium applies here as well, as does the obvious dependence of the payoffs on the size of the errors.

We can see from this illustration that reciprocity can prove an unprofitable strategy when there is uncertainty in the system. Generalized reciprocity, in which retaliation is less than one-for-one, is more amenable to use in this situation than pure Tit-for-Tat, but even then the nations will be observing the treaty only a small fraction of the time. Thus, these strategies can hardly be said to enforce the treaty; rather, they diminish the consequences of violations compared to an abrogation strategy.

5.4.3   Trigger Strategies

Both Ikle's abrogation strategy and Tit-for-Tat can be faulted for reacting too quickly and too strongly to perceived treaty violations that may be due only to uncertainty. Although complex alternative strategies could be designed that depend on the entire sequence of past actions of both sides, it is important that they

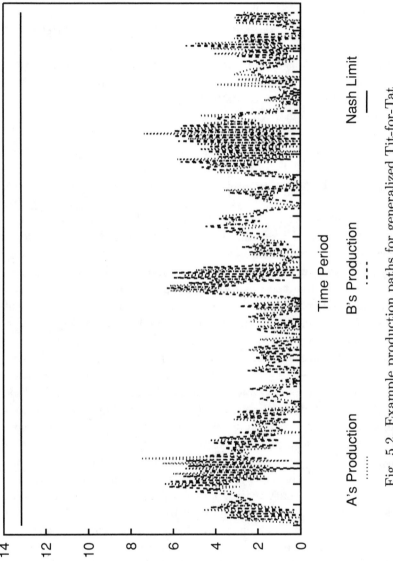

Production

14

12

10

8

6

4

2

0

Time Period

A's Production   B's Production   Nash Limit
                        · · · · ·   ———

Fig. 5.2. Example production paths for generalized Tit-for-Tat

be as simple to understand and implement as abrogation and Tit-for-Tat. Otherwise, their actual use would be problematic. In this section we address a behaviorally simple and attractive class of strategies that we call *trigger strategies*, inspired by the trigger price literature in oligopoly theory.[12] Developed by Green and Porter (1984; Porter 1983) a trigger price strategy is a method by which an oligopoly can enforce adherence to the restricted production levels that allow the oligopoly to reap excess profits over what would occur if each pursued its own optimal production level (Cournot reversion).

To see how a trigger strategy works in the context of oligopoly theory, suppose that each producer observes only his own production level and the market price, which is determined by aggregate production plus a stochastic factor. Whenever the market price dips below a trigger price $\tilde{p}$, the oligopolists revert for $T - 1$ periods to the Cournot production levels and then return to cooperation. Green and Porter determined the optimal level of cooperative production for identical oligopolists with fixed values of $\tilde{p}$. Porter (1983) determined the optimal values of $\tilde{p}$ and T, assuming that the oligopolists are identical and that production automatically adjusts. Here "optimal" means the values of $\tilde{p}$ and T that maximize the expected payoff to the oligopoly as a whole, as distinguished from "optimal" response in the sense of Nash equilibrium. If each member of the oligopoly were to choose individual values for $\tilde{p}$ and T as well as current production, then the optimal choice of $\tilde{p}$ and T may not be in a Nash equilibrium.

The treaty maintenance situation differs in some respects from oligopoly theory. We make no assumption that the parties have the same utilities, either in preference for arms advantage or in cost, and the signaling structure that comes from price determination by demand also is not relevant here. Nonetheless, a comparable approach to treaty maintenance is also plausible as a potential instrument to enforce an arms agreement. The idea of "drawing a line in the dirt," which is the hallmark of trigger strategies, has considerable intuitive appeal. As opposed to more complex strategies, its parsimony makes it intelligible to policymakers and domestic constituencies. It is also more easily communicated to

---

12. See Shapiro (1987) for a review.

and understood by the decision makers of a rival state. Finally, its simplicity makes it easy to implement, which minimizes the potential for failures of control.

Another significant difference between our analysis and that of oligopoly theorists is that we permit each of the nations to choose trigger levels independently. Although it may be reasonable to assume that all the firms in an oligopoly are identical and that the optimal choice of parameters is the one that maximizes the expected payoff to the oligopoly as a whole, this is less reasonable for nations. Since we are not assuming that utilities are comparable across nations, the concept of maximizing the aggregate benefit to the two nations makes no sense in our context. Instead, we define a two-step equilibrium in a modified Nash sense, so that each of the participants will wish to maintain its strategy given that the other side does so.

Assume that the treaty calls for the production of no more than $\bar{\Delta}^A$ and $\bar{\Delta}^B$ respectively. Because the time homogeneity of the decision process still remains, we will assume that the strategy of each side also remains constant. Assume that A will produce $\Delta_1^A \geq \bar{\Delta}^A$ in each period.[13] Assume also that A monitors B's apparent production choice and will abrogate the treaty at time $\tau + 1$ whenever $\tilde{P}_\tau^B > T_A$. Nation B is assumed to follow an equivalent strategy. The strategic problem for side A is to choose the two strategy parameters Δ_1^A and T_A so that, together with B's choices, a stable equilibrium is formed.

An important issue is the meaning of *equilibrium* in this context. As the utilities are defined, no pair $[(\Delta_1^A, T_A), (\Delta_1^B, T_B)]$ of strategies forms a Nash equilibrium. To see this, suppose that B's strategy as the pair (Δ_1^B, T_B) is fixed and one asks for the optimal reply (Δ_1^A, T_A). Clearly, A would have an incentive to raise the trigger T_A so that an accidental arms race would not occur, given that B's strategy remains the same. However, it is only A's trigger that is holding B to the level of production Δ_1^B; if T_A were

---

13. Under the assumption that $\bar{\Delta}^A < \Delta_0^A$, A will always prefer to produce $\bar{\Delta}^A$ rather than a smaller quantity. Once again, we are assuming here that norms of international diplomacy would prevent B from forcing A's production below the amount dictated in the treaty. Also, we will derive the results mostly for the case $\bar{\Delta}^A = \bar{\Delta}^B = 0$, although the results remain qualitatively similar in other cases.

raised, B's production would soon follow. Thus our concept of equilibrium has two requirements.

1. Given the triggers T_A and T_B, the production levels are in a Nash equilibrium.
2. If the production levels are considered as a function of the triggers through the process described in the first requirement, the choices T_A and T_B form a Nash equilibrium.

The best justification for this concept of equilibrium is that the two states will possess the minimal amount of foresight to realize that an increase in the trigger level will be shortly followed by an increase in the opponent's production level. The fundamental policy variable is the trigger that one will employ—the production level then follows as a response essentially to the opponents's trigger. This idea of equilibrium is essentially different from that used by oligopoly theorists such as Porter (1983). In oligopoly theory, it may be reasonable to assume (with Porter) that the oligopoly chooses a common value of the trigger, defection level, and defection time, so as to maximize the aggregate income of the oligopoly. In the context of an arms treaty, a trigger would consist of an announced level above which the treaty would be considered abrogated or a given punishment inflicted. There is no concept equivalent to aggregate income (in the absence of assumptions about interpersonal comparison of utilities) and it is unreasonable to require that the two sides must accept a common set of parameters.

The proposition below verifies the existence of an equilibrium that supports a treaty.

Proposition 5. *Assume that both A and B would prefer a treaty at $(\bar{\Delta}^A, \bar{\Delta}^B)$ to mutual total defection; that is, assume condition (5.12) for A and B.*

1. *For any values of T_A and T_B, the values $\Delta_1^A = \Delta_0^A$ and $\Delta_1^B = \Delta_0^B$ form an equilibrium.*

2. *For any values of T_A, T_B, and $\Delta_1^B < \Delta_0^B$, there exists $\Delta_1^A < \Delta_0^A$ that maximizes the utility of A.*

3. *If σ_A and σ_B are not too large, there exist triggers T_A and T_B such that the values $\Delta_1^A = \bar{\Delta}^A$ and $\Delta_1^B = \bar{\Delta}^B$ form an equilibrium.*

4. *If σ_A and σ_B are not too large, the triggers T_A and T_B determined in 5-3 form a Nash equilibrium.*

Proof. See Appendix.

Essentially, this proposition states that there is a trigger-strategy equilibrium supporting any arms treaty if the noise level is not too large. Of course, *too large* is a vague term. Some modest restriction on the level of noise is necessary, since each side must be able to distinguish full cooperation from an all-out arms race, for example. Fortunately, the requirement on the values of σ_A and σ_B may not be severe in practice. As an example, with the parameter values used in the previous examples, the level for total defection is 13.2 and the critical level of $\sigma_A = \sigma_B$ is about 4.5.[14] This amount of noise—34 percent of the defection level—is quite enormous. In this sort of environment, each side could barely be certain that the other side has defected from a zero-level arms treaty to a total arms race. In practice, estimates of the opponent's production level will usually be sufficiently good that the requirements of this Proposition will be satisfied. In cases of great uncertainty, no solution may exist except an all-out arms race.

Unlike the full-information case, any treaty maintenance strategy that operates in an environment where knowledge of a rival's activity is subject to some error or misestimation must incur some cost. This confronts a nation with the tradeoff between punishing transgressions that have not occurred, or allowing the other side to cheat. Any realistic strategy is going to do both—the question is what precise tradeoff is optimal. Further examination of this example shows that the trigger defection strategy can achieve most of the benefits that could be attained by the unrealizable ideal of costless enforcement of the treaty. If $\sigma_A = \sigma_B = 1$, then

---

14. The calculations were made for logistically distributed errors. These were used instead of normally distributed errors because the logistic distribution permits the occurrence of a greater number of unusual observations (outliers). This gives a better test of the robustness of the conclusions.

the utility of a zero-level treaty is -264.2 compared to a utility of 0 for a treaty that would be upheld without need for enforcement, and -2181.4 for an all-out arms race at the maximal production level of 13.2. This means that the trigger equilibrium just derived achieves almost 90 percent of the benefit that could be achieved by costless enforcement of a perpetual equilibrium. The equilibrium value of $T_A = T_B = 2.68$ results in a very large chance $p = .985$ that the treaty will continue on any one round (in the Appendix it is shown that $p \to 1$ as $\sigma_A, \sigma_B \to 0$). The expected length of the treaty is $1/(1 - p) = 65.3$ years.[15] Thus the treaty will be quite stable, although its life will be finite.

Readers may be disappointed that this strategy does not provide perpetual security for a treaty. However, to put this in perspective, it is useful to compare the expected treaty length of 65 years with the likelihood of a leadership change that would bring about the kind of differences that would, by themselves, upset the treaty. It is true that 65 years is a finite period, but nineteenth- and twentieth-century history provides little evidence that the strategy itself, rather than changes in national goals and leadership, will destroy a treaty.

It is also notable that the expected length of the treaty can be increased by improving intelligence. Using trigger strategies, the trigger is placed above the treaty level by a certain number of standard deviation units. As the noise level declines, the trigger becomes closer to the treaty level, but it is set *further* away if measured in standard deviation units, so that the chance of accidentally exceeding the trigger is lessened. This point is more easily seen by means of an example. If the noise standard deviation is 1, then the trigger is 2.68, which is 2.68 standard deviations above the treaty level. If the noise were reduced to one-tenth its previous size, so that the standard deviation is 0.1, the trigger would be reduced to 0.40, which is substantially closer to the treaty level than 2.68. However, this is over 4 standard deviations from the treaty level, so that the chance of the treaty being accidentally

---

15. The interpretation of a period as a year is reasonable given the discount rate of .90 and the deterioration rate of 10 percent assumed for arms stocks. If one assumed a shorter period such as a month to be the basic unit, then α and the δs would be closer to one and the expected length of the treaty in years would be similar.

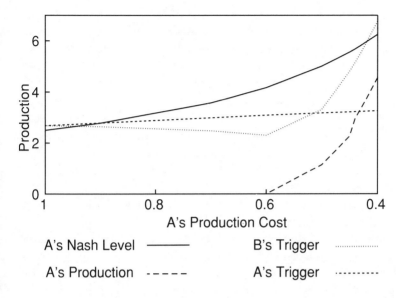

Fig. 5.3. Results of varying A's costs

violated is reduced from .015 to .0013. If intelligence were further improved so that σ_A and σ_B were reduced to 0.01, then the trigger would be 0.053, which is 5.3 standard deviations above the treaty level. Thus the chance of accidental abrogation would be only .00013.

It is interesting at this point to investigate what happens to the equilibrium when A and B have disparate preferences or costs. We showed earlier that the range of preferences within which an equal treaty can be upheld is fairly wide. However, within that range, the *kind* of strategy needed to enforce a treaty can vary substantially. For simplicity, we examine only one case—disparity in costs. Although we argued above that disparities large enough to make a treaty unattractive would be unusual, differences of smaller magnitude are quite common. For example, it is cheaper for the Soviets to maintain troops than for the United States to do so, while some kinds of high-technology weapons may be cheaper for the United States. Suppose that B has the preferences and costs as above, so that $a_B = 6$ and $b_B = c_B = 1$. Suppose that A has $a_A = 6$ and $b_A = 1$ but that c_A is lower, so that weapons production is correspondingly cheaper. Figure 5.3 shows the results of varying c_A on the resulting equilibrium. The uppermost line gives the one-period Nash value for A's production (proportional to the noncontingent Nash level), which increases steadily as A's costs decrease. At first, the only effect of this lowered cost is that B must lower the trigger value slightly to deter A from the now more attractive alternative of mutual defection. When A's costs decline to about 0.55, however, A prefers mutual defection to the strict observance of the treaty. B still has the ability to present A with a more attractive choice than mutual defection by raising the trigger to the point where A can produce more than 0. This situation continues to escalate in this direction until A's costs decline to 20 percent of B's, at which point the situation becomes too unstable to compute the equilibrium.

Thus, when costs (or preferences) are asymmetric, the weaker side can preserve a kind of alternative treaty by allowing the other side to "cheat." By allowing an unequal treaty, the weaker side can obtain an outcome better than reverting to an all-out arms race. This will necessitate accepting that the other side will be allowed to produce more arms, which can be done either in the context of an altered treaty or by constructing a de facto treaty by ignoring violations.

5.5   Conclusions

While much of the discussion about how to maintain arms treaties has been even more technical than that associated with obtaining an arms agreement, the analysis points in some provocative directions for the practical decision maker who is concerned about the fragility of arms agreements, and who must grapple with the problem of how to get a rival nation to comply with their provisions. One notable finding is that, under most circumstances, it is possible to assume that both of the nations that have achieved a tacit or formal arms agreement would prefer that the agreement survive than be replaced by an intense arms race. In order for one of the nations to prefer an arms race, it must value arms advantage twice as much as its rival or it must have a technological advantage of about the same magnitude.

This robustness of the preference for treaty maintenance implies that the common assignment of treaty failure to changes in technology, changes in economic conditions, and changes in national priorities may be overdrawn. These factors can destroy a treaty, but not as easily as we tend to imagine. On the other hand, there is good reason for believing that a primary cause of the collapse of treaties is the failure to develop a treaty maintenance (or enforcement) strategy that balances the deterrence of violations with the appreciation that information problems may cause the appearance of a violation where none exists. A mistake in this area may be precipitated by biased perception, but it does not have to be. A combination of nothing more than simple uncertainty (with no bias attached to it whatsoever) and a misconceived treaty maintenance strategy can be enough to set in motion an inexorable process that will precipitate a new arms race.

Most of the remaining findings relate to how the level of uncertainty affects the choice of treaty maintenance strategies. When verification procedures and intelligence information produce highly reliable information about the opponent's preferences and actions, then an arms treaty can be preserved by threats of reciprocity. The expectation of a one-for-one response to any violation will always be sufficient to deter cheating or defection and a lower level of response will often suffice. The added point that a lower level of threat may be enough is notable because pure reciprocity leads to poor results when there are serious problems of perception and control—even when these problems are not biased in the manner described by the heuristics literature in psychology.

When the treaty environment has stochastic elements brought about by imperfect information about the opponent's actions, an alternative to the "less than Tit-for-Tat" strategy is a strategy based on the use of "trigger levels." These involve a nation setting a level of arms production such that if it observes the trigger to be exceeded, it will abrogate the treaty and resume the arms race. A major attribute of this strategy is that a trigger can be set that takes uncertainty into consideration. This strategy possesses cognitive and political advantages over a graduated Tit-for-Tat schedule of punishments that might be mathematically equivalent. First, it permits a nation to announce the limits of its toleration for violations in a language that is far more simple than a carefully calculated series of escalating gestures that can easily be misunderstood. Second, it provides decision makers with an institutionalized mechanism to cope with the dysfunctional heuristics that are used to deal with uncertainty. While it will never be easy for politicians to resist the risk-aversion-inspired tendency to respond to the mere suspicion of a treaty violation, a trigger can provide a justifiable rationale for restraint. It works like a significance test. It restricts the judgment that a violation has taken place by defining a level of evidence that must be exceeded before such a judgment can be legitimized. At the same time, it prevents exploitation.

A careful choice of triggers can enforce a treaty with only a small chance that the treaty will break down by accident. This is true even if the treaty is not equal or if the two sides have somewhat different preferences and costs. The triggers and production levels, when chosen optimally, adapt themselves to the differing costs and preferences so as to provide exactly the threat needed to deter cheating or violation. Note that this strategy is markedly different from that associated with proportionate response or Tit-for-Tat, which call for a much larger response to small violations and a more modest response to large violations.

Among all trigger strategies, the best outcomes are generated by threatening defection to an all-out arms race rather than by more modest retaliation. This eliminates cheating because its benefits are always overwhelmed by the prospect of the treaty's disappearance. It also reduces the chance that the treaty will be abrogated accidentally to the lowest level. This last point may appear to be insensitive to the problem of overreaction. Total abrogation is likely to be far greater than the suspected violation. Yet to look at it this way is to ignore the role of the trigger. The success of both trigger strategies and generalized Tit-for-Tat rests on the fact that they do not overreact to relatively small departures from the treaty. In the case of the trigger strategy, the moderation lies in the fact that it is not set off by low levels of apparent treaty violations.

Chapter 6

Not by Words Alone

At a time when the INF treaty has been negotiated and the prospects for new formal agreements in both conventional and strategic arms seem excellent, attention to tacit bargaining may appear gratuitous. It is not. Regardless of their considerable merits, formal negotiations and the treaties that they produce cannot easily deal with every aspect of an arms race. No formal treaty has ever included the full range of weapons systems that existed at the time it was signed and future agreements are not likely to do so. To design a treaty that will cope with innovations that are still on the drawing board or yet to be imagined is still more difficult. Tacit bargaining provides a fast and flexible means of dealing with these problems and extending the range of cooperation.

The value of tacit bargaining for maintaining a treaty is even greater than for promoting cooperation outside its boundaries. However rigorous the verification procedures, the only sources of treaty integrity in a system of independent states lie in the preferences of the actors and their expectations about the response that treaty violations will elicit. No tacit bargaining will be necessary if states learn to devalue the policy leverage that an arms advantage confers or come to believe that their rival shares their own peaceful intentions. Spontaneous arms cooperation will flourish. Unfortunately, if such conditions do not evolve, and history provides us with an ample number of cases where they have not, then the sanctity of a treaty must rest on expectations about the cost of violations. These expectations are inevitably established through some combination of rhetoric and tacit bargaining.

The importance of tacit bargaining in promoting or preserving arms cooperation is easy to establish. The task of moving from the level of abstract justification to concrete policy prescriptions is more difficult. The historical record is thin and hard to interpret. Historians have focused little attention on tacit bargaining strategies and the success or failure of such strategies depends on variables such as the underlying preference structure of decision makers and uncertainty that are difficult to access. While doubtless there are cases where the data are quite good, there is no reason to believe that these cases constitute a representative sample from which to generate complicated inferences. Nor could they illuminate the strengths and weaknesses of promising tacit bargaining strategies that have never been employed.

Faced with these problems we elected to base our analysis on axiomatic modeling and simulation. Specific cases were referred to but their use was restricted to testing the reasonableness of the assumptions used in the formal models and in estimating the robustness of some of the more prominent findings. The amount of effort devoted to evaluating the realism of the assumptions is somewhat unusual in formal modeling. Often an author will simply refer to Friedman's well-known contention that the realism of a model's assumptions is irrelevant; the only standard of evaluation is predictive ability. This strategy was not chosen for a variety of reasons. One reason is that we tend to side with Samuelson's protestation that the fact that assumptions are invariably imperfect representations of reality does not mean that the degree of imperfection is irrelevant. Rhetoric aside, many other economists appear to hold the same view. Even in the absence of empirical falsification, the desire to make reasonable assumptions about information uncertainty and transaction costs has motivated a number of profound changes in economic theory.

The other motivation for paying special attention to the assumptions upon which the formal modeling must rest is related to the data problems that helped persuade us to adopt this mode of inquiry. For Friedman's contention that the only measure of a theory is its predictive performance to have any meaning, there has to be a way to estimate predictive performance. This requires a substantial number of cases. The fact that these do not exist necessitates that the evaluation of a theory must rest on other grounds. It is difficult to argue against the contention that another plausible basis for confidence in a model in a data-poor world involves the realism of the assumptions. Very few theories in the natural sciences, let alone economics, have emerged triumphant when propelled by demonstrably incorrect assumptions that have a large effect on the predictions that they generate.

A critical assumption in any treatment of the role of tacit bargaining in arms control is that which defines the nature of an arms race. All that we require is that increases in the arms stocks of two nations have been inspired to *some* extent by each nation observing the behavior of the other. This vision of an arms race is far more general than those found in the literature. It requires no Richardsonian trajectory of increases. It acknowledges that a substantial proportion of arms behavior can have exclusively domestic determinants that might be associated with a politically powerful military-industrial complex. There are no information assumptions: intelligence data about the arms activity of the rival can range from excellent to very poor. Most important, it does not restrict the underlying structure of the game that motivates the arms race to a single game with dichotomous choices such as Prisoner's Dilemma, Stag Hunt, Chicken, or Deadlock. As we persistently argue, there is no way that a student of arms races can examine four or five historical races and come away with the impression that the underlying pattern of motives was identical. Nor is it possible to assume that all nations behave as if they were playing a single game and deduce characteristics of arms races that are consistent with the limited case study data that are available.

The model we selected to represent an arms race can take on the properties of a variety of these games. The utility of an arms increase is assumed to be a function of four components: the relative advantage associated with arms superiority; the costs of maintaining a force level that includes all expenditures on maintenance, repair, and staffing; the cost associated with changing the level of an arms stock or level of force capability; and a domestic constituency factor capable of reflecting the fact that the least cost of production in political terms may not occur at zero. These components are broad enough to encompass the effects on innovation and leadership changes. Innovation can be viewed as a means of lowering the cost of acquiring a given increase in capability. Leadership changes affect arms races by changing the utility associated with arms superiority.

If the two sides in an arms race are roughly equivalent with respect to these dimensions, then this model shares certain features with the Prisoner's Dilemma. However, if the two sides are not equal in all respects it allows for the possibility that one side may prefer mutual defection to mutual cooperation because the advantage it can extract from a continued (or escalated) arms race is sufficient to make up for the costs.

Any theory that is built on a less general definition of an arms race will inevitably face limitations. One is that it will only apply to arms races that possess a particular underlying incentive structure. We will have a theory of Prisoner's Dilemma-like arms races or a theory of Deadlock-like arms races, etc. If there are enough races that fall into a particular category, the theory can still be quite useful, just as a theory of urban poverty would be valuable in the absence of any relevance to rural areas.

A more serious limitation is that a theory based on a single game will be insensitive to the critical problem of what decision makers should do in the absence of knowledge about *what* game is being played. To extend the previous analogy, it is as if the policymaker were asked to devise a poverty project without being told whether the location was urban or rural. Such an example sounds ridiculous because this sort of uncertainty does not exist in the realm of poverty policy. The policymaker always possesses information about where the policy will be implemented. Unfortunately, the national security decision maker must often operate with a high degree of uncertainty about information that is just as critical: information about the motives and behavior of the rival nation.

Of course, it is one thing to contend that uncertainty about motivations and information is commonplace and another to show when it is important and estimate how important it is. Here we turn from assumptions to analysis. The results from both the axiomatic modeling and the simulation are unambiguous: strategy selection is sensitive to very modest levels of uncertainty. Perhaps this should not surprise us. When the possible alternatives are so different in their implications and the strategies that can best deal with them are just as different, a little uncertainty goes a long way.

There are many scholars who would concur with our belief in the centrality and importance of uncertainty but contend that an understanding of its effects is not accessible to formal models that assume rationality or utility maximization. They would argue that there is an impressive experimental literature in psychology that suggests that individuals cope with uncertainty by applying heuristics that have little in common with the tenets of microeconomics. We are not completely unsympathetic with this position and show in chapter 4 how the employment of such heuristics can help explain the early stages of arms race behavior and the infrequency of successful tacit bargaining.

Yet it is important not to exaggerate the role of decision heuristics to the point that we are tempted to dispense with the implications of research that rests on optimization assumptions. Predictions that are suggested by the cognitive psychology literature are rarely fully realized. Most arms races do not escalate at the ever-increasing pace that a simple interpretation of the fundamental attribution bias and the tendency to overestimate the level of the rival state's hostility would suggest. For example, even when business cycles are taken into account, the arms race between the United States and Soviet Union has never consumed as great a portion of national income as a heuristic-driven model would predict.

One reason for this predictive inaccuracy may stem from the fact that the heuristics literature has focused on individual behavior rather than on that of institutions. Institutions can and do create procedures and incentive systems to overcome biases that are organizationally dysfunctional. These may be imperfect and slow to evolve, but they do emerge and become refined. Insurance companies estimate risk on an actuarial basis, not by intuition, and the techniques they use produce more accurate estimates than the ones that were employed fifty years ago.

If insurance companies and investment bankers can learn to cope with dysfunctional heuristics, perhaps states can as well. Certainly, if cognitive psychologists are successful in convincing decision makers that they are employing methods of policymaking that are making them worse off than they could be, we would expect to see less misperception and misinterpretation in the international system. As a consequence, tacit bargaining would evolve in the direction of the microeconomic ideal. Indeed, it is doubtful that political scientists with a psychological persuasion would be as aggressive as they sometimes are in trying to affect policy unless they believed that decision makers were educable and that effects of some of the more dysfunctional heuristics could be attenuated.

Taken together, the broad definition of an arms race, the emphasis on uncertainty, and the commitment to evaluating specific tacit bargaining strategies distinguish our analysis from its predecessors. Schelling, for example, was sensitive to the fact that arms races varied and to the importance of uncertainty, but spent little time defining or evaluating the merits of different tacit bargaining strategies. Thus, while he is careful to tell the policy community that imperfect monitoring can generate false impressions of violations as well as allowing real violations to go unnoticed, he does not go on to address all of the questions that this insight inspires. We do not learn where the balance between false positives and detection failures should be set or what should determine it. Nor do we know how vulnerable a balance capable of coping with purposeful violations will be to overdetection caused by noise. Should we expect a treaty that is conservative in its ability to avoid exploitation to last five years or fifty years? Schelling deals still less with how a state should respond to suspected violations. Should it deal with the noise problem by retaliating at a rate less than Tit-for-Tat would prescribe in order that a false positive not lead to an intensified arms race? Or, should it threaten to abrogate the treaty in order to maximize the disincentive for violations? These sorts of specific questions are left unanswered.

Axelrod's research on the evolution of cooperation addresses some of these issues by focusing on the relative merits of different strategies. In this sense it is a complement to Schelling's work. The problem is that the context in which the strategies are evaluated is very different than the one created by an arms race. Axelrod deals with a specific game and omits any extended treatment of information or utility uncertainty. The players in his tournament may not know the strategy that their rivals will employ, but they know their rivals' utility functions and have perfect information about the events that are occurring. States in the midst of an arms race or trying to maintain an arms agreement do not have these advantages.

Osgood's advocacy of GRIT shares some of the same problems. He believes that arms races are all driven by an underlying logic formed by mutual mistrust and the belief that security is a function of arms stocks. A policy of GRIT can dispel both illusions. The possibility that some arms races are driven by an inexorable desire on the part of one state to dominate another state is never seriously entertained. This is why he never investigates complicated implementation issues such as what a state should do if its rival argues that the state's cooperative initiative is too trivial to warrant a response. Should it increase the size of gesture and risk exploitation or withdraw?

More importantly, Osgood does not address uncertainty and interpretation problems. He suggests that a nation reduce risk by implementing GRIT across a diverse set of military, cultural, and economic policy initiatives without considering the confusion that would likely result. The history of events leading to both World Wars is filled with gestures that are both cooperative and aggressive, and this pattern has characterized superpower relations in the post-World War II period. A pattern of gestures that is spread across a number of policy areas is difficult to distinguish from business as usual and comparability questions abound. There is little evidence that the strategy of trying to precipitate a troop withdrawal by declaring a test ban moratorium or increasing the availability of credit will be effective. There is even less evidence that *responding* to a test ban moratorium by engaging in some unrelated cooperative action will be correctly interpreted. Tacit bargaining has always succeeded best when conducted in highly circumscribed policy areas such as satellite reconnaissance.

6.1 The Achievement of Arms Control

In chapter 4 a variety of tacit bargaining strategies designed to promote arms control were examined. While quite different in many respects, they are all cooperative: a state signals its desire to stabilize or end the arms race by reducing its rate of arms growth. This reliance on an initial cooperative gesture distinguishes these strategies from punishment-based strategies that rely on escalation to convince a rival nation that it is in its best interest to slow its growth in armaments. Our focus on cooperative strategies is not justified by the frequency with which they have been employed. The use of punishment-based strategies has always been more prevalent. The attractiveness of cooperative strategies stems from their potential ability to reduce the intensity of an arms race without requiring the risk that it first be escalated, potentially leading to a still more intensive arms race.

The problem of achieving arms cooperation was approached through the application of two different modeling techniques. The first involved the development of a simple sequential equilibrium model to examine the impact of utility uncertainty (i.e., uncertainty about the intentions of the rival nation). This issue is obviously critical because if Nation A believes that Nation B is irrevocably committed to the present arms race, there is no incentive for Nation A to make a cooperative gesture. Nation B will simply ignore the gesture and Nation A will experience a relative decline in military strength.

In the stylized game we examined, Nation A can be either weak or strong and Nation B can be one of three types: weak, strong, or Deadlocked. These ideal types characterize, in declining order, the extent to which the states prefer a tacit arms reduction to the present arms race. The analysis reveals how each type of Nation A should deal with each type of Nation B. The analysis is too complex to recapitulate here but it leads to some straightforward conclusions. One is that uncertainty about a rival's intentions will often lead to an outcome that is not optimal. For example, a weak nation A might yield too much to a weak nation B if it thinks that B is strong or refuse to make any cooperative gesture at all if it thinks B has Deadlock preferences. In the first case, uncertainty leaves Nation A worse off and in the second case both nations would be worse off than they would be in the presence of perfect information about intentions. The case where nation A is dissuaded from initiating a cooperative gesture because of its lack of faith that B will respond is notable because it suggests that there is a limit to the frequency with which states will adopt tacit bargaining strategies.

Another implication is that an increase in the certainty of one nation about the intentions of the other may make things worse instead of better. In international as well as interpersonal relations, one less fool is not enough. Suppose that A is strong and discovers correctly that B is weak. This makes a particular kind of tacit arms treaty both optimal and achievable. The problem is that if B thinks that there is much chance that A is weak, B will bluff and pretend that it is strong. In this case, it will demand a second conciliatory gesture on the part of A before it will respond. If A possessed imperfect information about B's character, it might be taken in by this ruse. But when A has perfect information, it will not be fooled and the arms race will continue.

The results of the equilibrium analysis corroborated our contention that utility uncertainty must play a major role in determining the choice of tacit bargaining strategy, but there are other factors that the literature suggests are also significant. Three of the most important are (1) the information uncertainty associated with assessing the size and capability of a rival state's weapons stocks, (2) the range of options available for cooperative initiatives and responses, and (3) the relative value that players place on the future as compared to the present. The last factor is what economists refer to as the discount rate and Axelrod calls the "shadow of the future."

The impact of these three factors together with utility uncertainty on the choice of tacit bargaining strategies was then investigated through the use of a simulation model. The model is designed to represent a situation in which a new administration assumes power in one of two states (referred to as Nation A) that are currently engaged in an arms race. This administration sees substantial advantages to be gained by slowing the arms race, but appreciates the policy leverage that arms superiority occasionally permits and the dangers of losing ground to the rival (Nation B). To capture the effect of variations in the perceived benefits and costs of arms superiority, we looked at two different sets of payoffs: a Base Case that is typical of Prisoner's Dilemma studies and a Low-Benefit Case where less value is placed on arms superiority.

The status of each side is its level of armaments. On each move, each side may increase or decrease its arms level by any amount. This represents the major policy variable and the instrument through which cooperation or defection is signaled. After both sides have moved, each side attains a benefit that is proportional to the difference in arms, minus a maintenance cost associated with its own arms stock. A building cost is also included to avoid a situation where an instantaneous, infinite arms buildup would be the optimal move.

To simplify matters, we depicted the results of a small number of simulation experiments graphically using only two or three values of each parameter. For example, we examined the impact of two dramatically different discount rates rather than all possible rates, and three archetypal arms strategies that a rival nation might employ instead of twenty or thirty. This allowed the clear demonstration of major effects; intermediate results can be inferred by interpolation.

One of the first relationships that was examined was the effect of uncertainty about the rival's intentions on the magnitude of the initial cooperative gesture. Clearly, the more a state is convinced that its rival will respond in kind to a cooperative gesture, the larger the gesture should be. Indeed, if there is no uncertainty, complete disarmament would occur in a few moves. The issue is: What size gesture is optimal when a state is uncertain about a rival's response and has to contend with the possibility that none will be forthcoming? To what extent does this uncertainty lead a rational actor to make more modest and tentative unilateral gestures?

It turns out that if the probability of nonresponsiveness is greater than 23 percent—a relatively low figure in a world of mutual suspicion—then the optimal concession level is never greater than a one-year moratorium on weapons increases. If the estimated probability that the rival will ignore a cooperative gesture reaches 55 percent, the optimal strategy is to make no gesture at all, not even a small one. Jointly these suggest that generous tacit bargaining gestures will be rare. They also suggest that it will not be difficult for a rational but uncertain administration that is slightly risk averse to talk itself out of initiating any serious tacit bargaining.

Detailed analysis of the different decision environments in which information uncertainty and the discount rate are varied suggest that even the equivalent of a one-year moratorium will be rare. It represents something closer to the maximum, rather than the median, gesture. The strategies that are the most robust across different decision environments prescribe a gesture that is less than one-half of one year's weapons growth.

When the decision makers adopt a very short time-horizon—or short shadow of the future—everything deteriorates further. A cooperatively minded state controlled by decision makers with a short time-horizon will make no gesture if it thinks that there is even a 10 percent chance that it will be ignored. A high level of noise and misperception brought about by problems of weapon comparability or poor intelligence will lead to similar problems. Under such conditions a 20 percent chance that the rival nation may have Deadlock preferences will make it optimal to make no cooperative gesture. If a gesture is made, it will be small and may go unnoticed by the rival.

A notable implication of the simulation is that no specific strategy is always dominant. The optimal strategy changes as the decision environment changes. At a minimum, decision makers need to estimate the intentions of the rival nation and the arms strategy that it is employing, the extent to which they value the benefits that will not be realized for some time (i.e., the discount rate), the amount of noise in the system and the likelihood of misinterpretation, and the strategic cost associated with making a cooperative gesture that is ignored by the other side. It would be conceptually neater and more reassuring to be able to formulate a tacit bargaining strategy that is optimal under all circumstances and requires no intelligence input, but no such strategy exists.

This is not to say that certain guidelines do not emerge. The absence of a dominant strategy together with the ever-changing character of the factors that determine the "best" strategy suggest that it would be unwise to pursue a single strategy over a long period. Different administrations in the rival state are likely to have slightly different discount rates or different views about the benefits associated with being slightly ahead in the arms race.

It is also clear that in the face of the uncertainty that characterizes most arms races, the optimal tacit bargaining strategy will be conservative. Even when the likelihood of constant defection is relatively low, the magnitude of the conciliatory gesture should be modest. This will still be true in those rare instances when other conditions for tacit bargaining are almost ideal (i.e., when there is a small benefit associated with an arms advantage and a strong possibility that the rival is engaging in a strategy of pure or cautious reciprocity).

The pervasive and conservative effect of uncertainty is best exemplified by what we call the basic paradox of tacit bargaining: A state will rarely be certain enough about an opponent's response to make a large cooperative gesture; the opponent will rarely be trusting enough to respond enthusiastically to a small one.

Decision makers in a cooperatively minded state must also decide how patient they will be in dealing with responses that do not match their initial gestures. Not surprisingly, it turns out to be unwise to be extremely impatient if the initial gesture is very small, or extremely patient if it is large. The former risks failing to communicate the message of cooperation; the latter is vulnerable to exploitation. Between these two extremes, simulation reveals a rule of thumb that is quite robust: Reduce your offer by half in the face of nonresponse.

The sensitivity of tacit bargaining to intelligence and interpretation problems also generates a conservative effect. In this case, the conservatism refers to the complexity (rather than the magnitude) of the tacit initiatives and responses. Our analysis suggests that it is probably wise to avoid tacit bargaining across weapons systems as well as in areas where estimates of weapon effectiveness are likely to be far apart. Either situation creates an environment analogous to the High-Noise Case where there is a real possibility that any cooperative response will be misinterpreted. Of course, the natural affinity of tacit bargaining for decomposable problems is not always a disadvantage. It opens the possibility for tacit cooperation in connection with a single weapon system or policy area even when most interactions between the nations continue to be uncooperative.

The prediction that noise and interpretation problems will restrict most tacit bargaining efforts to a specific weapon system or policy area seems borne out by experience. In the nineteenth and early-twentieth century, the most conspicuous examples of tacit bargaining in the area of arms control are associated with

the Anglo-German and Anglo-French naval races rather than total military forces. Usually, only one type of ship was involved.
In the U.S.-Soviet arms race, tacit bargaining has been similarly
restricted to satellite reconnaissance, nuclear weapons in space,
the use of biological and chemical weapons, nuclear testing, and,
more recently, the number of conventional forces in Europe.

There is some empirical corroboration for the formally derived
propositions that predict that cooperation-based tacit bargaining under conditions of uncertainty will be a conservative and
problematic method of achieving arms control. First, there is the
infrequency with which the technique is employed. The vast majority of tacit bargaining schemes that we see employed in actual
arms races (e.g., the British Two Power Standard) are based on
escalating punishments rather than cooperative gestures. Despite
the apparent virtues of strategies such as GRIT, there are few
documented instances where cooperation-based tacit bargaining
has been used in, for example, the Anglo-French, Anglo-German,
U.S.-Japanese, or even the U.S-Soviet arms races. This is consistent with the prediction that if a nation believes that there is a
substantial chance that its rival will ignore a cooperative gesture,
the rational course is to refrain from making such a move.

Historical evidence is also consistent with the prediction that
when tacit initiatives are offered they will be modest is size. In the
model we use, the offer will rarely be greater than the equivalent
of six months to one year of arms growth and it is difficult to
find many counterexamples from the real world. Actions such
as test ban moratoriums and the destruction of biological and
chemical weapons that have characterized tacit bargaining in the
U.S.-Soviet arms race may be meaningful, but they are certainly
not dramatic in comparison with the consequences of year-to-year
growth in military budgets.

Finally, we are confronted with the apparent fact that while
attempts to conduct cooperation-based tacit bargaining are rare,
successes are even rarer. More often then not, gestures such as test
ban moratoriums and troop withdrawals have not precipitated a
spiral of ever-increasing arms control. This is consistent with the
predictions of the formal model. It reveals that the same uncertainty that makes initiatives relatively rare and modest in size,

leads the target nation to be slow to recognize that an initiative has been offered, skeptical about the motives that produced it, and unclear about the nature of response that is required.

This is not to say, of course, that bold—or apparently bold— tacit initiatives will never be made, only that they will be relatively rare and take place in a fashion consistent with the basic model. Gorbachev's troop reduction and force restructuring that took place in Eastern Europe in 1989 provides a good example. To oversimplify slightly, the model says that the Soviet Union might initiate such a gesture if there was (1) a decrease in the utility it attached to arms superiority; (2) an increase in the probability that the United States would respond positively to such an initiative; (3) a reduction in misperception and misinterpretation; or (4) a change in the time preferences of key decision makers. Arguably, at least numbers one and two occurred during Gorbachev's administration. He evidenced less inclination to seek offensive advantage on the European front and he had reason to believe that public opinion in West Germany and other countries had shifted in such a way that it would be impossible for NATO not to respond to a Soviet troop reduction with a troop reduction of its own.

6.2   The Maintenance of Arms Agreements

Much of the agenda for the research on tacit bargaining and arms cooperation was laid out by the work of scholars such as Tom Schelling, Robert Osgood, and Robert Axelrod. The equally critical question of how to best maintain a treaty once it has been formally or tacitly arrived at has not had the benefit of such attention. There is a general appreciation that arms control efforts are fragile structures that are often disregarded soon after they are constructed, but there has been little theoretical or empirical research on questions such as what pattern of sanctions best deters violations and how the problems of displacement and innovation can be minimized.

At the present time, the small number of individuals who have pondered the matter of treaty maintenance can be divided into two camps. The first, associated with Fred Ikle, favors responding to a suspected treaty violation by stepping up the arms race. The logic is that the expected cost of the stepped-up race will deter a rival from engaging in such behavior or that incurring such a "fine" will keep it from being repeated. Ikle realizes that this strategy may lead the aggrieved nation to pay a penalty itself by spending more than it otherwise would, but argues that this cost is less than the aggression that might come from another nation exploiting the advantage that it had acquired by breaking an arms treaty.

The second camp recommends a Tit-for-Tat strategy that is sometimes referred to as "proportionate response." As the names imply, this strategy prescribes responding to a treaty violation by engaging in some equivalent behavior. While it offers less of a deterrent than Ikle's abrogation plus punishment approach, this strategy risks less escalation.

Curiously, proponents of one strategy have not spent time criticizing the other. The two simply exist as noncompetitive and untested policy alternatives. When a decision maker or policy adviser chooses between them, the basis for the choice is usually ideology and intuition. The punishment strategy is generally favored by conservatives and the proportionate response strategy generally supported by liberals. Theory or reference to historical experience rarely plays a role.

The first phase of our investigation of treaty maintenance consisted of an equilibrium analysis of the relative merits of these two types of strategies when each state possesses perfect information about the other's arms behavior and capabilities. Because we felt that Ikle's punishment strategy suffered from credibility problems (i.e., convincing another nation that you are willing to hurt yourself in order to punish it is difficult), we limited the level of the punishment response to simple treaty abrogation. That is, if a violation is detected, a state returns to a rate of arms production that is equal to the rate it would pursue in the absence of any cooperation.

Somewhat to our surprise, under these perfect conditions both the abrogation strategy and the reciprocity strategy proved capable of supporting an equilibrium in which an arms treaty would be preserved. Moreover, in equilibrium the outcomes and payoffs are identical. In some sense, this result justifies the lack of competition between the two strategies in the literature: a supporter of either strategy has little justification for criticizing a rival that leads to the same result. Of course, if there is any possibility that the equilibrium will fail, their relative strengths and weaknesses begin to emerge. Abrogation minimizes the chance of such a failure by providing the greater threat. Reciprocity minimizes the cost of such failures.

In order to say something more about the relative merits of the two strategies and the tradeoff between the probability and cost of failure, it was necessary to develop a more sophisticated model that incorporated a mechanism that could cause an arms agreement to break down. The mechanism that was selected was capability uncertainty. This concept has both a qualitative and a quantitative dimension. The first refers to uncertainty about the physical quantity of weapons that a rival is producing: how many cruise missiles, how many tanks, etc. The qualitative dimension involves uncertainty about the effectiveness of these weapons in time of war: whose missiles are more accurate, whose tanks are most reliable, etc.

No student of arms control would deny the prevalence of either type of uncertainty in most nineteenth- and twentieth-century arms races, and the arms race between the United States and Soviet Union is no exception. On the quantitative side, the United States has, at various times, wildly misestimated the number of Soviet ICBMs and doubtless the Soviets have made similar errors. On the qualitative side, there is a strong argument that the United States was uncertain about the importance of Soviet ABM research and the Krasnoyarsk radar installation, while the Soviet Union was equally uncertain about the significance of Star Wars.

When two stochastic factors are added to the arms race model to represent these two capability dimensions, the performance of both the abrogation and reciprocity strategies deteriorates. This deterioration is most apparent in the case of Ikle's abrogation strategy. Even if we assume that each side is just as likely to underestimate as to overestimate the other side's force level (an assumption that history suggests is hopelessly optimistic), any level of error in force assessment will lead to a 50 percent chance that the treaty will be abrogated after only one period if one side employs a strict abrogation strategy. If both sides employ this strategy and observe each other with some degree of error, the chance that the treaty will end after a single period rises to 75 percent. Under either condition, there is virtually no chance that the treaty will endure for a significant length of time.

A reciprocity strategy fares somewhat better because it responds less strongly to small observational errors. While it is true that overestimations of the rival's activities will be common in an uncertain world, if the overestimation is only slight, the response that it provokes will also be small. Thus, in a repeated game with small observational errors, the drift from the optimal treaty level would be quite slow. If we think in terms of discounted expected utility instead of simply long-run equilibrium behavior, the cost of this drift will be very modest and the value of the treaty will not be appreciably different than one that could be enforced with no error.

Unfortunately, the performance of a reciprocity strategy deteriorates rapidly when we move into a world where observational and interpretive errors are large. The nations' arms behaviors will conform to the requirements of the treaty only a small percentage of the time and the departures from the treaty level will no longer be small. The resultant situation will be better than an all-out arms race or the result of mutual adherence to an abrogation strategy, but it will be far poorer than what would be optimal. The performance of the reciprocity strategy in the kind of environment that likely characterizes most arms races prompted the search for a more effective treaty maintenance strategy. One approach is to employ what we called generalized reciprocity in which the response is proportionate to, but less than, the violation. This performs better than simple reciprocity because it tends to dampen spirals of escalation inspired by misperception and misinterpretation. However, it still leads to a situation where nations will be observing the treaty only a small fraction of the time.

It is possible to develop more sophisticated generalized reciprocity strategies in which the ratio of the response to the violation changes with the magnitude of the perceived violation, or where the size of the punishment is a function of the entire sequence of past actions of both sides. This would doubtless lead to a theoretical improvement in performance. The problem is that the complexity of such strategies makes their implementation problematic. Decision makers rarely implement—or communicate to a rival nation—strategies that they cannot comprehend.

Rather than refine generalized reciprocity, we chose to develop a trigger strategy approach inspired by the trigger price literature in oligopoly theory. Members of an oligopoly risk exploitation by a firm that chooses to produce more than would be optimal for the group as a whole. Ideally, discipline could be enforced by observing production levels, but trustworthy information is not usually available. All that a given firm knows with certainty are its own level of production and the market price, which is determined by aggregate production and a stochastic factor. To cope with potential exploitation and the uncertainty produced by the stochastic factor, the members of the oligopoly determine what market price will provide a fairly reliable signal that some member firm is cheating the other members of the oligopoly by producing at too high a level. Whenever the market price dips below this trigger price, the oligopolists all produce at a higher rate and the offending firm is punished (although all the others suffer as well).

The translation of the trigger price strategy as it is employed in oligopoly theory to the world of arms control is somewhat complicated, but the basic idea remains the same. The object is to recognize that intelligence and interpretation problems exist and take them into consideration by not yielding to the temptation to see a treaty violation until a certain threshold of increased capability is estimated to have been reached.

From a formal modeling perspective, our first task was to demonstrate that a trigger strategy could support a treaty when there was a significant amount of uncertainty about the number or effectiveness of a rival's weapons. Proposition 4 shows that a trigger strategy equilibrium can be maintained up to the point where there is so much noise and uncertainty in the environment that each side can barely distinguish whether its opponent is obeying the treaty or engaging in an all-out arms race.

A trigger strategy is also attractive with respect to the cost that it exacts. In the presence of uncertainty, a nation is confronted with the tradeoff between needlessly provoking an arms race by punishing the rival nation for a violation that did not occur and allowing the other side to exploit it by systematically cheating at some low level that could simply be the product of inaccurate intelligence information or interpretation errors. Any strategy is going to be plagued with both problems; the question is how much.

Numerical calculation of equilibrium values reveals that even with a fairly large amount of uncertainty, the trigger equilibrium achieves 90 percent of the benefit that is possible with perfect information. In terms of its ability to stabilize an arms race for an appreciable period of time, the same calculation shows that the trigger strategy leads to a treaty life that averages sixty-five years. As one might expect, performance increases still further as uncertainty is reduced.

Thus, triggers can be chosen so that there is only a small probability that the treaty will break down by accident and, if carefully selected, they can avoid the problem of exploitation to a high degree. If the treaty is not equal (e.g., the Washington Naval Treaty of 1923) or if the two sides have somewhat different preferences and costs, trigger strategies can still be used and still produce outcomes that are substantially better than the alternatives of abrogation or reciprocity. While it is true that their relative benefit depends on estimates of information uncertainty, even a crude approximation will lead the trigger strategies to outperform these two alternatives. It is important to remember that the performance of *every* treaty maintenance strategy depends on the level of information/capability uncertainty. Trigger strategies simply make this link explicit and incorporate it into the design of the strategy.

The simplicity of trigger strategies also offers advantages over the sort of complex Bayesian reciprocity strategy that is probably its closest rival in terms of effectiveness. Trigger strategies can easily be comprehended by the decision makers asked to employ them and are easily communicated to the rival nation. They are far less likely to cause confusion than a large number of carefully graduated punishments that would be open to misinterpretation at every level of escalation.

The fact that a very finely graduated response strategy has considerable cognitive disadvantages does not mean that there may not be times when it might make sense to have a series of two or three triggers (each with its own set of associated responses) instead of only one. This would reduce the probability of a serious escalation caused by an error in estimating the amount of uncertainty in the system at the cost of providing slightly less disincentive for violation. However, the most important advantage of multiple triggers lies in their ability to "educate" a rival about the likelihood that its behavior will have the promised consequences. A state that is promptly punished for a small violation may increase its estimation of the probability that it will be punished for a larger violation. We would thus expect the wisdom of such a multiple trigger strategy to hinge on the necessity of convincing the other side that the violation of a trigger will have the promised consequences and the availability of qualitatively distinct and communicable trigger thresholds.

Just as theoretical work on treaty maintenance is in short supply, empirical research that might be used to reinforce these conclusions is also scarce. While it would be nice to have a large number of treaties in which the strategies of abrogation, reciprocity, and trigger strategies were each employed and about which we possessed reliable information about levels of capability uncertainty, the benefits and costs associated with violations, and so forth, such information is not available. Even if it existed and we could cope with the attendant selection bias, we would be left with all of the inferential problems that plague the empirical study of deterrence. In equilibrium, a successfully maintained treaty is the same sort of nonevent.

Until more case studies are completed with the relevant variables in mind, empirical corroboration must be limited to fragmentary information on two indirect tests. The first concerns the role of technological innovation in overturning formally negotiated or tacit arms agreements. Contrary to the literature that implies that a nation will willingly withdraw from an agreement if it believes that a technological breakthrough in the design of the weapon system that is being controlled will give it a modest advantage in any ensuing arms race, our model suggests that the innovation will have to lead to cost or effectiveness differences on the order of 50 percent or more before this step is beneficial. Since innovations capable of producing such differences in the short run are rare, the theory would predict that nations will be more likely to break arms treaties because: (1) they have been rendered useless by the displacement of resources to weapons systems that are not covered by the treaty and the exploitation of loopholes, (2) there has been a change of leadership that has led to a dramatic reassessment of the benefits and costs associated with arms control, or (3) one or both nations have employed a treaty maintenance strategy that was too sensitive to uncertainty or could be exploited.

There is partial evidence supporting all of these expectations. Evangelista's work (1988) plays down the role of a U.S.-Soviet arms race fueled by technology, and Goldman (1989) suggests that most of the technological advances that eroded the significance of the Washington Naval Treaty of 1923 occurred in areas that were not covered by the treaty. No less interestingly, significant violations of Versailles, the Washington Naval Treaty of 1923, and both SALT agreements were all more closely associated with new leaders than with new weapons technology. With respect to the application of the incorrect treaty maintenance strategy, one could argue that both the Washington Naval Treaty of 1923 and the tacit slowdown in the U.S.-Soviet arms race in the 1970s fell apart partly because of a downward spiral of mutual overreaction.

The second indirect test of the theory involves the circumstances in which trigger-like strategies evolve. Ceteris paribus, we would expect to see them employed with increasing frequency as information uncertainty increases. The logic is simple. When uncertainty is low, a variety of strategies will be equally effective; when it is high, the advantages of a trigger strategy (or a more complicated equivalent) become substantial.

Unfortunately, while the simplicity of this test is attractive, it suffers from two problems. First, unless we have some assurance that trigger strategies are included in the repertoire of strategy choices available to decision makers, the results of the test may be biased. If the literature in the area is any indication, trigger strategies are less well-known than the polar alternatives of abrogation and reciprocity. Second, the task of estimating the amount of information uncertainty associated with a given treaty is no easy matter. If an outside observer makes this estimation, he or she must be aware that there are a number of organizations within a nation that are likely to bias the estimate downward. Just as it is often in the interest of the military and intelligence communities

to overestimate the size of the threat, it is usually in the interest of
intelligence agencies to underestimate the amount of uncertainty
that should be attached to these estimates. Like stockbrokers,
they are not paid to be uncertain.

These problems notwithstanding, the enforcement of the ABM
treaty seems to indicate an increased tendency to adopt a trigger-
like strategy or some close relative in the presence of capability uncertainty.[1] Despite some inflammatory rhetoric, the United
States did not renounce the treaty or retaliate because of the Krasnoyarsk radar facility, and the Soviet Union has not done so in the
face of Star Wars experimentation or funding. Were either move
thought to represent a clear improvement in capability, some response would probably have been forthcoming. Yet it seems that
in both countries, there was simultaneous skepticism about the
military implications of these actions—which is equivalent to a
high degree of uncertainty about whether these actions consti-
tuted a capability change—and a continuing belief in the value of
the treaty. These are the conditions that we expect to inspire the
use of a trigger strategy and they appear to have done so.

---

1. In the case of the ABM treaty, the effect of the bias of the intelligence
community is somewhat mitigated because the critical uncertainty lies less
with the quantitative aspects of weapon estimation than with the qualitative
aspects. That is, not so much with what one side has done, but with what it
means in terms of increased military effectiveness or changes in the balance
of power. The greater the importance of the qualitative dimension, the less
influence an intelligence agency is likely to have, and the more likely that
an outside observer's estimation of uncertainty will coincide with that of key
decision makers.

Appendix

Proof of Proposition 5

Proposition 5. *Assume that both A and B would prefer a treaty at $(\bar{\Delta}^A, \bar{\Delta}^B)$ to mutual total defection; that is, assume condition (5.12) for A and B.*

1. *For any values of T_A and T_B, the values $\Delta_1^A = \Delta_0^A$ and $\Delta_1^B = \Delta_0^B$ form an equilibrium.*

2. *For any values of T_A, T_B, and $\Delta_1^B < \Delta_0^B$, there exists $\Delta_1^A < \Delta_0^A$ which maximizes the utility of A.*

3. *If σ_A and σ_B are not too large, there exist triggers T_A and T_B such that the values $\Delta_1^A = \bar{\Delta}^A$ and $\Delta_1^B = \bar{\Delta}^B$ form an equilibrium.*

4. *If σ_A and σ_B are not too large, the triggers T_A and T_B determined in 5-3 form a Nash equilibrium.*

Proof. Consider A's optimal response to a fixed trigger defection strategy of B's. Suppose that A and B choose the strategies (Δ_1^A, T_A) and (Δ_1^B, T_B) and suppose that the treaty lasts from period 1 to period τ, at which time one trigger or the other is exceeded and the two parties defect at their noncontingent Nash rates thereafter. Then from Equation (5.1), we have

$$S_t^A = \alpha^t S_0^A + \Delta_1^A (1 - \alpha^t)/(1 - \alpha)$$

215

for $t \leq \tau$ and

$$S^A_{\tau+t} = \alpha^{\tau+t} S^A_0 + \Delta^A_1 \alpha^t (1 - \alpha^\tau)/(1 - \alpha)$$

$$+ \Delta^A_0 (1 - \alpha^t)/(1 - \alpha) \tag{A.1}$$

for $t > 0$, and similarly for B. The utility to A of this outcome is

$$V^A_\tau = \sum_{t=1}^{\tau} \delta^t_A [\alpha^t S^A_0 + \mathcal{D}^A_1 (1 - \alpha^t)/(1 - \alpha) - \mathcal{Q}^A_1]$$

$$+ \sum_{t=1}^{\infty} \delta^{\tau+t}_A [\alpha^{\tau+t} S^A_0 + \mathcal{D}^A_1 \alpha^t (1 - \alpha^\tau)/(1 - \alpha)$$

$$+ \mathcal{D}^A_0 (1 - \alpha^t)/(1 - \alpha) - \mathcal{Q}^A_0]$$

$$= S^A_0 \left(\frac{\alpha \delta_A}{1 - \alpha \delta_A} \right) + \mathcal{D}^A_1 \left(\frac{\delta_A}{(1 - \delta_A)(1 - \alpha \delta_A)} \right)$$

$$+ (\mathcal{D}^A_0 - \mathcal{D}^A_1) \left(\frac{\delta^{\tau+1}_A}{(1 - \delta_A)(1 - \alpha \delta_A)} \right)$$

$$- \mathcal{Q}^A_1 \left(\frac{\delta_A}{(1 - \delta_A)} \right) - (\mathcal{Q}^A_0 - \mathcal{Q}^A_1) \left(\frac{\delta^{\tau+1}_A}{(1 - \delta_A)} \right) \tag{A.2}$$

where

$$\mathcal{D}^A_0 = a_A (\Delta^A_0 - \Delta^B_0) - b_A \Delta^A_0$$

$$\mathcal{D}^A_1 = a_A (\Delta^A_1 - \Delta^B_1) - b_A \Delta^A_1$$

$$\mathcal{Q}^A_0 = c_A (\Delta^A_0)^2$$

$$\mathcal{Q}^A_1 = c_A (\Delta^A_1)^2.$$

Now the probability that the defection occurs after time τ depends on the chance of the apparent production exceeding the trigger levels. Under this model, eventually one or both sides will exceed the other side's trigger level. On the next turn both sides will defect (under the assumption that the two sides' strategies are common knowledge). If we let $F_A = F_A(\epsilon^A/\sigma_A)$ and $F_B = F_B(\epsilon^B/\sigma_B)$ be the distribution functions of ϵ^A and ϵ^B respectively, then the chance of neither side passing the other side's trigger level is $p = F_A(T_B - \Delta_1^A)\,F_B(T_A - \Delta_1^B).$[1]

With this convention, the expected utility to A of the strategies used is

$$
\begin{aligned}
V^A &= \sum_{\tau=1}^{\infty}(1-p)p^{\tau-1}V_\tau^A \\[2mm]
&= \mathcal{S}_0^A\left(\frac{\alpha\delta_A}{1-\alpha\delta_A}\right) + \mathcal{D}_1^A\left(\frac{\delta_A}{(1-\delta_A)(1-\alpha\delta_A)}\right) \\[2mm]
&\quad + (\mathcal{D}_0^A - \mathcal{D}_1^A)\left(\frac{\delta_A^2(1-p)}{(1-\delta_A)(1-\alpha\delta_A)(1-p\delta_A)}\right) \\[2mm]
&\quad - \mathcal{Q}_1^A\left(\frac{\delta_A}{(1-\delta_A)}\right) \\[2mm]
&\quad - (\mathcal{Q}_0^A - \mathcal{Q}_1^A)\left(\frac{\delta_A^2(1-p)}{(1-\delta_A)(1-p\delta_A)}\right) \qquad \text{(A.3)}
\end{aligned}
$$

and similarly for nation B.

In order to investigate the potential equilibria with this model and class of strategies, we begin by examining the first-order condition for A to choose a level Δ_1^A of production given fixed levels of the other decision variables. We have

$$
\begin{aligned}
\frac{\partial V^A}{\partial \Delta_1^A} &= \frac{2c_A\delta_A(\Delta_0^A - \Delta_1^A)}{1-p\delta_A} \\[2mm]
&\quad - \frac{\partial p}{\partial \Delta_1^A}\frac{\delta_A^2}{(1-p\delta_A)^2}\left(\frac{\mathcal{D}_0^A - \mathcal{D}_1^A}{1-\alpha\delta_A} - (\mathcal{Q}_0^A - \mathcal{Q}_1^A)\right) \text{(A.4)}
\end{aligned}
$$

1. We are considering the case when $\mu_A = \mu_B = 0$ without loss of generality. We will also assume F_A and F_B to be absolutely continuous with unimodal twice continuously differentiable densities f_A and f_B having mean zero and finite variance. Candidate distributions include the normal, logistic, and the t-distribution with at least three degrees of freedom in the symmetric case, as well as asymmetric distributions such as the lognormal and gamma.

where

$$\frac{\partial p}{\partial \Delta_1^A} = -\sigma_A^{-1} f_A((T_B - \Delta_1^A)/\sigma_A) \, F_B((T_A - \Delta_1^B)/\sigma_B). \quad \text{(A.5)}$$

First note that

$$\lim_{\Delta_1^A \to \infty} \frac{\partial V^A}{\partial \Delta_1^A} = -\infty$$

$$\lim_{\Delta_1^A \to -\infty} \frac{\partial V^A}{\partial \Delta_1^A} = \infty. \quad \text{(A.6)}$$

Consequently, there must be at least one local maximum. If $\Delta_1^A = \Delta_0^A$, then

$$\left[\frac{\partial V^A}{\partial \Delta_1^A}\right]_{\Delta_1^A = \Delta_0^A} = \frac{\partial p}{\partial \Delta_1^A} \frac{\delta_A^2 a_A (\Delta_0^B - \Delta_1^B)}{(1 - \alpha \delta_A)(1 - p \delta_A)^2}. \quad \text{(A.7)}$$

If $\Delta_1^B = \Delta_0^B$, then this is zero, proving 5-1. If $\Delta_1^B < \Delta_0^B$, then this is negative, so there must be a maximum value as stated in 5-2.

For part 3, we need to show that there exist triggers T_A and T_B such that levels of production chosen by each side in response are $\bar{\Delta}^A$ and $\bar{\Delta}^B$. For there to exist T_B that is a root of (A.4) with fixed (Δ_1^A, Δ_1^B), two things are necessary. First, the last parenthesized term must be negative. This condition is easily seen to be the same as that in Equation (5.12), the condition for A to prefer mutual treaty adherence to mutual total defection. Thus, this imposes no additional requirement. The second condition is that $\partial p/\partial \Delta_1^A$ must be sufficiently large in magnitude so that the second term, which is negative, cancels the first term, which is positive. Clearly, if T_B is very large, then $\partial p/\partial \Delta_1^A$ is small so (A.4) is positive. If there is any value of T_B for which (A.4) is negative, then there must be at least one root by continuity. Considering the value $T_B = \Delta_1^A$ we have $\partial p/\partial \Delta_1^A = -\sigma_A^{-1} f_A(0) F_B((T_A - \Delta_1^B)/\sigma_B)$, and it is easily seen that $\partial p/\partial \Delta_1^A$ can be made as large as desired by making σ_A small. Now this shows the existence of a root T_B of Equation (A.4) for each fixed value of T_A and similarly the existence of a root T_A of the corresponding equation for a fixed value of T_B. It is still necessary to show that there exists a pair (T_A, T_B) that is a simultaneous solution of the two equations. We do this and the remainder of the theorem using asymptotic analysis as σ_A and σ_B tend to zero.

Define $\tilde{T}_A$ and $\tilde{T}_B$ by $\tilde{T}_A = (T_A - \Delta_1^B)/\sigma_B$ and $\tilde{T}_B = (T_B - \Delta_1^A)/\sigma_A$. Then as σ_A and σ_B go to zero for fixed $\tilde{T}_A$ and $\tilde{T}_B$, the right hand sides of Equation (A.4) and its equivalent for B go to $-\infty$. If we wish to maintain the possibility of a solution, we must let $\tilde{T}_A$ and $\tilde{T}_B$ increase at such a rate that $\partial p / \partial \Delta_1^A$ goes to a finite limit. In particular, it is easily seen that $T_B, T_A \to 0$ and $\tilde{T}_A, \tilde{T}_B \to \infty$ as $\sigma_A, \sigma_B \to 0$. Also, as σ_A and σ_B tend to 0, we get

$$F_A(\tilde{T}_B) \rightarrow 1$$

$$F_B(\tilde{T}_A) \rightarrow 1$$

$$p \rightarrow 1. \tag{A.8}$$

Using (A.5), we can solve (A.4) for $f_A(\tilde{T}_B)$ as

$$f_A(\tilde{T}_B) = \frac{-2c_A\sigma_A(\Delta_0^A - \Delta_1^A)(1 - p\delta_A)}{\delta_A F_B(\tilde{T}_A)\mathcal{E}^A} \tag{A.9}$$

where

$$\mathcal{E}^A = \frac{\mathcal{D}_0^A - \mathcal{D}_1^A}{1 - \alpha\delta_A} - (\mathcal{Q}_0^A - \mathcal{Q}_1^A). \tag{A.10}$$

For small σ_A and σ_B we may use the fact that $F_B(\tilde{T}_A)$, $F_A(\tilde{T}_B)$, and p are all near one to obtain the approximate solution

$$\tilde{T}_B^0 = f_A^{-1}\left(\frac{-2c_A\sigma_A(\Delta_0^A - \Delta_1^A)(1 - \delta_A)}{\delta_A \mathcal{E}^A}\right). \tag{A.11}$$

This solution is correct up to terms that are small compared to $\sigma_A^{1/2}$ and $\sigma_B^{1/2}$—more accurate approximations that are good to order σ_A^2 and σ_B^2 are easily developed.[2] Since we are now only

---

2. The exact order of these approximations depends on the tail behavior of F_A and F_B. When the tails are as fat as possible (algebraic with exponent 3), then the error declines as $\sigma_A^{2/3}$. For exponential tails, the decline is at the rate of σ_A.

showing the existence of a solution, this extra level of analysis is not needed.

Finally, we need to show that the choices of (T_A, T_B) that force production (Δ_1^A, Δ_1^B) to the treaty amounts $(\bar{\Delta}^A, \bar{\Delta}^B)$ form a Nash equilibrium. If A contemplated lowering the value of the trigger, then the convention that B cannot be forced to go below the treaty amount means that the change in utility is given by

$$\frac{\partial V^A}{\partial T_A} \;=\; -\frac{\partial p}{\partial T_A}\frac{\delta_A^2 \mathcal{E}^A}{(1 - p\delta_A)^2} > 0 \qquad (A.12)$$

so the decrease would be counterproductive. On the other hand, if A contemplated raising the value of the trigger, then B could profitably raise the production level Δ_1^B, so this needs to be accounted for. Thus, we treat the production levels (Δ_1^A, Δ_1^B) as functions of T_A and compute the partial derivatives under that assumption. This yields

$$\frac{\partial V^A}{\partial T_A} \;=\; \frac{\partial \mathcal{D}_1^A}{\partial T_A}\left[\frac{\delta_A}{(1 - \delta_A)(1 - p\delta_A)}\right] - \frac{\partial \mathcal{Q}_1^A}{\partial T_A}\left[\frac{\delta_A}{1 - p\delta_A}\right]$$

$$- \frac{\partial p}{\partial T_A}\left[\frac{\delta_A^2 \mathcal{E}^A}{(1 - p\delta_A)^2}\right] \qquad (A.13)$$

where

$$\frac{\partial \mathcal{D}_1^A}{\partial T_A} \;=\; (a_A - b_A)\frac{\partial \Delta_1^A}{\partial T_A} - a_A\frac{\partial \Delta_1^B}{\partial T_A} \qquad (A.14)$$

$$\frac{\partial \mathcal{Q}_1^A}{\partial T_A} \;=\; 2c_A\Delta_1^A\frac{\partial \Delta_1^A}{\partial T_A} \qquad (A.15)$$

$$\frac{\partial p}{\partial T_A} \;=\; -\sigma_A^{-1}\frac{\partial \Delta_1^A}{\partial T_A}f_A(\tilde{T}_B)F_B(\tilde{T}_A)$$

$$+ \sigma_B^{-1}(1 - \frac{\partial \Delta_1^B}{\partial T_A})F_A(\tilde{T}_B)f_B(\tilde{T}_A). \quad (A.16)$$

There remain the partial derivatives of Δ_1^A and Δ_1^B with respect to T_A that need to be determined. Using our asymptotic approximation we have

$$f_A(\tilde{T}_B^0) = \frac{2c_A\sigma_A(\Delta_0^A - \Delta_1^A)(1 - \delta_A)}{\delta_A \mathcal{E}^A} \qquad (A.17)$$

$$f_B(\tilde{T}_A^0) = \frac{2c_B\sigma_B(\Delta_0^B - \Delta_1^B)(1 - \delta_B)}{\delta_B \mathcal{E}^B} \qquad (A.18)$$

so that, treating (Δ_1^A, Δ_1^B) as functions of T_A and T_B, we have

$$-\sigma_A^{-1} f_A'(\tilde{T}_B^0)\frac{\partial \Delta_1^A}{\partial T_A}$$

$$= \delta_A^{-1}(\mathcal{E}^A)^{-2} 2c_A\sigma_A(1 - \delta_A)$$

$$\times \left[-\frac{\partial \Delta_1^A}{\partial T_A}\mathcal{E}^A - (\Delta_0^A - \Delta_1^A)\frac{\partial \mathcal{E}^A}{\partial T_A} \right] \quad (A.19)$$

and

$$-\sigma_B^{-1} f_B'(\tilde{T}_A^0)(1 - \frac{\partial \Delta_1^B}{\partial T_A})$$

$$= \delta_B^{-1}(\mathcal{E}^B)^{-2} 2c_B\sigma_B(1 - \delta_B)$$

$$\times \left[-\frac{\partial \Delta_1^B}{\partial T_A}\mathcal{E}^B - (\Delta_0^B - \Delta_1^B)\frac{\partial \mathcal{E}^B}{\partial T_A}) \right] \quad (A.20)$$

Since $f_A'(\tilde{T}_B^0)$ and $f_B'(\tilde{T}_A^0)$ are of order σ_A and σ_B, respectively,[3] we must have that

$$\frac{\partial \Delta_1^A}{\partial T_A} \rightarrow 0 \qquad (A.21)$$

$$1 - \frac{\partial \Delta_1^B}{\partial T_A} \rightarrow 0. \qquad (A.22)$$

---

3. Again, the exact order of the approximation depends on the tail behavior of F.

Substitution into (A.13) gives the asymptotic approximation

$$\frac{\partial V^A}{\partial T_A} = \frac{-a_A \delta_A}{(1 - \delta_A)(1 - p\delta_A).}$$

(A.23)

Since this is negative, A must lose by increasing the trigger. ∎

Bibliography

Abreu, Dilip. 1986. "Extremal Equilibria of Oligopolistic Supergames." *Journal of Economic Theory* 39:191–225.

Abreu, Dilip; Pearce, David; and Stacchetti, Ennio. 1986. "Optimal Cartel Equilibria with Imperfect Monitoring." *Journal of Economic Theory* 39:251–69.

Achen, Christopher H. 1988. "A state with Bureaucratic Politics is Representable as a Unitary Rational Actor." Presented at the annual meeting of the American Political Science Association, Washington, D.C.

Adelman, Kenneth. 1984–85. "Arms Control with and without Agreements." *Foreign Affairs* 63:240–62.

Allison, Graham T. 1971. *Essence of Decision: Explaining the Cuban Missile Crisis.* Boston: Little, Brown and Company.

Altfeld, Michael F. 1983. "Arms Races?—And Escalation? A Comment on Wallace." *International Studies Quarterly* 27:225–31.

Arrow, Kenneth J. 1951. *Social Choice and Individual Values.* New York: John Wiley. 2d ed. 1963.

Axelrod, Robert. 1984. *The Evolution of Cooperation.* New York: Basic Books.

223

Bendor, Jonathan. 1987. "In Good Times and Bad: Reciprocity in an Uncertain World." *American Journal of Political Science* 31:531–58.

Bixenstein, V. E., and Gaebelein J. 1971. "Strategies of 'Real' Opponents in Eliciting Cooperative Choice in a Prisoner's Dilemma Game." *Journal of Conflict Resolution* 15:157–66.

Bixenstein, V. E.; Potash, H. M.; and Wilson, K. V. 1963. "Effects of Level of Cooperation by the Other Player on Choices in a Prisoner's Dilemma Game, Part I." *Journal of Abnormal and Social Psychology* 66:308–13.

Bixenstein, V. E., and Wilson, K. V. 1963. "Effects of Level of Cooperative Choice by the Other Player on Choices in a Prisoner's Dilemma Game, Part II." *Journal of Abnormal and Social Psychology* 67:139–47.

Black, D. 1948. "On the Rationale of Group Decision-Making." *Journal of Political Economy* 56:23–34.

Brams, Steven J. 1985. *Superpower Games: Applying Game Theory to Superpower Conflict.* New Haven: Yale University Press.

Brams, Steven J.; Davis, Morton D.; and Straffin, Philip D. 1979. "The Geometry of the Arms Race." *International Studies Quarterly* 23:567–88.

Brams, Steven J., and Kilgour, D. Marc. 1988. *Game Theory and National Security.* New York: Basil Blackwell.

Bueno de Mesquita, Bruce. 1981. *The War Trap.* New Haven: Yale University Press.

Bull, Hedley. 1961. *The Control of the Arms Race: Disarmament and Arms Control in the Missile Age.* New York: Praeger.

Caplin, Andrew, and Nalebuff, Barry. 1988. "On 64 Percent Majority Rule." *Econometrica* 56:787–814.

Caplin, Andrew, and Nalebuff, Barry. 1989. "Aggregation and Social Choice: A Mean Voter Theorem." Princeton University. Typescript.

Cobden, Richard. 1868. *The Political Writings of Richard Cobden.* London: William Ridgeway.

Cohen, Michael D., and March, James G. 1974. *Leadership and Ambiguity: The American College President.* New York: McGraw Hill.

Condorcet, Marquise de. 1785. *Essai sur l'application de l'analyse à probibilité des décisions rendues à la pluralité des voix.* Paris.

Cyert, R. M., and March, J. G. 1963. *A Behavioral Theory of the Firm.* Englewood Cliffs, NJ: Prentice-Hall.

Davis, O., and Hinich, M. 1967. "A Mathematical Model of Policy Formation in a Democratic Society." In *Mathematical Applications in Political Science*, ed. J. Bernd. Dallas: Southern Methodist University Press.

Deutsch, M.; Epstein, Y.; Canavan, D.; and Gumpert, P. 1967. "Strategies of Inducing Cooperation: An Experimental Study." *Journal of Conflict Resolution* 11:345–60.

Downs, George W., and Rocke, David M. 1987. "Tacit Bargaining and Arms Control." *World Politics* 39:297–325.

Downs, George W.; Rocke, David M.; and Siverson, Randolph M. 1985. "Arms Races and Cooperation." *World Politics* 38:118–46.

Duffy, Gloria. 1988. "Conditions that Affect Arms Control Compliance." In *U.S.-Soviet Security Cooperation*, ed. Alexander George et al. New York: Oxford University Press.

Eimer, Manfred, and Drell, Sidney. 1987. "Verification and Arms Control." *Science* 235:406–14.

Etzioni, Amitai. 1967. "The Kennedy Experiment." *Western Political Science Quarterly* 20:316–80.

Evangelista, Matthew. 1988. *Innovation and the Arms Race: How the United States and the Soviet Union Develop New Military Technologies.* Ithaca, NY: Cornell University Press.

Farley, Philip J. 1988. "Arms Control and U.S.-Soviet Security Cooperation." In *U.S.-Soviet Security Cooperation,* ed. Alexander George et al. New York: Oxford University Press.

Farrell, Joseph, and Maskin, Eric. 1988. "Renegotiation in Repeated Games." University of California, Berkeley. Typescript.

Ferejohn, John A. 1976. "On the Effects of Aid to Nations in Arms Races." In *Mathematical Models in International Relations,* ed. Dina A. Zinnes and John V. Gillespie. New York: Praeger.

Garwin, Richard. 1985. "Is There a Way Out?" *Harpers,* June, 35–47.

George, Alexander L.; Farley, Philip J.; and Dallin, Alexander, eds. 1988. *U.S.-Soviet Security Cooperation: Achievements, Failures, Lessons.* New York: Oxford University Press.

Gillespie, John U.; Zinnes, Dina A.; Tahim, G. S.; and Schrodt, Philip A. 1977. "An Optimal Control Theory of Arms Races." *American Political Science Review* 71:226–51.

Goldman, Emily. 1989. "The Washington Naval Treaty." Ph.D diss. Stanford University.

Gooch, George Peabody. 1923. *Franco-German Relations, 1817–1914.* London: Longmans.

Green, Edward J., and Porter, Robert H. 1984. "Noncooperative Collusion under Imperfect Price Information." *Econometrica* 52:87–100.

Halperin, Morton H., and Kantor, Arnold, eds. 1973. *Readings in American Foreign Policy: A Bureaucratic Perspective.* Boston: Little, Brown and Company.

Hirst, Francis Wrigley. 1913. *The Six Panics and Other Essays.* London: Methuen.

Hoover, Robert A. 1980. *Arms Control: The Interwar Naval Limitation Agreements.* Denver: Denver Monograph Series in World Affairs.

Howard, Nigel. 1971. *Paradoxes of Rationality: Theory of Metagames and Political Behavior.* Cambridge, MA: MIT Press.

Ikle, Fred Charles. 1961. "After Detection—What?" *Foreign Affairs* 39:208–20.

Isard, Walter. 1988. *Arms Races, Arms Control, and Conflict Analysis.* New York: Cambridge University Press.

Isard, Walter, and Anderton, Charles H. 1985. "Arms Race Models: A Survey and Synthesis." *Conflict Management and Peace Science.* 8(2):27–98.

Jervis, Robert. 1976. *Perception and Misperception in International Politics.* Princeton: Princeton University Press.

Jervis, Robert. 1978. "Cooperation under the Security Dilemma." *World Politics* 30:167–214.

Jervis, Robert. 1988. "War and Misperception." *Journal of Interdisciplinary History* 18:675–700.

Kahneman, Daniel; Slovic, Paul; and Tversky, Amos, eds. 1982. *Judgment Under Uncertainty: Heuristics and Biases.* Cambridge: Cambridge University Press.

Komorita, S. S. 1965. "Cooperative Choice in a Prisoner's Dilemma Game." *Journal of Personality and Social Psychology* 2:741–45.

Komorita, S. S., and Mechling, J. 1967. "Betrayal and Reconciliation in a Two-Person Game." *Journal of Personality and Social Psychology* 6:349–53.

Koshland, Daniel E. 1987. "Techniques and Strategies of Verification." *Science* 235:405.

Kreps, David M.; Milgrom, Paul; Roberts, John; and Wilson, Robert. 1982. "Rational Cooperation in the Finitely Repeated Prisoners' Dilemma." *Journal of Economic Theory* 27:245–52.

Kreps, David M., and Wilson, Robert. 1982a. "Reputation and Imperfect Information." *Journal of Economic Theory* 27: 253–79.

Kreps, David M., and Wilson, Robert. 1982b. "Sequential Equilibria." *Econometrica* 50:863–94.

Kriesberg, Louis. 1987. "Carrots, Sticks, De-escalation: U.S.-Soviet and Arab-Israeli Relations." *Armed Forces and Society* 13:403–23.

Larson, Deborah. 1989. "Order under Anarchy." Presented at the annual meeting of the American Political Science Association, Atlanta, Georgia.

Laudan, Larry. 1977. *Progress and Its Problems: Towards a Theory of Scientific Growth.* Berkeley, CA: University of California Press.

Lee, William T. 1977. *Understanding the Soviet Military Threat.* New York: National Strategy Information Center.

Leng, R. J., and Wheeler, H. G. 1979. "Influence Strategies, Success, and War." *Journal of Conflict Resolution* 23:655–84.

Lindskold, Svenn, and Collins, M. G. 1978. "Inducing Cooperation by Groups and Individuals." *Journal of Conflict Resolution* 22:679–90.

Lindskold, Svenn; Walters, Pamela S.; and Koutsourais, Helen. 1983. "Cooperators, Competitors, and Response to GRIT." *Journal of Conflict Resolution* 27:521–32.

Livermore, Seward. 1944. "Battleship Diplomacy in South America, 1905–1925." *Journal of Modern History* 16:31–48.

Luce, R. D., and Raiffa, H. 1957. *Games and Decisions.* New York: John Wiley.

McCloskey, Donald. 1985. *The Rhetoric of Economics.* Madison: University of Wisconsin Press.

Majeski, Stephen J. 1984. "Arms Races as Iterated Prisoner's Dilemma Games." *Mathematical Social Sciences* 7:253–66.

Majeski, Stephen J., and Jones, David L. 1981. "Arms Race Modeling." *Journal of Conflict Resolution* 25:259–88.

March, J. G., and Simon, H. A. 1958. *Organizations.* New York: John Wiley.

Milgrom, Paul, and Roberts, John. 1982. "Limit Pricing and Entry under Incomplete Information: An Equilibrium Analysis." *Econometrica* 50:443–59.

Nalebuff, Barry. 1989. "Minimal Nuclear Deterrence." Princeton University. Typescript.

Nash, J. F. 1951. "Noncooperative Games." *Annals of Mathematics* 54:289–95.

Nisbett, R. E., and Ross, L. 1980. *Human Inference: Strategies and Shortcomings of Social Judgement.* Englewood Cliffs, NJ: Prentice-Hall.

Ordeshook, Peter C. 1986. *Game Theory and Political Theory.* New York: Cambridge University Press.

Osgood, C. E. 1962. *An Alternative to War or Surrender.* Urbana: University of Illinois Press.

Oskamp, S. 1971. "Effects of Programmed Strategies on Cooperation in the Prisoner's Dilemma and Other Mixed-Motive Games." *Journal of Conflict Resolution* 15:225–59.

Oskamp, S., and Perlman, D. 1965. "Factors Affecting Cooperation in a Prisoner's Dilemma Game." *Journal of Conflict Resolution* 9:359–74.

Patchen, Martin. 1987. "Strategies for Eliciting Cooperation from an Adversary." *Journal of Conflict Resolution* 31(1):164–85.

Pilisuk, Marc. 1984. "Experimenting with the Arms Race." *Journal of Conflict Resolution* 28:296–315.

Pilisuk, M.; Potter, P.; Rapoport, A.; and Winter, J. A. 1965. "War Hawks and Peace Doves: Alternate Resolutions of Experimental Conflicts." *Journal of Conflict Resolution* 9:491–508.

Pilisuk, M., and Skolnick, P. 1968. "Inducing Trust: A Test of the Osgood Proposal." *Journal of Personality and Social Psychology* 8:121–33.

Porter, Robert H. 1983. "Optimal Cartel Trigger Price Strategies." *Journal of Economic Theory* 29:313–38.

Powell, Robert. 1985. "The Theoretical Foundations of Strategic Nuclear Deterrence." *Political Science Quarterly* 100:75–96.

Powell, Robert. 1987. "Crisis Bargaining, Escalation, and MAD." *American Political Science Review* 81:717–35.

Powell, Robert. 1988. "Nuclear Brinksmanship with Two-Sided Incomplete Information." *American Political Science Review* 82:155–78.

Powell, Robert. 1990. *Deterrence and Credibility: Nuclear Deterrence Theory and the Problem of Credibility.* Cambridge: Cambridge University Press.

Rapoport, A. 1964. *Strategy and Conscience.* New York: Harper & Row.

Rapoport, A., and Chammah, A. M. 1965. *Prisoner's Dilemma.* Ann Arbor: University of Michigan Press.

Rattinger, Hans. 1976. "Econometrics and Arms Races." *European Journal of Political Research* 4:421–39.

Richardson, Lewis F. 1939. *Generalized Foreign Politics.* British Journal of Psychology, Monographs Supplement 23. Cambridge: Cambridge University Press.

Richardson, Lewis F. 1960a. *Arms and Insecurity.* Pittsburgh: Boxwood Press.

Richardson, Lewis F. 1960b. *Statistics of Deadly Quarrels.* Pittsburgh: Boxwood Press.

Ross, Lee, and Anderson, Craig. 1982. "Shortcomings in the Attribution Process: On the Origins and Maintenance of Erroneous Social Assessments." In *Judgment Under Uncertainty: Heuristics and Biases,* ed. Daniel Kahneman, Paul Slovic, and Amos Tversky. Cambridge: Cambridge University Press.

Ross, M., and Sicoly, F. 1979. "Egocentric Biases in Availability and Attribution." *Journal of Personality and Social Psychology* 37:322–36.

Schear, James A. 1985. "Arms Control Treaty Compliance: Buildup to a Breakdown?" *International Security* 10:141–82.

Schelling, Thomas C. 1960. *The Strategy of Conflict.* Cambridge, MA: Harvard University Press.

Schelling, Thomas C. 1966. *Arms and Influence.* New Haven: Yale University Press.

Schelling, Thomas C., and Halperin, Morton. 1962. *Strategy and Arms Control.* New York: Pergamon-Brassey.

Schrodt, Philip A. 1978. "Statistical Problems Associated with the Richardson Arms Race Model." *Journal of Peace Science* 3:159–72.

Scodel, Alvin; Minas, J. Sayer; Ratoosh, Philburn; and Lipetz, Milton. 1959. "Some Descriptive Aspects of Two-Person Non-Zero-Sum Games." *Journal of Conflict Resolution* 3:114–19.

Scodel, Alvin. 1962. "Induced Collaboration in Some Non-Zero-Sum Games." *Journal of Conflict Resolution* 6:335–40.

Selten, R. 1975. "Reexamination of the Perfectness Concept for Equilibrium Points in Extensive Games." *Journal of Game Theory* 4:25–55.

Selten, R. 1978. "The Chain-Store Paradox." *Theory and Decision* 9:127–59.

Sermat, V. 1964. "Cooperative Behavior in a Mixed-Motive Game." *Journal of Social Psychology* 62:217–39.

Sermat, V. 1967. "The Effect of an Initial Cooperative or Competitive Treatment upon a Subject's Response to Conditional Cooperation." *Behavioral Science* 12:301–13.

Shapiro, Carl. 1987. "Theories of Oligopoly Behavior." Discussion Papers in Economics no.126, Woodrow Wilson School, Princeton University.

Shure, G. H.; Meeker, R. J.; and Hansford, E. A. 1965. "The Effectiveness of Pacifist Strategies in Bargaining Games." *Journal of Conflict Resolution* 9:106–16.

Simaan M., and Cruz, J. 1975. "Formulation of Richardson's Model of Arms Race from a Differential Games Viewpoint." *Review of Economic Studies* 42:67–77.

Smith, R. Jeffrey. 1985. "Administration at Odds over Soviet Cheating." *Science* 228:695–96.

Snyder, Glen H. 1971. " 'Prisoner's Dilemma' and 'Chicken' Models in International Politics." *International Studies Quarterly* 15:66–103.

Snyder, Glenn H., and Diesing, Paul. 1977. *Conflict Among Nations.* Princeton: Princeton University Press.

Solomon, L. 1960. "The Influence of Some Types of Power Relationships and Game Strategies upon the Development of Interpersonal Trust." *Journal of Abnormal and Social Psychology* 61:223–30.

Terhune, K. W. 1968. "Motives, Situation, and Interpersonal Conflict within Prisoner's Dilemma." *Journal of Personality and Social Psychology* 8: monograph 3, part 2.

Wagner, David L.; Perkins, Ronald T.; and Taagepera, Rein. 1975. "Complete Solution to Richardson's Arms Race Equations." *Journal of Peace Science* 1:159–72.

Wagner, R. Harrison. 1983. "Theory of Games and the Problem of International Cooperation." *American Political Science Review* 77:330–46.

Wallace, Michael D. 1982. "Armaments and Escalation." *International Studies Quarterly* 26:37–56.

Waltz, Kenneth N. 1979. *Theory of International Politics*. Reading, MA: Addison-Wesley.

Weber, Steven, and Drell, Sidney. 1988. "Attempts to Regulate Military Activities in Space." In *U.S.-Soviet Security Cooperation*, ed. Alexander George et al. New York: Oxford University Press.

Weede, Erich. 1980. "Arms Races and Escalation." *Journal of Conflict Resolution* 24:285–87.

Wilson, W. 1971. "Reciprocation and Other Techniques for Inducing Cooperation in the Prisoner's Dilemma." *Journal of Conflict Resolution* 15:196–98.

Wittman, Donald. 1989. "Arms Control Verification and Other Games Involving Imperfect Detection." *American Political Science Review* 83:923–45.

Index